*Agendas, Alternatives,
and Public Policies*

Agendas, Alternatives, and Public Policies

Second Edition

John W. Kingdon
THE UNIVERSITY OF MICHIGAN

HarperCollins*CollegePublishers*

Acquisitions Editor: *Leo A. Wiegman*
Project Coordination, Text and Cover Design: *York Production Services*
Art Coordination: *York Production Services*
Electronic Production Manager: *Christine Pearson*
Electronic Page Makeup: *R. R. Donnelley & Sons Company*
Printer and Binder: *R. R. Donnelley & Sons Company*
Cover Printer: *R. R. Donnelley & Sons Company*

Agendas, Alternatives, and Public Policies, 2/e

Library of Congress Cataloging-in-Publication Data

Kingdon, John W.
    Agendas, Alternatives and public policies / John W. Kingdon. --
    2nd ed.
        p.   cm.
    Includes bibliographical references and index.
    ISBN 0-673-52389-6
        1. United States—Politics and government.   2. Political planning—United States.
    3. Policy sciences.   I. Title.
    JK274.K62 1995
    320.973—dc20   94-17762
                                                                                CIP

98 99 00 01 02   12 11 10 9 8

This book is dedicated to

Ralph K. Huitt
and
John D. Lewis

CONTENTS

PREFACE TO THE FIRST EDITION

Some years ago, I became convinced that scholars had learned quite a bit about such authoritative decisions in government as legislators' roll call votes and presidents' final decisions. It seemed to me that we knew something about how issues were decided, but that we knew much less about how they got to be issues in the first place. Several questions emerged, and this book was written to grapple with them. How do subjects come to officials' attention? How are the alternatives from which they choose generated? How is the governmental agenda set? Why does an idea's time come when it does?

In these pages, I report the results of a research project designed to follow the rise and fall of items on the agenda, and to determine why some agenda items and alternatives are prominent and others are neglected. I explore how problems are recognized and defined, how policy proposals are developed, how political events enter in, and how these things become joined at critical junctures. This book draws from interviews I conducted over four years with people in and around the United States federal government who deal with health and transportation policy. I also used information from case studies, government documents, party platforms, press coverage, and public opinion surveys. The Appendix contains an account of the study's design.

My very considerable debts are scattered far and wide. They begin with my profound gratitude to the many congressional staffers, administration appointees, civil servants, lobbyists, journalists, researchers, and consultants who agreed to talk with me during long interviews over several years. I guaranteed them their anonymity, so cannot acknowledge their help by name. But this book could not have been written without their generous cooperation.

Various faculty colleagues at the University of Michigan and elsewhere have contributed their time, thought, and insights far beyond any reasonable expectation. Michael Cohen's many hours of stimulating conversation and reflective reviews of my writings have affected every chapter, and I am most grateful. Robert Putnam and Jack Walker have supported my efforts and provided me with wise counsel, encouragement, and helpful criticism from the beginning of the project through their reading of an earlier version of the manuscript. Richard Fenno, Charles Jones, and reviewers for Little, Brown—Allan P. Sindler, Edmund Beard, Robert L. Lineberry, Burdett Loomis, and Herbert Jacob—have read the manuscript with great care and have given me the benefit of frank and full appraisals. Robert Axelrod, Joel Aberbach, and John Campbell have shared many fruitful periods of discussion and have criticized portions of the manuscript most helpfully. Other colleagues and students across the country, including Edie Goldenberg, Paul Light, Carolyn Kawecki, and others too numerous to list by name, have been sounding boards and thoughtful contributors at various stages. Some of them may not even have realized the major effect that a seemingly casual conversation might have had on my thinking. Of course, none of these people should be held responsible for the contents of this book.

I have enjoyed the highly professional services of many research assistants. For various tasks of coding, case study research, editing, substantive commentary, and many other jobs extremely well done, I am happy to thank Emma Gross, Cathy Johnson, Edward Kutler, Paul Light, Roy Meyers, H. W. Perry, Mark Peterson, and Carmine Scavo. Personnel of the Institute of Public Policy Studies at the University of Michigan, including Helene McCarren, Judy Jackson, Charlotte Nametz, and Jackie Brendle, have helped in many ways. I have been delighted with the cooperation, attention, and helpfulness of the people at Little, Brown, and particularly want to thank Will Ethridge and Don Palm for their interest and thoughtfulness from beginning to end.

This research has been supported by several institutions. Faculty grants from the Rackham Graduate School and support from the Institute of Public Policy Studies, both at the University of Michigan, helped launch the project. A grant from the National Science Foundation helped me to complete the field work and analysis. A fellowship from the John Simon Guggenheim Foundation enabled me to obtain time free for writing. I also have been a Guest Scholar at the Brookings Institution for several periods, and want to thank the people there for their hospitality and good offices.

I have tried to express my love and appreciation to my parents, my wife, and my sons in many ways over the years. This book is dedicated to Ralph K. Huitt and John D. Lewis, the former my major adviser when I was working on my Ph.D. at the University of Wisconsin and a good friend since, the latter an important professor of mine at Oberlin College during my undergraduate days. Both of them were fine teachers and advisers, and had very important effects on my professional and personal development.

John W. Kingdon
Ann Arbor, Michigan

PREFACE TO THE SECOND EDITION

This book first appeared in print in 1984. Much has happened since then, both in the real world of policy formation and in scholars' understandings of that world. Thus, a second edition seems a logical opportunity to update the book by introducing a consideration of events during the 1980s and 1990s, and to present some reflections on the lines of argument and the theories which were developed in the first edition.

In the main, the picture of agenda-setting, alternative specification, and policy formation presented in the first edition remains accurate and useful. The notice which the book has received and continues to receive seems to confirm that judgment. The process described in this book seems highly fluid and loosely coupled, various streams—problems, policies, and politics—seem to flow through and around the federal government largely independent of one another, and big policy changes occur when the streams join. Since the understandings of the processes presented in these pages seem roughly right, I have elected to follow the old maxim, "If it ain't broke, don't fix it." So, I have kept the body of the book exactly the same as it was in the first edition.

But I do want to add some reflections on the theory and some descriptions of events that took place since the primary field work for the book was completed in 1979. I accomplish those aims by adding Chapter 10, entitled "Some Further Reflections." In that chapter, I present some thoughts about the concepts and theories in the book which I have developed since the book was first written, some discussion of the literature as it has evolved since this book first appeared, and some responses to comments that have been made by readers of the book as they have discussed it in reviews, conferences, and conversations. In addition, the new Chapter 10 uses some events from the 1980s and 1990s to illustrate the workings of the theory and to show that the original concepts continue to be useful for understanding contemporary events. I hope the resulting book, unchanged except for the addition of Chapter 10, will remain pleasing and useful to scholars, students, and general readers.

My debts remain largely as I presented them in the Preface to the First Edition. I am constantly amazed and delighted that very busy people in

Washington are willing to take some time to talk with me and to educate me about what they do. They are my greatest help, and I'm most grateful. My colleagues and graduate students at the University of Michigan are a tremendous fund of ideas, suggestions, and companionship. John Holland and Michael Cohen helped me think about several theoretical issues for Chapter 10. I appreciate very much the times I have spent at the Center for Advanced Study in the Behavioral Sciences at Stanford and at the Brookings Institution in Washington. My family continues to provide the kind of supportive and loving environment that's crucial to my professional and personal well-being. I lead a good life in many ways, and feel very lucky to receive all of this largesse from so many people.

John W. Kingdon
Ann Arbor, Michigan

CHAPTER 1

How Does an Idea's Time Come?

Greater than the tread of mighty armies is an idea whose time has come.

—Victor Hugo

The phrase "an idea whose time has come" captures a fundamental reality about an irresistible movement that sweeps over our politics and our society, pushing aside everything that might stand in its path. We feel that such an event can be recognized by signs like sustained and marked changes in public opinion, repeated mobilization of people with intensely held preferences, and bandwagons onto which politicians of all persuasions climb. Members of Congress are fond of trotting out the phrase whenever they are advocating a piece of landmark legislation. And policy activists of all kinds often attempt to account for the emergence of an issue to the forefront of attention with such comments as, "I don't know—it was an idea whose time had come, I guess."

But what makes an idea's time come? That question is actually part of a larger puzzle: What makes people in and around government attend, at any given time, to some subjects and not to others? Political scientists have learned a fair amount about final enactment of legislation, and more broadly about authoritative decisions made at various locations in government. But predecision processes remain relatively uncharted territory. We know more about how issues are disposed of than we know about how they came to be issues on the governmental agenda in the first place, how the alternatives from which decision makers chose were generated, and why some potential issues and some likely alternatives never came to be the focus of serious attention.

If academics find these subjects rather murky, practitioners of the art of government scarcely have a clearer understanding of them. They are able to de-

1

scribe the subjects occupying their attention with some precision, and, in specific instances, can set forth a convincing account of the reasons for their focus on those subjects. But with some exceptions, they are neither inclined nor obliged to develop a more general understanding of the forces that move policy formation processes in one direction or another. As I was reminded by respondents in the study reported in this book, "You're the political scientist, not me" and, "It's your job to put this thing together, so that's not my worry." Yet the subject remains an absolutely critical puzzle for them. As one well-informed individual high in the federal executive branch put it:

> It's a fascinating question that you're dealing with. Why do decision makers pay attention to one thing rather than another? I've seen situations in which the Secretary has been dealing with absolute junk when he should be working on some really significant issue. I've always wondered why.

This book attempts to answer that question. In these pages, we will consider not how issues are authoritatively decided by the president, Congress, or other decision makers, but rather how they came to be issues in the first place. We will try to understand why important people pay attention to one subject rather than another, how their agendas change from one time to another, and how they narrow their choices from a large set of alternatives to a very few. This introductory chapter outlines the research on which this book is based; discusses the definitions, ideas, hypotheses, and theories with which the study began; presents an overview of several findings and case studies; and outlines the intellectual journey upon which we embark through the rest of the book.

Let no reader begin with the illusion that the journey is easy. In contrast to many areas of study in the social sciences, this one is particularly untidy. Subjects drift onto the agenda and drift off, and it is difficult even to define agenda status. When a subject gets hot for a time, it is not always easy even in retrospect to discern why. The researcher thinks one case study illuminates the process beautifully, only to discover another case study that behaves very differently. Conceptual difficulties often rise up to ensnare the traveler.

But the journey is also rewarding because the phenomena involved are so central to our comprehension of public policy outcomes and governmental processes, yet they are so incompletely understood. The patterns of public policy, after all, are determined not only by such final decisions as votes in legislatures, or initiatives and vetoes by presidents, but also by the fact that some subjects and proposals emerge in the first place and others are never seriously considered.[1] This book tries to contribute to a more complete understanding of these predecision public policy processes.

CONCEPTS AND DEFINITIONS

Though a drastic oversimplification, public policy making can be considered to be a set of processes, including at least (1) the setting of the agenda, (2) the

---

[1]Schattschneider's oft-quoted statement, "The definition of the alternatives is the supreme instrument of power," aptly states the case. See E. E. Schattschneider. *The Semi-Sovereign People* (New York: Holt, Rinehart, and Winston, 1960), p. 68.

specification of alternatives from which a choice is to be made, (3) an authoritative choice among those specified alternatives, as in a legislative vote or a presidential decision, and (4) the implementation of the decision.[2] Success in one process does not necessarily imply success in others. An item can be prominently on the agenda, for instance, without subsequent passage of legislation; passage does not necessarily guarantee implementation according to legislative intent. This study concentrates on the first two processes. We seek to understand why some subjects become prominent on the policy agenda and others do not, and why some alternatives for choice are seriously considered while others are neglected.

The word "agenda" has many uses, even in the context of governmental policy. We sometimes use the word to refer to an announced subject for a meeting, as in the sentence, "The agenda before the committee today is H.R. 1728 and proposed amendments thereto." At other times, we might mean the kind of plan an organizer wants participants to adopt, as in the phrase, "a hidden agenda." And sometimes the word "agenda" refers to a coherent set of proposals, each related to the others and forming a series of enactments its proponents would prefer, as in "an agenda for the 1980s." It is thus important to define with some precision how the word will be used in this book.

The *agenda,* as I conceive of it, is the list of subjects or problems to which governmental officials, and people outside of government closely associated with those officials, are paying some serious attention at any given time. Within the general domain of transportation, for instance, the Secretary of Transportation and the members of the congressional committees of jurisdiction could be considering, at any given time, a range of problems like the cost of mass transit construction, the deterioration of highway surfaces, the inefficiencies produced by economic regulation of the airlines, and tanker spills in the ports of the country. Out of the set of all conceivable subjects or problems to which officials could be paying attention, they do in fact seriously attend to some rather than others. So the agenda-setting process narrows this set of conceivable subjects to the set that actually becomes the focus of attention. We want to understand not only why the agenda is composed as it is at any one point in time, but how and why it changes from one time to another.

We have been speaking of a governmental agenda, the list of subjects to which governmental officials and those around them are paying serious attention. Of course, this list varies from one part of the government to another. The president and his closest advisers, for instance, have as their agenda the "biggest" items, things like international crises, major legislative initiatives, the state of the economy, and major budgetary decisions. Then there are more *specialized* agendas, including agendas for health officials or transportation officials. Even within an area like health, there are still more specialized agendas,

---

[2]When discussing decision-making models, Simon distinguishes between directing attention, discovering or designing possible courses of action, and selecting a particular course of action. These categories roughly correspond to agendas, alternatives and choice. See Herbert Simon, "Political Research: The Decision-Making Framework," in David Easton, ed., *Varieties of Political Theory* (Englewood Cliffs: Prentice-Hall, 1966), p. 19. For another use of similar distinctions, see John W. Kingdon, *Congressmen's Voting Decisions,* 3rd ed. (Ann Arbor: University of Michigan Press, 1989), Chapter 12.

lists of subjects that dominate the attention of people in areas like biomedical research or direct delivery of medical services. We should also distinguish between the *governmental* agenda, the list of subjects that are getting attention, and the *decision* agenda, or the list of subjects within the governmental agenda that are up for an active decision. As we will see later in this book, governmental and decision agendas are affected by somewhat different processes.

Apart from the set of subjects or problems that are on the agenda, a set of *alternatives* for governmental action is seriously considered by governmental officials and those closely associated with them. If the cost of medical care is a prominent agenda item, for instance, officials could seriously consider a number of alternatives related to that problem, including directly regulating hospital costs, introducing incentives into the system to encourage market regulation, paying consumers' costs through comprehensive national health insurance, enacting such partial insurance plans as catastrophic insurance, nationalizing the system in a scheme of socialized medicine, or doing nothing. Out of the set of all conceivable alternatives, officials actually consider some more seriously than others. So the process of specifying alternatives narrows the set of conceivable alternatives to the set that is seriously considered.

This distinction between agenda and alternatives will turn out to be quite useful analytically. In much of the current literature, "agenda setting" refers to both of them at once, and the distinction between agenda and alternatives is not very sharply drawn. One scholar will argue that professionals, experts, and technicians dominate "the agenda," for example, while another will argue that highly visible crises and the public positions of presidents and key Senators dominate "the agenda." Perhaps agenda setting and alternative specification are governed by quite different processes. Experts might then be more important in generating alternatives, and presidents might be more important in setting the agenda. Presidents can dominate the congressional agenda, for example, but they have much less control over the alternatives members of Congress consider. We will return to this distinction between agenda and alternatives repeatedly.

A BRIEF ACCOUNT OF THE RESEARCH

The research on which this book is based was designed to follow the development of public policy over time, concentrating on the areas of health and transportation in the federal government of the United States. I gathered two kinds of information for the study. The first consisted of four waves of interviews, in 1976, 1977, 1978, and 1979, with people close to decision making in health and transportation. Over the four years, I conducted 247 lengthy and detailed interviews, 133 in health and 114 in transportation. One-fifth of them were with congressional staff, either committee staff or people located in support agencies. About a third were in the executive branch, including upper-level civil servants, political appointees in departments and bureaus, and presidential staff. The remaining interviews were with people outside of government, including lobbyists, journalists, consultants, academics, researchers, and other "important" people in health and transportation. Many respondents carried over from one year to the next; others were replacements. My aim was to tap into entire policy communities, not just parts like Congress, the presidency, the bureaucracy, or lobbies.

I asked these respondents many questions, but among the central ones were the following: "What major problems are you and others in the health (transportation) area most occupied with these days? Why? What proposals are on the front burner? Why?" I also asked about some problems and proposals that were not prominent, and why they were not. I then could compare one year to the next. If a previously prominent item fell by the wayside, or if a new item came to the fore during the year, I asked why. We can thus trace the rise and fall of items on policy agendas, and discover why items get hot or fade.

In addition to these interviews, research assistants and I developed a series of case studies of policy initiation and noninitiation, drawing from my interviews and from such publicly available sources as government documents, popular and specialized accounts, and academic writings. We identified for detailed analysis twenty-three case studies, covering many policy changes in health and transportation over the last three decades. Finally, we also gathered information on subjects that were currently prominent, from such sources as congressional hearings and committee reports, presidential State of the Union addresses and other messages, party platforms, press coverage, and public opinion data.

The appendix to this book discusses the study's methods in more detail.

THE LAY OF THE LAND

What do the agendas in health and transportation look like? To give a view of the events we seek to understand, let us examine four brief case studies. Each will describe the events and pose some questions that represent the sorts of questions we want to answer. We will then return to these and other case studies throughout the book.

Health Maintenance Organizations

In the early 1970s, people in the Nixon administration were concerned about the dramatically rising cost of medical care, and particularly of Medicare and Medicaid.[3] Rapidly rising cost was a problem not only in absolute dollar terms; it also created a tremendous budgetary pressure on other programs in the Department of Health, Education, and Welfare (HEW). In addition, administration officials saw Senator Edward Kennedy as at least one of the prominent potential presidential challengers in 1972. Since Kennedy was quite visible in the health area, administration officials felt that they too should be known for

[3]For fuller treatments of the HMO case, see Lawrence D. Brown, *Politics and Health Care Organization: HMOs As Federal Policy* (Washington, D.C.: The Brookings Institution, 1983); Joseph L. Falkson, *HMOs and the Politics of Health System Reform* (Bowie, MD: Robert J. Brady, 1980); and Patricia Bauman, "The Formulation and Evolution of the Health Maintenance Organization Policy," *Social Science and Medicine* 10 (March–April 1976): 129–142.

health initiatives. Both the cost problem and the political considerations produced a receptivity to ideas for health initiatives. As the political appointees in the Nixon administration cast about for ideas, they ran into some difficulty finding possible initiatives that would meet their requirements, including low cost and compatibility with their values of less regulation and smaller government.

Enter Paul Ellwood, the head of a Minneapolis-based policy group called InterStudy. Ellwood was a firm believer in the virtues of prepaid group practice, an arrangement that has been operating successfully in a number of locations for many years. Instead of paying a provider a fee for services rendered at every encounter, patients and their employers pay a yearly fee, in return for which the organization furnishes care as needed. Ellwood was well-known in the community of health policy specialists. He was known, among others, to Thomas Joe, then a top assistant to HEW Undersecretary John Veneman. In the words of one of my respondents:

> The story goes that Ellwood was in town, and when he left, he happened to sit on the plane next to Tom Joe. They got into a conversation, and Joe started bitching about how they have this problem and nobody has any ideas. So Ellwood says, "I've got an idea," and laid it out for him.

Ellwood proposed federal assistance for what he called Health Maintenance Organizations (HMOs). But instead of presenting it as a liberal do-gooder idea, Ellwood rather cleverly packaged it as a way of introducing marketplace competition into the medical care system. Different kinds of HMOs could compete both with each other and with traditional fee-for-service and insurance systems, and the resultant competition in the marketplace would regulate expenditures. Thus the administration could propose the desired initiative while avoiding a major new dose of government regulation. This twist on the idea made the proposal congruent with the ideology of the Nixon administration. Joe arranged for Ellwood to meet with Veneman and several other top-level HEW officials. They were sold on the idea. The proposal grew from a conversation to a memo, then from a very thick document to the status of a major presidential health initiative, all in a matter of a few weeks.

This story poses a number of intriguing questions. Given that prepaid practice had been established and well-known for years, why did the HMO idea suddenly take off as a federal government initiative at this particular time? Did events really turn on a chance airplane meeting? How important was the proposal's packaging? What underlying forces drove the events? This book tries to provide answers to questions like these.

National Health Insurance During the Carter Administration

National health insurance proposals are hardy perennials.[4] Public discussion of the idea in the United States stretches back at least to Teddy Roosevelt. It received some consideration during the New Deal period. Harry Truman pro-

---

[4]Most of the information about this case study is drawn from my interviews and from contemporary press accounts.

posed national health insurance in the late 1940s and early 1950s. Medicare and Medicaid, health insurance targeted toward the elderly and the poor, were passed in the mid 1960s. The idea of a more general national health insurance received considerable attention once again in the 1970s. There was a serious flurry of activity in 1973 and 1974, when Senator Edward Kennedy sponsored a scaled-down proposal together with Wilbur Mills, the chairman of the House Ways and Means Committee.

Interest rose once again during the Carter administration. Jimmy Carter was publicly committed to some version of national health insurance during the 1976 campaign. The United Automobile Workers (UAW) had been ardent proponents of comprehensive national health insurance for years. When Carter was elected with UAW support and with a hefty Democratic majority in both houses of Congress, many advocates thought that the time had come for another push.

National health insurance proposals are famous for their diversity. Even when it was clear that the subject would be on the agenda in 1977 through 1979, dramatically different proposals were put forward by their advocates. Some called for a plan that would be financed and administered entirely by the government; others provided for substantial doses of mandated private insurance. Some plans provided for comprehensive benefits, so that virtually all medical expenses would be covered; others were more selective in the benefits they would provide. Some provided for universal coverage of the entire population; others targeted subsets of the population. Some had the insurance foot the entire bill; others provided for patients to pay for a portion, either a portion of each year's expenses or a portion of each encounter with a medical care provider. Aside from the disputes, the complexities of the various proposals were staggering. Even among the advocates of national health insurance, there was considerable dispute over very fundamental features of their desired plans.

Early in the tenure of the Carter administration, Kennedy and labor entered into a series of conversations with the top policy makers and political advisers in the White House over the salient features of the administration's proposal. The labor-Kennedy coalition very much wanted the proposal to be formulated and announced before the 1978 congressional elections, reasoning that if there actually were an administration plan on the table, their people in each congressional district could firm up commitments from legislators and future legislators as a part of the campaign process. Several months into the new administration, the major supporters of comprehensive national health insurance, including Kennedy and organized labor, revised their insistence on the comprehensive plan they had held out for all these years. Here they had a president committed to national health insurance and a Democratic Congress. They reasoned that a similar opportunity might not come around again for another decade or even another generation. So while maintaining their proposal for comprehensive benefits and universal coverage, they dropped their insistence on a totally government program, and worked up a proposal for both underwriting and administration by private insurance companies. They claimed this gave Carter two features he wanted: a place for private insurers, and a way to get much of the cost off the federal budget. The critics of the new plan claimed it was still too costly and administratively unworkable, but compromise seemed to be in the air.

Meanwhile, a conflict developed within the administration between those (especially in HEW and in the president's Domestic Policy staff) who favored a proposal with comprehensive benefits and universal coverage, phased in over several years, and those (especially in Treasury and in the Office of Management and Budget) who favored much more limited initiatives providing for catastrophic insurance and some improved coverage for poor people, if there was to be any plan at all. The latter advisers were worried about the impact of a more ambitious plan on inflation and on the federal budget, particularly in light of what they perceived to be the more conservative national mood exemplified by such occurrences as the passage of Proposition 13 in California. Other administration figures, both in HEW and in the president's Executive Office, took the role of negotiating between the factions.

The resultant delay in announcing the administration's proposal made labor restive. Indeed, Douglas Fraser, the head of the United Auto Workers, referred in a late 1977 speech to his displeasure with the administration over this and several other issues. In a not-so-veiled reference to a potential Kennedy challenge, he raised the possibility of labor seeking "new allies" in their struggle. By some time in 1978, there was a fairly pronounced break with the labor and Kennedy people, and to the extent that the administration was consulting on the Hill, they did so with such other important actors in the process as Russell Long, the chairman of the Senate Finance Committee; Dan Rostenkowski, chairman of the House Ways and Means health subcommittee; and his successor, Charles Rangel.

Shortly after the 1978 elections, Senator Long made quite a dramatic move; he decided to mark up national health insurance in early 1979, before the administration's plan was announced, and proceed to actual drafting sessions. Long's move prodded administration officials into an accelerated timetable for their proposal. They had been actively working on the proposal, at President Carter's personal insistence, through 1978. After Long's action, they announced a first-phase proposal that included catastrophic coverage, help for the poor and near-poor, maternal and child benefits, and several other features; all in the rubric of a government plan that appealed to some liberals more than the revised Kennedy-labor approach.

So in 1979, there were several serious proposals under consideration: Long's, the administration's, the revised Kennedy-labor plan, and some others. Figure 1-1 shows the degree to which my health respondents paid attention to various types of proposals. There can be little doubt that they were indeed receiving a great deal of notice.

The rest of the story goes beyond the agenda-setting phase. But in brief, the whole thing fell through. National health insurance ran afoul of (1) substantial worries in the administration that the enactment of any plan would create imposing pressures on the federal budget, (2) a national mood that seemed to prefer smaller government, and (3) the inability to gather a unified coalition around one proposal.

What accounts for these ebbs and flows of attention to national health insurance? What conditions would increase the chances for enactment? How impor-

Figure 1-1

Discussion of Catastrophic, Kennedy-Labor, and Administration National Health Insurance Proposals

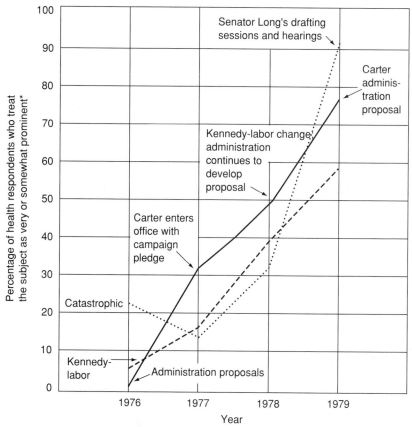

* For coding details, see Appendix.

tant are such prominent figures as Carter, Kennedy, and Long? In retrospect, given the budget constraints and perceived national mood, how could advocates have thought this was the right time? Indeed, how can one tell when an idea's time is coming?

Deregulation: Aviation, Trucking, Railroads

Our third case study describes the progress of proposals for economic deregulation in various transportation modes—aviation, trucking, and railroads.[5] We concentrate on economic, not safety, regulation: government regulation of routes, service, entry into markets, and rates. In transportation, these activities

[5]There is quite a bit of writing on deregulation. For an excellent overview, see Martha Derthick and Paul J. Quirk, *The Politics of Deregulation* (Washington, D.C.: The Brookings Institution, 1985). An earlier statement of some of their results is in Paul J. Quirk and Martha Derthick, "Congressional Support for Pro-Competitive Regulatory Reform," paper at the annual meeting of the American Political Science Association, 1981.

centered on the Civil Aeronautics Board (CAB) for aviation and on the Interstate Commerce Commission (ICC) for trucking and rail.

Government regulation of these industries started with the founding of the ICC to regulate the railroads, back in the nineteenth century. Regulation was supposedly started to protect consumers and shippers from gouging by the rail monopolies, and to protect fledgling industries from cutthroat competition until they became established. Regulations developed and were extended to trucking and to aviation, a formidable body of administrative law and bureaucratic superstructure evolved, and carriers of regulated commodities found themselves laboring under (and protected by) a considerable corpus of regulations and regulators. In the 1960s and 1970s, complaints mounted about the effects of this regulatory apparatus. Some carriers who wanted to enter new markets were prevented from doing so by government regulation. In some instances, regulated carriers protested that they were being forced to serve marginally profitable or even unprofitable markets. Public policy analysts wrote of the inefficiencies produced by regulation. And everybody complained about the red tape.

During the 1960s, there was a burgeoning of academic work on subjects relating to regulation, springing from economists' work on natural monopoly and economies of scale. This substantial body of academic theory essentially argued that economic regulation by government in an industry that could be regulated by marketplace forces only produces inefficiencies. If entry into markets is naturally easy, then marketplace competition could regulate rates and services provided. In the case of trucking, for instance, the economists argued that it is relatively easy to enter markets and compete with established carriers because the cost of obtaining a truck is much lower than the cost of, say, starting a railroad. Hence, if government were to stop regulating entry, rates, and service, the natural forces of competition would do the regulating for the consumer, and society would save the costs of the regulatory apparatus.

The 1960s and 1970s also saw an increasingly anti-government mood in the public at large, or so seasoned politicians perceived. With the shocks that such occurrences as the Vietnam War, busing, urban unrest, and economic difficulties brought to the political system, politicians detected a feeling among their constituents that government can't solve every problem or, at the extreme, that government can't do anything right. The mood seemed to swing, after the enactment of Lyndon Johnson's great society programs, away from support for ambitious new government programs toward a feeling that government is too big, too cumbersome, and too expensive. Taxpayer revolts in California and elsewhere reinforced this interpretation.

The Nixon administration drew up a package of transportation deregulation proposals designed to ease restrictions on entry and to reduce government control over rates and service. But the Ford administration started the major legislative push. President Gerald Ford himself gave the advocates of deregulation in his administration a great deal of support in their effort to formulate, publicize, and push for congressional enactment of their proposals. He sent up bills dealing with each of the transportation modes, and while not successful in obtaining enactment, he did set the stage for an effort that ultimately would bear fruit.

Sensing the potential popularity of deregulation as a consumer issue, Senator Edward Kennedy also made aviation deregulation one of his major projects. He used his chairmanship of the Judiciary Subcommittee on Administrative Practices and Procedures to hold hearings into the stewardship of the Civil Aeronautics Board and to give national exposure to advocates of regulatory reform. Then Senator Howard Cannon, the chairman of the Commerce Subcommittee on Aviation, felt obliged to hold hearings as well, partly in response to the administration and partly to seize back his jurisdiction over aviation within the Senate which he felt Kennedy had usurped.

Cannon's hearings, mostly dominated by airline after airline opposing deregulation, were noteworthy for two unusual elements. First, a few airlines broke the united front of opposition and favored some version of deregulation. Second and more dramatic, the CAB itself testified in favor of drastically curtailing its own jurisdiction. CAB's senior staff had studied the issue and concluded that the economic arguments for deregulation did appropriately apply to the aviation industry, and John Robson, President Ford's appointee as chairman, agreed. Apparently, the simple weight of the ideas persuaded them.

In 1976, Jimmy Carter made the general theme of "getting government off your back" one of the major selling points of his campaign. Once he got into office, his administration was primed for suggestions about how government intrusion in the private sector might be reduced. Because of the groundwork laid by both the Ford administration and Congress, aviation deregulation was ready to go. Railroad deregulation had been addressed to some degree in the acts dealing with the Penn Central collapse. Trucking was widely perceived as more difficult than aviation, due to the united and formidable opposition of the regulated truckers and the Teamsters. So the administration chose to concentrate on aviation deregulation and, furthermore, chose to use the Kennedy-Cannon bill as their vehicle, rather than working up their own proposal from scratch. For a time, the Department of Transportation dragged their heels, but Carter's personal commitment to aviation deregulation simply steamrollered them into acquiescence.

Carter also named Alfred Kahn to head the CAB and appointed several proreform members to the board. Kahn and his associates moved very vigorously in the direction of deregulation on their own, granting airlines permission to experiment with competitive pricing and market entry. It is possible that they went farther than the law technically allowed, or at least interpreted the law rather creatively. The results of the deregulation started by the CAB looked at first blush to be extremely promising: lower fares for consumers, higher profits for airlines, and little diminution of service. Given the groundwork laid by the Ford administration, the consensus developing on Capitol Hill, the new push from the Carter administration, the division within the industry, and the seemingly successful foray into the field by the CAB, an aviation deregulation bill did pass the Congress and was signed by President Carter in 1978.

At that point, policy makers' attention turned with a vengeance to the other transportation modes, as Figure 1-2 shows. After its success in aviation, the administration could take on the truckers and Teamsters more easily than they could have as the first battleground. The appropriateness of the lessons from aviation as applied to other areas could be debated at length, but politically the

Figure 1-2

Discussion of Deregulation: Aviation, Rail, Trucking

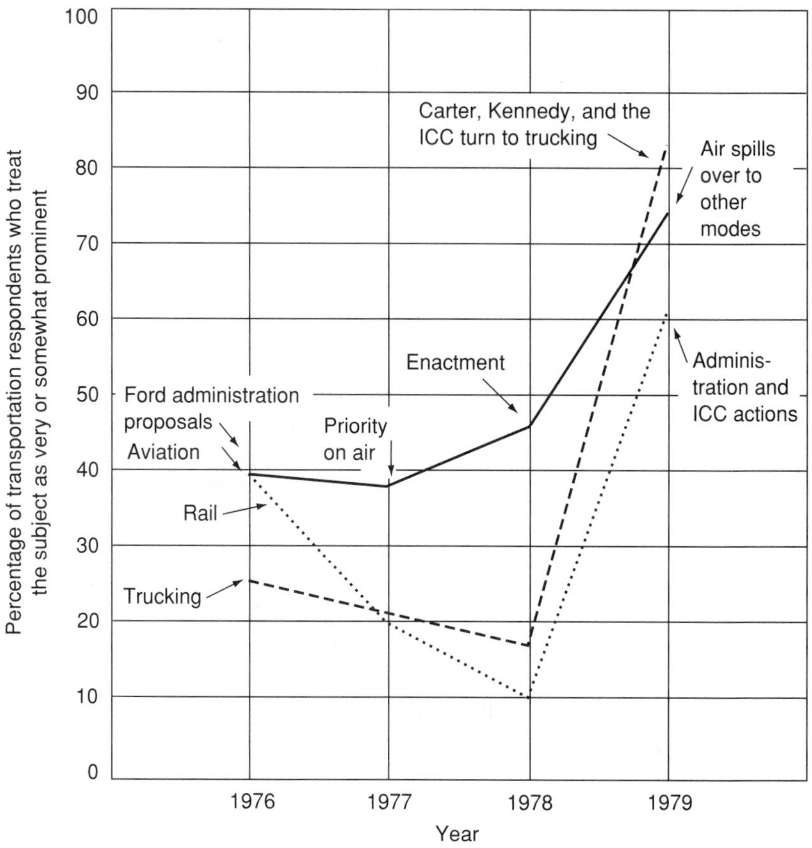

momentum seemed irresistible. Thus aviation broke the floodgates, resulting in movement in the other transportation modes and the extension of deregulation talk into communications, health, occupational safety, and many other areas. Toward the end of the Carter administration, both trucking and rail deregulation bills were approved by Congress and signed by the president.

Was this momentum actually irresistible? What made it so powerful? Did arcane academic theories really affect these events? Why did the national mood seem more receptive to these proposals in the 1970s than in the 1960s?

Waterway User Charges

Our last case study is the imposition of a waterway user charge, enacted in 1978.[6] Waterways were the last transportation mode to be provided to users without a charge. Highways were built with fuel taxes paid by commercial and

---

[6]For an account of the development of the issue during the late 1970s, see T. R. Reid, *Congressional Odyssey: The Saga of a Senate Bill* (San Francisco: W. H. Freeman, 1980).

pleasure users. Airports were constructed with the aid of a trust fund financed by a ticket tax. Railroad rights-of-way were furnished by land grants, but then built and maintained through expenditures by the railroads. When it came to waterway improvements, however, all of the work of the Army Corps of Engineers—dams, locks, channels, dredging, and canals—was paid for by general taxpayers. Proposals for some form of user charge—fuel taxes, lockage fees, or license fees—had been advanced for decades. But they had always run into the opposition of the owners of barges, pleasure boaters, the partisans of the Corps on the Hill, and the shippers of such bulk commodities as grain and coal who would eventually pay higher shipping costs if a user charge were enacted. Railroads supported a waterway user charge, reasoning that free use of government-financed facilities gave their waterway competitors an unfair advantage. The policy arguments surrounding the issue were very familiar through this long process of debate.

Some of the waterway facilities were falling into serious disrepair. In particular, attention during the late 1960s and early 1970s centered on Lock and Dam 26, on the Mississippi River at Alton, Illinois. This facility, a bottleneck that affected shipping for the entire length of the river, was in such serious disrepair that something needed to be done. Water leaked through it, parts of it were crumbling, it was repeatedly closed for repairs, and after a few more years of use, it could give way altogether. The required rebuilding would cost more than $400 million. So barge owners and operators pushed hard for the federal funding to rebuild Lock and Dam 26.

As the hearings droned on through the summer of 1976 before the Senate subcommittee of Public Works, Senator Pete Domenici, a first-term Republican from New Mexico, started to toy with the idea of imposing a user charge as a way to pay for a new Lock and Dam 26. He knew that taking on this cause would put him at odds with some powerful senators, including Russell Long of Louisiana, the chairman of the Finance Committee, so for some time Senator Domenici resisted the urgings of his staffers that he push for the user charge. But the story goes that he became so infuriated at the testimony of the barge interests, who were asking for federal money for Lock and Dam 26 while staunchly resisting any talk of a user charge, that he decided to introduce and push hard for a bill. His strategy was to tie the user charge to the rebuilding that the barge interests and shippers wanted so badly: no user charge, no Lock and Dam 26. He and his staffers plunged into the fight with great energy, reams of information and argumentation, and great political acumen.

In the incoming Carter administration, policy makers in the Department of Transportation saw this as an opportunity to impose a waterway user charge for the first time in history. President Carter was persuaded to announce that he would veto any authorization for Lock and Dam 26 that was not accompanied by a user charge bill. With the combination of senators, the Department of Transportation, and the president linking Lock and Dam 26 to the revenue issue, even the barge and shipping interests ended up supporting a less ambitious version of a user charge. See Figure 1-3 for my transportation respondents' attention to the issue.

The intricacies of enactment are a story by themselves. At many points, Domenici's project was threatened with defeat. Major compromises were

Figure 1-3

Discussion of Waterway User Charges and Lock and Dam 26

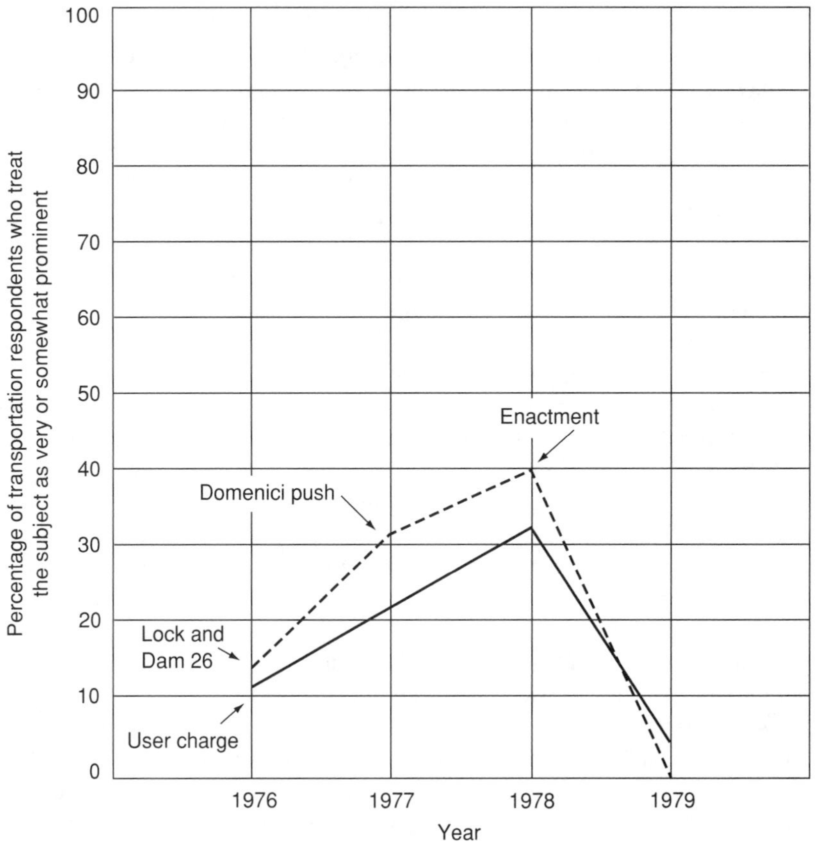

needed to obtain sufficient votes to pass any user charge bill, so the version finally passed in 1978 was less ambitious than Domenici's original proposal. But
since this is a book on agenda setting rather than enactment, we needn't tarry
long on this portion of the story, fascinating as it is. Opponents figured the bill
was the best they could get under the circumstances. Proponents felt they had at
least established the principle of imposing a charge, and looked forward to
years and decades of ratcheting it up.

Did this case really turn on the anger of one junior, minority senator? How
critical was the happenstance of a crumbling Lock and Dam 26? Why, after
years of familiarity with the issue, did this particular time prove to be right?

Some Subjects Never Get onto the Agenda

Consider Table 1-1, which shows some subjects in health and transportation
that were discussed very infrequently. These figures present several interesting
puzzles. Why do items that deserve attention never receive it? Everybody real-
izes that the population is aging, and that long-term medical care will increasingly be a pressing problem for the society. In view of these demographic pro-

Table 1-1

Subjects Discussed Infrequently*

Health	
Maternal and child care	14%
Long-term care	13
Government delivery (Community Centers, Veterans Administration, Public Health Service)	11
Fraud and abuse	11
FDA and drugs	9
Mental health	5
Transportation	
Environmental impact	16
Pipeline (including coal slurry)	15
Safety	14
Buses	13
Rail nationalization	7

*For each subject, the number is the percentage of health or transportation respondents who treated the subject as very or somewhat prominent, adding across all four years, for the highest-valued variable associated with the subject. See discussion of groupings in the footnote to Table 6-1. Health N = 133: Transportation N = 114.

jections, why was the subject of long-term care discussed so infrequently by health specialists in the late 1970s? In view of the tremendous amount of attention the media gave to fraud and abuse during this very period, why did health policy makers and those around them refer so little to that subject when discussing issues that were occupying their attention? Why are intercity buses so far out of sight? Why does a subject like transportation safety, so prominent only a few years earlier, fade so quickly from high agenda status?

By contrast, the cost of medical care was prominently discussed in over 80 percent of my health interviews in most of these years. Why does a subject like cost come to dominate an agenda like health so completely?

Some subjects receive a lot of attention, while others are neglected. This book tries to understand why.

SOME EXPLANATIONS

Our discussion so far has presented a series of interesting descriptions of policy changes and subjects that never rise on the agenda. It has also left us with many questions about *why* changes occur and why some subjects are more prominent than others. In general, two categories of factors might affect agenda setting and the specification of alternatives: the participants who are active, and the processes by which agenda items and alternatives come into prominence.

Participants

The president, the Congress, bureaucrats in the executive branch, and various forces outside of government (including the media, interest groups, political parties, and the general public) could all be sources of agenda items and alternatives. Thus agenda setting may involve the transfer of items from a non-governmental, "systemic" agenda to a governmental, "formal" agenda, partly through the mobilization of the relevant publics by leaders.[7] Or issues may reach the agenda through diffusion of ideas in professional circles and among policy elites, particularly bureaucrats.[8] Or changes in the agenda may result from a change in party control or in intraparty ideological balances brought about by elections.[9] Thus a critical locus of initiative may be parties and elected officials. One of the purposes of this study is to ascertain how frequently and under what conditions each of these participants is important, and to determine what sorts of interactions there might be among them.

This book sheds some light on the long-smoldering topic of the sources of initiative, partly by tracking the progression of ideas from one place to another over the years under observation, and partly by learning how seriously the people close to policy making treat these possible influences. What is the relative importance of president and Congress? Within the executive branch, how important are political appointees as opposed to career civil servants? In Congress, what are the respective contributions of staff and members? Do agenda items well up from the public, or is the process better understood as a "top-down" sequence? Within the public, what is the place of general public opinion, as contrasted with organized interest groups? How often do ideas come from people like policy analysts, researchers, academics, and consultants, or are such people regarded as quaint irrelevancies? How important are the mass media in focusing officials' attention on some problems and contributing to their neglect of other problems, or do media report attention rather than create it?

Processes of Agenda Setting and Alternative Specification

It would surely be unsatisfying to end the story with the importance of various players in the game. We want to know something about the game itself. So aside from the participants, we are interested in the processes by which agendas are set and alternatives are specified. We will deal in this book with three kinds of processes: problems, policies, and politics.

One influence on agendas might be the inexorable march of problems pressing in on the system. A crisis or prominent event might signal the emergence of such problems. The collapse of the Penn Central Railroad or the crash of a DC-

[7]For a statement of this perspective, see Roger W. Cobb and Charles D. Elder, *Participation in American Politics: The Dynamics of Agenda-Building* (Boston: Allyn and Bacon, 1972), pp. 14–16, 34–35, 85–89.

[8]For a treatment of such a process, see Jack L. Walker. "The Diffusion of Innovations Among the American States," *American Political Science Review* 68 (September 1969): 880—899.

[9]For treatments of the effects of realignments on policy agendas, see Benjamin Ginsberg, "Elections and Public Policy," *American Political Science Review* 70 (March 1976): 41–49; Barbara Deckard Sinclair, "Party Realignment and the Transformation of the Political Agenda," *American Political Science Review* 71 (September 1977): 940–953; and David Brady, "Congressional Party Realignment and Transformations of Public Policy in Three Realignment Eras," *American Journal of Political Science* 26 (May 1982: 333–360.

10, for example, result in some focus on the financial problems of the railroads or on issues in air safety. Another way of becoming aware of a problem might be change in a widely respected indicator: costs of medical care or the size of the Medicare budget increase; energy consumed per ton mile decreases with the application of a given technology; the incidence of rubella or polio inches up; the number of highway deaths per passenger mile rises or falls. How often is governmental attention to problems driven by such indicators, by dramatic events, or by other suggestions that there might be a problem which needs addressing? Indeed, how does a given condition get defined as a problem for which government action is an appropriate remedy?

A second contributor to governmental agendas and alternatives might be a process of gradual accumulation of knowledge and perspectives among the specialists in a given policy area, and the generation of policy proposals by such specialists. Academics' arguments that economic regulation of trucking or airlines only produces inefficiencies, or studies that suggest a greater supply of doctors increases rather than decreases medical costs might gradually diffuse among policy makers, producing perspectives that might make them more receptive to some proposals than to others. The development of a new technology, such as a shunt making renal dialysis possible or a markedly more efficient storage battery for electric automobiles, might create considerable pressure for policy change. But independent of science or knowledge, ideas may sweep policy communities like fads, or may be built gradually through a process of constant discussion, speeches, hearings, and bill introductions. What part does each of these communication or diffusion processes play in agenda setting and alternative specification?[10]

The foregoing suggests that at some points in this book we will forsake the usual political science preoccupation with pressure and influence, and instead take excursions into the world of ideas. One inquiry of the study, indeed, is the extent to which arm-twisting, muscle, and other such metaphors of pressure realistically describe the forces that drive the agenda, and the extent to which persuasion and the diffusion of ideas, good or bad, affect the subjects of attention. How much do ideas like equity or efficiency affect the participants? More broadly, what values affect the processes, and how much are people motivated by their desire to change the existing order to bring it into line with their conception of the ideal order? How much do they acquire new ideas by studying situations similar to their own in states or other countries? How much do they learn through experimentation, either formally designed experiments or cruder personal experiences? How much does feedback from the operation of existing programs affect the agenda?

Third, political processes affect the agenda. Swings of national mood, vagaries of public opinion, election results, changes of administration, and turnover in Congress all may have powerful effects. How much change in the agenda and in the seriously considered alternatives is produced by a change of administration, a change of congressional committee chairs, or a marked

---

[10]On diffusion in policy communities, see Walker, "Diffusion of Innovations," op. cit.; and Hugh Heclo, "Issue Networks and the Executive Establishment," in Anthony King, ed. *The New American Political System* (Washington, D.C.: American Enterprise Institute, 1978), pp. 87–124.

turnover of personnel in Congress through retirement or defeat at the polls? How much does politicians' receptivity to certain ideas depend on such considerations as maintaining or building electoral coalitions, being reelected, or running for higher office? How much do important people compete for policy turf, and what effect does such competition have? How do important people judge such a vague phenomenon as a shift in national mood?

Each of the three processes—problem recognition, generation of policy proposals, and political events—can serve as an impetus or as a constraint. As an impetus, items are promoted to higher agenda prominence, as when a new administration makes possible the emergence of a new battery of proposals. As a constraint,[11] items are prevented from rising on the agenda, as when a budget constraint operates to rule out the emergence of items that are perceived as being too costly. Some items may not rise on the agenda because of the financial cost, the lack of acceptance by the public, the opposition of powerful interests, or simply because they are less pressing than other items in the competition for attention.

Finally, the study began with several general musings on the nature of the processes to be examined. Does change take place incrementally, in gradual, short steps, or does one observe sudden, discontinuous change? If both are present, does one pattern describe one part of the process better than another part?' Do the participants seem to proceed in an orderly process of planning, in which they identify problems, specify goals, and attend to the most efficient means of achieving these goals? Even if some single participants proceed in this orderly, rational manner, does the process involving many participants take on a less orderly character, with the outcome a product of bargaining among the participants? Or is the process even more free from than that, with problems, proposals, and politics floating in and out, joined by fortuitous events or by the appearance on the scene of a skillful entrepreneur who assembles the previously disjointed pieces? Instead of problem solving, do advocates first generate their pet solutions and then look for problems coming along to which to attach their proposals? How often is plain dumb luck responsible?

A BRIEF PREVIEW OF THE BOOK

The last few pages have presented a rather formidable array of puzzles. Not all of them will be completely assembled in the pages of this book. But answers to many of these questions and partial answers to others, combined with attempts to build theory about these processes from careful empirical observation, will advance our understanding.

We are now ready to begin our journey through the labyrinth of policy formation. We first distinguish between participants and processes. In principle, each of the active participants can be involved in each of the important processes—problem recognition, policy generation, and politics. Policy is not the sole

[11]An excellent summary of constraints on agenda change is in Roger W. Cobb and Charles D. Elder, "Communications and Public Policy," in Dan Nimmo and Keith Sanders, eds. *Handbook of Political Communications* (Beverly Hills: Sage, 1981), Chapter 14, particularly pp. 402–408.

province of analysts, for instance, nor is politics the sole province of politicians. In practice, as we will see, participants specialize to a degree in one or another process, but participants can be seen as conceptually different from processes.

We will begin with participants in Chapter 2 and 3. We will discover, perverse as it might sound to some readers, that textbooks are not always wrong: If any one set of participants in the policy process is important in the shaping of the agenda, it is elected officials and their appointees, rather than career bureaucrats or nongovernmental actors. We will also discuss the clusters of the actors which emerge, arguing that a visible cluster made up of such actors as the president and prominent members of Congress has more effect on the agenda, while a hidden cluster that includes specialists in the bureaucracy and in professional communities affects the specification of the alternatives from which authoritative choices are made.

We will then turn our attention in the remaining chapters of the book to the processes which govern the system. In Chapter 4, an overview of these processes, we first discuss the limitations of three common approaches. A search for origins of public policies turns out to be futile. Comprehensive, rational policy making is portrayed as impractical for the most part, although there are occasions where it is found. Incrementalism describes parts of the process, particularly the gradual evolution of proposals or policy changes, but does not describe the more discontinuous or sudden agenda change. Instead of these approaches, we use a revised version of the Cohen-March-Olsen garbage can model of organizational choice to understand agenda setting and alternative generation.[12] We conceive of three process streams flowing through the system—streams of problems, policies, and politics. They are largely independent of one another, and each develops according to its own dynamics and rules. But at some critical junctures the three streams are joined, and the greatest policy changes grow out of that coupling of problems, policy proposals, and politics.

Each of the three next chapters discusses one of the three streams. In Chapter 5, we consider how problems come to be recognized and how conditions come to be defined as problems. Problems are brought to the attention of people in and around government by systematic indicators, by focusing events like crises and disasters, or by feedback from the operation of current programs. People define conditions as problems by comparing current conditions with their values concerning more ideal states of affairs, by comparing their own performance with that of other countries, or by putting the subject into one category rather than another.

The generation of policy proposals, the subject of Chapter 6, resembles a process of biological natural selection. Many ideas are possible in principle, and float around in a "policy primeval soup" in which specialists try out their ideas in a variety of ways—bill introductions, speeches, testimony, papers, and conversation. In that consideration, proposals are floated, come into contact with one another, are revised and combined with one another, and floated again. But the proposals that survive to the status of serious consideration meet several criteria, including their technical feasibility, their fit with dominant val-

---

[12]Michael Cohen, James March, and Johan Olsen, "A Garbage Can Model of Organizational Choice," *Administrative Science Quarterly* 17 (March 1972): 1–25.

ues and the current national mood, their budgetary workability, and the political support or opposition they might experience. Thus the selection system narrows the set of conceivable proposals and selects from that large set a short list of proposals that is actually available for serious consideration.

The political stream described in Chapter 7 is composed of such factors as swings of national mood, administration or legislative turnover, and interest group pressure campaigns. Potential agenda items that are congruent with the current national mood, that enjoy interest group support or lack organized opposition, and that fit the orientations of the prevailing legislative coalitions or current administration are more likely to rise to agenda prominence than items that do not meet such conditions. In particular, turnover of key participants, such as a change of administration, has powerful effects on policy agendas. The combination of perceived national mood and turnover of elected officials particularly affects agendas, while the balance of organized forces is more likely to affect the alternatives considered.

The separate streams of problems, policies, and politics come together at certain critical times. Solutions become joined to problems, and both of them are joined to favorable political forces. This coupling is most likely when policy windows—opportunities for pushing pet proposals or conceptions of problems—are open. As we argue in Chapter 8, windows are opened either by the appearance of compelling problems or by happenings in the political stream. Thus agendas are set by problems or politics, and alternatives are generated in the policy stream. Policy entrepreneurs, people who are willing to invest their resources in pushing their pet proposals or problems, are responsible not only for prompting important people to pay attention, but also for coupling solutions to problems and for coupling both problems and solutions to politics. While governmental agendas are set in the problems or political streams, the chances of items rising on a *decision* agenda—a list of items up for actual action—are enhanced if all three streams are coupled together. Significant movement, in other words, is much more likely if problems, policy proposals, and politics are all coupled into a package.

Chapter 9 then summarizes what we have learned and states our major conclusions. Chapter 10, written for the second edition, adds new case studies and further reflections. Some readers, if they prefer to preview the larger picture before seeing the details, may wish to skip to Chapters 4 and 9 before reading the rest of the book. Readers who wish to be more fully informed of the study's methods are advised to examine the Appendix before proceeding. Those who are more interested in processes than in participants may wish to skim Chapters 2 and 3, proceeding to Chapters 4 through 9. Many readers will follow the order of chapters as they are presented.

The processes we will discuss are extraordinarily complex, and the telling of the story is thus complicated. Unlike the juggler who keeps several bowling pins in the air at once, we will concentrate on one pin at a time, allowing the rest to clatter to the floor. If readers are patient, they will notice that the seemingly neglected pins will each receive attention in their turn, and that we will finally assemble them into a pattern as coherent as is allowed by the actual character of the observed processes. We will follow Einstein's sage advice: "Everything should be made as simple as possible, but not simpler."

CHAPTER 2

Participants on the Inside of Government

One logical place to begin our story is with the players in the game. That discussion will establish which players are important, which players are thought to be important but turn out not to be, and the ways they relate to each other and to the agenda-setting process. We will discuss three subjects: (1) the importance of each participant, (2) the ways each is important (e.g., whether each affects agendas, alternatives, or both), and (3) the resources available to each participant. We start with this chapter on actors inside of government, including the administration, civil servants, and Congress. In the next chapter, we turn to actors outside of government: interest groups, academics, media, and public opinion. That inside-outside distinction is partly artificial, but it serves as a rough way to organize the discussion.

THE ADMINISTRATION

People in and around federal policy making are often preoccupied with "the administration." When the administration considers a given issue a top-priority item, many other participants do too. And when advocates of a given proposal find that they do not have a receptive ear in the administration, they often must downgrade their chances for a serious hearing, at least for the time being. Although it would be overstating the matter to say that the administration always dominates the government's policy agenda, the administration still figures very prominently indeed in agenda setting.

Actually, when people refer to "the administration," they may have in mind one of, or a combination of, three actors: the president himself, the staff in the

Executive Office that is responsible to the president, and the political appointees in departments and bureaus who are responsible to the president. We will turn presently to a consideration of each of the three separate components of the administration. But the administration in some guise—either the president himself, or the presidential staff, or political appointees in departments and bureaus—were discussed as being important in 94 percent of my interviews.[1] This same combination of actors was coded as important in 22 of the 23 case studies used in this research. (See the Appendix for coding details.) These figures, the highest for any set of actors we will discuss in these two chapters, suggest the large extent to which the administration is a player to be reckoned with in the policy formation process.

As far as the relative importance of each of the three components of the administration is concerned, Table 2-1 shows that respondents treated all three of them as important in a bit over one-third of the interviews. Sorting through the comparisons among them, the president himself and his political appointees in departments and bureaus are mentioned with about equal frequency, while the staff in the White House and in the Executive Office of the President is discussed less often as being of serious consequence, independent of the others. The prominence of the departments in these figures speaks not so much to dominance over the other two but rather to the frequency with which an administration agenda is defined by the participants as primarily a department concern. Reform of the food and drug law during the Carter administration, for instance, was primarily the responsibility of the Secretary of Health, Education, and Welfare and the head of the Food and Drug Administration, working with the

---

[1]When citing such statistics, we will use the coding categories discussed in the Appendix. "Important" in the text of the book refers to the combination of "very" or "somewhat" important coding categories, unless otherwise noted. Similarly, a "prominent" agenda item is the combination of the "very" and "somewhat" prominent categories.

Table 2-1

*Importance of Administration Components**

President himself	Department appointees very or somewhat important		Department appointees, little or no importance	
	President's staff very-some	President's staff little-no	President's staff very-some	President's staff little-no
Very or somewhat important	36%	27%	4%	8%
Little or no importance	4%	15%	0%	6%

*The percentage in each cell is the percentage of all interviews (n = 247) that falls into the cell. The eight entries total to 100 percent. Thus 36 percent of all interviews treated president, appointees, and staff as very or somewhat important. Add cells to determine totals for each of the three components. Thus 75 percent (36 + 27 + 4 + 8) treat president himself as very or somewhat important, or 44 percent (36 + 4 + 4 + 0) treat staff as very or somewhat important.

relevant staffers and members on the Hill. Many agenda items are left to the departments in this fashion, with "the administration" in effect defined as the department or even its subunits. But as we shall see, there is little doubt in the minds of the participants concerning the ability of the president to dominate the agenda-setting process within the administration if he chooses to do so.

The President Himself

The old saw goes that "the president proposes and Congress disposes." There is certainly plenty of confirmation in the interviews that the president can single-handedly set the agendas, not only of people in the executive branch, but also of people in Congress and outside of government. As a lobbyist said, "Obviously, when a president sends up a bill, it takes first place in the queue. All other bills take second place." No other single actor in the political system has quite the capability of the president to set agendas in given policy areas for all who deal with those policies. In quantitative terms, the president himself, as opposed to "the administration" or "the White House," is considered very or somewhat important in three-quarters of the interviews, and very important in 31 percent.

Examples of his importance abound in the interviews and case studies. The costs of medical care had always been a prominent agenda item through this period. But specific references to hospital cost containment as an agenda item of at least some prominence jumped from 18 percent of the 1976 health interviews to 81 percent in 1977. Costs had not jumped in that fashion during that one year, nor had policy makers' awareness of the general problem increased. Instead, the Carter administration made hospital cost containment their top priority in health and one of their top priorities in domestic policy. Their proposal then occupied a major portion of the time and energy of the relevant congressional committees. To take another instance, trucking deregulation was treated as important in 16 percent of the transportation interviews in 1978, and jumped to 83 percent in 1979. Although there were several reasons for that dramatic shift, a prominent explanation is that the Carter administration started its major push in the motor carrier area in 1979 after the success of airline regulatory reform in the previous year. Many respondents told me of President Carter's personal commitment to trucking deregulation.

The president, of course, does not totally control the policy agenda, for many events beyond his control impinge on the agendas of various participants and even on his own agenda. Every president—Carter with Iran, Johnson with Vietnam, Hoover with the depression—has discovered to his sorrow that events beyond his control impinge on his agenda. Still, there is little doubt that the president remains a powerful force in agenda setting, particularly compared to other actors.

Setting the agenda and getting one's way, however, are two very different things. The president may be able to dominate and even determine the policy agenda, but is unable to dominate the alternatives that are seriously considered, and is unable to determine the final outcome.[2] This is one place where our distinction between the agenda and the alternatives, discussed in Chapter 1, becomes useful. The hospital cost containment issue again provides an example. The Carter initiative set the agenda for the health-related congressional committees, whose members spent substantial portions of their hearing and markup time over three years on this subject. But the administration proposal, which provided for caps on inflation rates and limits on capital expenditures, was only one of several options considered. People on the Hill also considered defeating all proposals and doing nothing, providing for a voluntary effort by the hospitals with the imposition of government controls if the effort failed, and a longer-range strategy including reimbursement reforms. One Hill staffer said, "This particular piece of legislation is not near and dear to the heart of anyone on Capitol Hill. The ones that favor it, favor it only out of a sense of obligation and duty, out of a sense that they must do something about cost inflation, and out of loyalty to the White House." This sense of obligation and loyalty could carry the president's initiative as far as agenda status, but could not restrict the range of alternatives to his proposal that were seriously considered.

The reasons for the president's preeminent position in agenda setting are by now quite familiar to readers of the literature on the presidency. The first of these reasons is a set of institutional resources, including the veto and the prerogative to hire and fire. To fill key policy making positions, the president nominates people who are responsive to his conception of the agenda for their agencies. If he discovers that his appointees are not responsive concerning items of major importance to him, they usually don't last long in the job. The veto also looms large as an institutional advantage that powerfully affects policy agendas of all participants. Waterway user charges moved into prominence on the transportation agenda during 1977 and 1978, for example, partly because President Carter threatened to veto improvements for Lock and Dam 26 on the Mississippi River, a project the barge interests wanted very much, unless it was accompanied by a user charge bill. Or as an avid proponent of national health insurance told me in 1976, congressional initiative in the absence of presidential support takes two-thirds. "You couldn't get two-thirds of the Congress to vote for the Ten Commandments. With a president who was behind national health insurance, we'd only need half, and it would be a completely different ball game."

The second presidential resource is organizational. At least relative to Congress, the executive branch is a more unitary decision-making entity. The literature on the presidency and on bureaucratic politics appropriately cautions us not to overestimate the president's ability to command the executive branch.[3] Nonetheless, there remain times in the executive branch when bureaucratic conflict is resolved after a fashion. In particular, once the president

[2]For another study that suggests the president affects agendas more than outcomes, see Jeffrey Cohen, "Passing the President's Program," Ph.D. diss., University of Michigan, 1979, pp. 104–111.

[3]For example, see Richard E. Neustadt, *Presidential Power* (New York: Wiley, 1976), Chapter 2; Thomas E. Cronin, *The State of the Presidency,* 2nd ed. (Boston: Little, Brown, 1980). Chapter 3; and Graham T. Allison *Essence of Decision* (Boston: Little, Brown, 1971), Chapters 3 and 4.

makes clear his concept of the appropriate policy agenda, his conception is likely to carry the day. Many well-informed respondents, for instance, told me that President Carter had personally intervened in the intra-administration struggle between national health insurance advocates and economic advisors, personally deciding to present a plan and personally determining the major contours of the proposal. In such a case, some sniping by the losers through leaks or less-than-enthusiastic endorsements is still possible. But the president's involvement has at least determined the participants' agendas: they will be working on national health insurance.

In contrast, Congress operates with 535 members and 535 agendas, each with some claim on the institution. Some of the members are more important than others, to be sure, but Congress has no coordinating mechanisms or incentives to cooperate comparable to those operating in the executive branch. With a major issue like national health insurance, people wait for the president's proposal. As a Hill staffer put it:

> Why should we lay our lives on the line and our electoral popularity on the line when we don't know what the administration is going to propose? Is it going to be comprehensive? Is it going to be moms and kiddies? Is it going to be catastrophic? Is it going to be private or public or what mix? Is it going to be social security based? All of these uncertainties make people very nervous. They're being asked to support this cost containment thing and they don't know what they are saving the money for.

The third presidential resource is a command of public attention, which can be converted into pressure on other governmental officials to adopt the president's agenda. One health respondent used the example of the overbuilding of hospitals to make the point: "You know, Teddy Roosevelt said that the presidency is a bully pulpit. There's a tremendous ability for the president to get public attention. Too many beds were there all the time, but when the president of the United States says that we've got unnecessary beds, then people notice that." A congressional committee staffer illustrated the conversion of this advantage into concrete pressure by citing the flood of mail that ensues when the president goes on the offensive in a news conference.

There is also a partisan element to the president's ability to dominate the congressional agenda. In a period of divided government, congressional committee chairs feel less restraint in plunging ahead with their own agendas than they do when the White House is controlled by their own party. As a committee staffer said of national health insurance during the first year of the Carter administration. "We've decided that we're not going to fool around with this subject until we get the administration's proposal. We've waited around for eight years of Republican administrations anyway. We've held a lot of hearings in the past, and nothing has been enacted. Now that we've got a Democratic president telling us that he's going to do something about it, there's no way that we will go ahead with it on our own."

The public and partisan advantages depend on the state of presidential popularity, both in the mass public and among partisans and other elites in representatives' districts. The president is much more able to use that advantage when members of Congress perceive him as a popular figure than when he is seen as unpopular; there is less cost to crossing him and even a possible benefit when his popularity is low. This erosion of public and congressional support seems to plague all presidents after an initial honeymoon period. Paul Light argues persuasively that just as first-term presidents and their advisors are learning the ropes and acquiring the expertise in substance and in intra-Washington politics to be effective, their public popularity, favorable media coverage, and congressional support are slipping away.[4]

Finally, the president's impact on the agenda depends on his involvement. Official Washington has developed very sensitive antennae for measuring the subtleties of a presidential commitment. A president can mention an item in the State of the Union Address or in another public forum, but participants look for signs of commitment beyond the *pro forma* mention—phone calls, repeated requests to take up the issue, signs of actually using such powers of the office as the veto or the publicity advantages. A handwritten note from President Carter to Secretary of Transportation Brock Adams, for instance, expressing the president's reservations about large-scale, capital-intensive mass transit projects and his preference for lower-cost transit options, obviously set off a tremendous pattern of ripples throughout the transportation community, judging by how often it was mentioned in my interviews.

Presidential Staff

The second component of the administration is the staff in the White House and in the Executive Office which is responsible to the president. Some members of that staff are the top personal advisors to the president himself. Others are members of such Executive Office agencies as the Domestic Policy Staff, Council of Economic Advisors, and the Office of Management and Budget (OMB) who specialize in such subjects as health insurance and transportation deregulation. As Table 2-1 shows, presidential staff is discussed as being important in 44 percent of the interviews.[5] OMB is mentioned in similar terms in 26 percent of the interviews.[6] There are no differences of any consequence between health and transportation. In the case studies, White House and other presidential advisors were important in 11 of the 23 cases; OMB in 3 of the 23.

---

[4]See Paul C. Light, *The President's Agenda* (Baltimore: Johns Hopkins University Press, 1982), pp. 36–40.

[5]The 44 percent figure for presidential staff is a bit of an overestimate, since we coded undifferentiated mentions of "the administration" in the interviews as being both presidential staff and political appointees in departments and bureaus. Since there were many such references, that coding rule inflates the figure beyond literal mentions of White House advisors.

[6]Both presidential staff and OMB are coded as very or somewhat important in 15 percent, staff alone in 29 percent, OMB alone in 11 percent, and neither in 45 percent. A different administration with different priorities might produce greater OMB prominence. For example, David Stockman's OMB in the first year of the Reagan administration was clearly central.

In sum, these figures suggest that presidential advisors are quite important in agenda setting, but they are not among the most frequently discussed actors.

Presidential staffers are not discussed more frequently as important agenda-setting actors partly because many agenda items are delegated to a department or bureau level within the executive branch. But while some items are delegated downward, other items of greater importance are taken over by the president himself or by a handful of his closest advisors. As a former White House aide put it, "I discovered that at critical points I wouldn't necessarily be doing the deciding; it would be taken out of my hands." Or in the health area, a knowledgeable source discussed the national health insurance issue in 1978: "It's no secret that most of the presidential staff prefer delay because of the great press of unfinished items like welfare reform and so forth. But the president himself feels that he has a commitment to national health insurance and he insists on moving ahead."

That sort of information about national health insurance illustrates the place of the presidential staff in policy formation. To return to our distinction between the agenda and the alternatives, these staffers are more important in working on alternatives than in setting the agenda. The president and his top advisors, including top White House staff and cabinet appointees, generally establish a tone, which means setting the administration's agenda and deciding a few of the fundamental issues. Then it is up to the presidential staff to engage in the detailed negotiations—with the departments, the Hill, and the major interest groups—that will produce the administration's proposals and that will clarify the administration's bargaining positions as the proposals move through the legislative process. One HEW official used the 1978 national health insurance negotiations between President Carter and his top aides on the one hand, and Senator Kennedy and top representatives of organized labor on the other, to present a general perspective on the places of various actors:

> Those meetings are critical in settling a few large issues and in moving the whole subject matter along. But they are really dealing with the top one-half of one percent of the issues. They are really dealing with super macro questions, questions of general philosophy. So they're not too important in settling a lot of issues. They are more important in ordering people's perceptions. The secretary notices them, the undersecretary does, right down to the lower levels. It's not that Carter and Kennedy are going to sit down in a little room and write the bill. They couldn't possibly write the bill. But what these sessions do is create the impression of the priority that the administration is giving to the matter, so that the people further down who will write the bill will pay some attention to it. Out of the dozen or so things they could be working on, they will choose to write their health insurance paper first. And that's what really moves it along.

Political Appointees

The third component of the administration is the set of officials in departments and bureaus who are appointed by the president, ranging from cabinet secretaries and undersecretaries to heads of bureaus, administrations, or other such agencies. At least in traditional legal theory, such appointees should be critical policy makers since they presumably gain their authority from a presidential blessing and from the chain of command that it implies. But it has frequently been argued that presidential appointees become captured by their agencies, or that the professional civil servants find ways to circumvent the authority of their appointed superiors. Thus it is possible that appointees are less important than the traditional legal theory would indicate.

Actually, respondents in this study betrayed little of this revisionist thinking. Indeed, political appointees in departments and bureaus turn out to be among the most frequently mentioned actors in the political system. They were spontaneously treated as being very or somewhat important in 82 percent of the interviews, and very important in 26 percent.[7] As Table 2-1 shows, they are mentioned more frequently than staff in the White House or in the Executive Office of the President, and even slightly more frequently than the president himself. We coded these political appointees as very important in 7 of the 23 case studies, and as somewhat important in an additional 14.

One reason that attention to Health Maintenance Organizations increased from 3 percent of my 1977 interviews to 63 percent in 1979 was that the top-level appointees in the Department of Health, Education, and Welfare, particularly Undersecretary Hale Champion, undertook to promote HMOs as a major policy initiative of their administration. Or the department's 1978 war on smoking was seen as Secretary Joseph Califano's personal crusade, roundly criticized in some quarters as politically naive and the product of Califano's publicity-seeking, yet warmly approved in other quarters as an important move to change the public's health habits. Critics and proponents alike, though, attributed that spurt of the departmental promotion directly to Califano. As one respondent replied when asked why Califano took it on, alluding to the storm of controversy and the White House unease that it created, "I think it has come about because Califano is the first secretary in recent memory who has a set of certified bronzed testicles."

Even when the political appointees do not originate an idea, they still play a large part in placing it on the agendas of important people, both within and outside of their agencies. Many times, proposals and ideas float around within executive branch agencies for some time, without being taken very seriously. But should a high-level political appointee take an interest in the project, the issue suddenly attains much greater prominence. A high-level source from the Department of Transportation captured the essence of the process as "elevating" rather than creating issues:

> People at the secretary's level do not really discover issues. They elevate issues.
> The issues are all there. There is nothing that is new in what is available. The

---

[7]As with the case of presidential staff, the figures must be interpreted somewhat cautiously since undifferentiated mentions of "the administration" were coded as being both presidential staff and political appointees. So the importance of each is somewhat overestimated by these figures. Nevertheless, the noticeably greater frequency of discussion of political appointees indicates that respondents did regard them as important more often than White House or Executive Office staff.

question is, what will you elevate? The question is, what do you have sufficient
interest in to spend your time on?

Political appointees elevate issues from within their own agencies, but they
also arrive at some of their priorities from their interactions with the White
House. For the issues that demand presidential involvement, they generate substantial numbers of the alternatives from which White House people choose.
On those issues that interest the president or his immediate advisors, however,
there is little doubt on either side of the exchange where the ultimate authority
lies. There may be many attempts to convince the president of the justice of
one's position, and those attempts are often successful. But in the cases of disagreement between the president and his appointees over the major policy initiatives of the administration, the president's priorities—once they are made
clear—set the policy agendas for his appointees. For instance, many of my respondents reported that Transportation Secretary Brock Adams was lukewarm
about the Carter administration's priority on deregulation. When he let his
reservations be known, even in public, he "got run over" or "had the rug pulled
out from under him." He subsequently testified in favor of the proposal because
he had to be a "good soldier" or a "team player." On the other hand, one reputed reason that HEW Secretary Joseph Califano was fired in 1979 was that he
continued to whisper his opposition to Carter's new Department of Education
after the president's decision had been made.

One finds few instances of such confrontations because the parties avoid
them whenever possible. The appointee finds it prudent to bend with the presidential wind, and the president finds it politically embarrassing to be portrayed
as being at war with his major advisors. On occasion, cabinet secretaries and
other presidential appointees attempt to curry favor with the White House by
anticipating what the president would like to see and then moving decisively on
a proposal that will win presidential approval and gratitude, even though the
president did not order such action. Many of my informants portrayed
Secretary Califano's reorganization of HEW in that light. The basic ingredients
of the health part of the reorganization—the combination of Medicare,
Medicaid, and the Bureau of Quality Assurance into the new Health Care
Financing Administration—had been embodied in many proposals stretching
back for years, including memoranda internal to the department and legislation
introduced by Senator Herman Talmadge and others. Califano chose to "elevate" that issue for a complex of reasons, but a major reason was that it would
win approval for him at the White House. In respondent language:

> If you really want to look at the dynamics of the thing, here you had a president
> coming in who made a terrific emphasis in the campaign on reorganization of
> government, the supposed efficiencies that would come from reorganization,
> and so forth. So naturally, you have a set of cabinet officers who are vying with
> each other on who will make the best show of reorganization. This makes
> Califano look like the best, hardest working, most energetic, greatest go-getting
> cabinet officer.

Finally, notice a fundamental problem that political appointees have: their
impermanence. As one respondent put it, "Historically, secretaries don't last

very long." Their length of service is shorter than the president's two-term potential, and far shorter than the tenure of a senior member of Congress or a career civil servant. Among the many motivations of people like cabinet officers is their desire to have some effect on something, to "put their stamp on something." to "make their mark." One respondent encapsulated this desire to be remembered for some initiative by remarking, "All these guys get a little history-happy." If appointees are to make their mark, given their short tenure, they must make it quickly. The incentive thereby created to move rapidly is discussed in approving tones by those who want to see change, particularly change in the directions being advocated, and in disapproving tones by people like the respondent who said of a cabinet officer, "He wants to be the firstest with the mostest, and it doesn't matter if it's the bestest."

BY CONTRAST: CIVIL SERVANTS

Bureaucrats are often thought to be the source of many agenda items. They are alleged to have the necessary expertise, the dedication to the principles embodied in their programs, an interest in program expansion, and sheer staying power. These attributes might lead them to capture the political appointees in their agencies, to forge powerful relationships with interest groups and with members of Congress, to shape the flow of information essential to policy proposals.

Despite this formidable array of supposed advantages, my research does not find career civil servants to be nearly as influential in agenda setting as the executive branch officials who are part of the administration. They were important in 32 percent of the interviews, but "very" important only once. There were few differences between health and transportation, among the four years, or among types of respondents (i.e., civil servants did not attribute more importance to themselves than did others). Career bureaucrats fared a bit better in the case studies: very important in 2 of the 23, somewhat important in 10, with again no differences between health and transportation. These indicators of importance in agenda setting clearly are not as impressive as those for political appointees in departments and bureaus, suggesting that the appointees, not the career civil servants, are the movers and shakers in the executive branch.

These quantitative indicators are reinforced by the content of the interview responses. When a given subject apparently had a high priority in the executive branch, I asked why and asked specifically who in the executive branch was pushing it along. Respondents frequently discussed political appointees—the secretary, the undersecretary, assistant secretaries, and their deputies—and virtually never cited career civil servants as the ones responsible for the issue's prominence on the executive branch's agenda. One HEW civil servant who was extremely unhappy about the push for HMOs, when asked what would happen, replied, "Well, it's going to be full speed ahead on HMOs. The secretary wants it, the undersecretary is giving a lot of attention to it." Another said of his appointed superior, "You go in and tell him X and he wants to hear Y. You go back again and you tell him X and he says he wants to hear Y. The third time, you finally conclude that you'd better say Y."

Activities: Agendas, Alternatives, and Implementation

With respect to agenda setting, then, a top-down model of the executive branch seems to be surprisingly accurate. We discovered that the president can dominate his political appointees, and that the appointees can dominate the career civil servants. The model comports roughly with a traditional notion of hierarchy in organizations. That result is surprising and puzzling because of the tremendous volume of literature arguing that superiors in such organizations as the executive branch cannot command their subordinates, despite their formal position in the hierarchy.[8]

The solution to the puzzle lies in a differentiation among types of policy processes. We have been talking here of agenda setting, or the determination of the subjects to which subordinates will pay attention. We have not been discussing the content of the alternatives generated by the bureaucrats in response to their superiors' agendas, nor the implementation of the superiors' decisions. There is good reason to suspect that implementation and alternative generation may work quite differently from agenda setting, and that career civil servants may have a far greater impact on those processes than on the agenda.[9]

Implementation is one major preoccupation of career bureaucrats. Most of them are administering existing programs, not concentrating on new agenda items. The power of bureaucrats often is manifested in that implementation activity. Because careerists are so involved in administration, they have little time left for pushing new ideas. Through feedback from the operation of programs, however, implementation can lead to innovation. If bureaucrats find a program is not going well in some particular, that recognition might feed into a policy change. But even in that case, there is some incentive to protect the existing program rather than to open it up to criticism and a possible pandora's box of changes.

The customary distinction between line and staff bureaucrats is also important, because line people are particularly preoccupied with administering existing programs while staff people might have more time to concentrate on policy changes. Thus one does find staff people located in such places as planning and evaluation or legislation offices, who concentrate on legislative proposals, studies of future problems, and thinking about the directions public policy might take. But to return to our point about the dominance of political appointees, people in those staff positions are generally the very ones who are most responsive to the political appointees when it

---

[8]For examples of such writings, see Neustadt, *Presidential Power:* Cronin, *The State of the Presidency;* and Allison, *Essence of Decision,* op. cit. See also Hugh Heclo, *A Government of Strangers* (Washington, D.C.: The Brookings Institution, 1977).

[9]For a discussion of the importance of civil servants in these ways, see Hugh Heclo, *Modern Social Politics in Britain and Sweden* (New Haven: Yale University Press, 1974), pp. 301–304.

comes to the determination of their agendas. As one of them succinctly put it, "We are staff to the secretary."

Our distinction between the agenda and the alternatives is also useful, for the career civil servants may have more impact on the specification of alternatives. It is quite common for the higher-level appointees to define an agenda item and then to solicit the advice of careerists in drafting the proposals. Bureaucrats are not the only source of such advice, but they are an important source. As one of them said, "Usually, people from the bureaucracy and the career civil service do the scut work and write the position papers." A congressional staffer told me, "Bureaucrats are not so important with respect to the generation of ideas, but they're critical with respect to their professional advice and consultation in pursuing approaches which we have generated. For example, with manpower, if we want the definition of underserved areas to include Pittsburgh or other urban areas, technically how can we do that? The bureaucrats are in a position to tell us how."

This attention to the alternatives does not simply start afresh with the requests from higher authorities or from the Hill. Civil servants in locations like planning and evaluation offices continue to work on proposals of various kinds, keeping them ready for the opportunity that will be provided by a receptive administration to push the idea into prominence. As one long-term occupant of an important career position stated, "Our attitudes about the merits of the cases don't readily change. But that doesn't mean that there aren't any changes produced by the system. Sometimes the views of people like me will get a hearing in a given administration and sometimes they won't. The political process will move changes along, and sometimes political people will draw on our judgment and sometimes they won't." So lower-level bureaucrats in the Department of Transportation, for instance, keep working on approaches to peak-hour landing fees, prepared for the time when superiors evidence some interest in subjects to which their proposals could be related. The "Forward Plan for Health," a document issued annually by the assistant secretary for health during the Nixon and Ford administrations that discussed the nation's health needs and goals, was just such an attempt. Described as "just an exercise" or "the wishlist," it still was a way for people in the Public Health Service to keep their ideas alive and in circulation during lean times. As one of them candidly told me. "It was a way of getting our ideas about priorities out into the public without having to go through the administration."

This discussion about the importance of career bureaucrats in implementation and in alternatives specification, however, only highlights their weaknesses in agenda setting. If they work away on planning new approaches, they depend on political appointees, the president, or members of Congress to "elevate" their ideas to the point on the policy agenda of receiving serious attention. Or if they are particularly important in implementation, the programs they are implementing were generally started in the political arena. The general analytical strategy of distinguishing among various types of policy processes— agenda setting, alternative specification, authoritative decision, implementation—turns out once again to be better than trying to assess the global "importance" of civil servants.

Bureaucrats' Resources

To the extent that career civil servants are important in various policy formation processes, their impact can be understood as the product of several resources. Not the least of these resources is their longevity. As one Hill staffer put it, "Political appointees come and go, but the bureaucracy endures." Longevity of careerists might imply that they can capture the political appointees. One often finds instances of appointees who, once they take office, change in the direction advocated by the civil servants who have been in the agencies for a long time. Of course, one also finds many counter-examples, and it is not the purpose of this book to sort out the frequency with which political appointees "turn native" and become captured by their agencies. The point here is that the administration agenda still depends on the political appointees, and that civil servants are obliged to convince those appointees to highlight the subjects they prefer. If they are not convincing, they are not in a position to set a policy agenda for their department independent of the appointed officials, and their best bet is to wait out the storm until a more receptive set of appointees comes along. Thus for all the supposed failure of the Nixon administration to bring HEW to heel, my respondents in HEW repeatedly expressed their extreme frustration with that administration, describing times of dispiriting budget stringency, inability to move on desired initiatives, and drastic declines in morale. They simply did not sound like victors in any sense. Many left, and those who stayed seemed more like bare survivors of a devastating tornado than like triumphant conquerors of the Nixon appointees. The Reagan administration only underlines this point.

A second bureaucratic resource is expertise. There is a wealth of experience in administering current programs, in dealing with the interest groups and the congressional politics surrounding these programs, and in planning possible changes in government policy. Of course, the civil servants have no monopoly on expertise or information. As one said of higher-level administration officials, "They'll look around fairly widely, and they'll be hearing from people besides you. So you can't control the whole thing."

A final resource of career bureaucrats is their set of relationships with people in Congress and in the interest groups. An agency characteristically has a clientele they service and congressional committees with which they deal. The relationship between these three actors—bureaucrats, committees, and interest groups—is often called an iron triangle because their interests dovetail nicely and because they are alleged to be impenetrable from the outside and uncontrollable by president, political appointees, or legislators not on the committees in question. One observer attributed the early, rapid expansion of the National Institutions of Health (NIH) partly to its extremely close contacts with the biomedical research community:

> People called it "buccaneering." You know how secretaries have these little dividers in their desk drawers for different letterheads, carbon paper, bond, and so forth? Well, they had one in their drawer at NIH called "citizen witness bond." They would buy it at some drugstore, so as to be sure it didn't have the government watermark on it. Then when they were typing up the testimony of some supposedly outside impartial witness who wasn't connected to NIH, nobody on the Hill would be able to hold it up to the light and see that there was an NIH connection after all.

The contacts with Congress and clients sometimes take the form of leaks from bureaucrats. The game is well known in Washington: Bureaucrats locked in a battle within the executive branch leak embarrassing information or premature proposals to their allies as a part of the internal struggle. Various Hill staffers told me of instances in which they introduced legislative proposals fed them by bureaucrats without legislative clearance, got publicity for pieces of analysis that superiors had squelched, and used information leaked to them in questioning hearing witnesses and drafting speeches. One confided: "As soon as anybody in the bureaucracy is thinking about doing something, they write it down. As soon as they write it down, I get things in plain brown envelopes." Another staffer had been leaked the entire set of briefing papers that had been prepared for the secretary's hearing testimony even before the secretary received his own copy.

CAPITOL HILL

One comes to a consideration of the place of Congress in agenda setting with mixed expectations. On the one hand, Congress is the location of the people's representatives, the repository of many constitutionally established responsibilities, and the object of media and public attention. On the other, Congress may produce 535 individual agendas incapable of coordination, may lack control over implementation, may have deficiencies in the expertise necessary to draft detailed proposals, and may be at the mercy of interest groups, constituencies, and administration pressures that pull them hither and yon, preventing them from setting an agenda of their own.

No such ambiguity exists in the quantitative indicators drawn from my interviews. Respondents judge members of Congress to be important in 91 percent of the interviews, which places them right next to the administration and well ahead of any of the individual components of the administration. Hill members are coded as very important in 13 of the 23 case studies, and as somewhat important in the remaining 10. Again, these figures are far ahead of those of any other actor, and suggest strongly the central importance of senators and representatives.

People close to the process cite example after example of congressional involvement. Only 14 percent of my health respondents in 1977 treated catastrophic insurance as prominent on the agenda; that figure had risen to 33 percent in 1978 and catapulted to 92 percent in 1979. The dominant explanation for that dramatic change in such a short period of time was that Russell Long, the chairman of the Senate Finance Committee, had scheduled mark-up sessions for national health insurance during which his proposals to cover catastrophic medical bills were prominently featured. In other words, a key congressional committee chairman single-handedly set a major portion of the policy agenda in health by his intention to move on health insurance. Accounts of Senator Long's motivations varied, and some respondents approved of his actions while others were upset. But all informants—within and outside government, in the administration and on the Hill—agreed that his decision to start marking up national health insurance legislation suddenly moved the issue from the planning stage to serious front-burner status. One administration source attributed the timing of the announcement of the administration's plan to Long's prodding:

> He says that it was when he scheduled his markups that the administration was really galvanized into action. And I think there probably is something to that. You know, in one of the markup sessions he told the story about this, and he said, "It's a little like the game you played when you were kids when you count to ten and then say, 'Ready or not, here I come.'" He says that's what he did to the administration; he counted to ten and he said, "Ready or not, I'm going to mark up a bill."

Senator Long's action did not mean that anything would necessarily pass, nor that if something were to pass, it would be catastrophic insurance. But it did set agendas for important people all over town.

Nor is that example an isolated exception. Senator Wallace Bennett, the Finance Committee's ranking Republican, pushed a proposal for Professional Standards Review Organizations onto the agenda and into law. Senator Warren Magnuson became interested in health manpower maldistribution and pushed the Health Service Corps into being. Interviews in both health and transportation were filled with references to Senator Edward Kennedy's proposals for national health insurance, health manpower changes including a doctor draft, food and drug reform, airline and trucking deregulation, and a host of other subjects. As one Hill staffer acknowledged, "Kennedy is into so many issues, many of which are technically not within his jurisdiction. He just snarfs up issues right and left."

Senators and representatives are discussed frequently partly because they are among the few actors in the political system who have marked impacts on both the agenda and the alternatives that are seriously considered. Of course, because uncontrollable events, presidential requests, and lobbying forces all impinge on the legislative agenda as well, it is difficult to pinpoint any one source, even including the members themselves, as exclusively in control of their agendas. But members of Congress, in contrast to most other actors, have the unusual ability to combine some impact on the agenda with some control over the alternatives.

The prominent place of Congress in the policy formation process sends ripples throughout the policy system. Advocates of policy changes attempt to anticipate what they can expect from Congress, and adjust their proposals or sometimes drop subjects altogether. My interviews with people in the executive branch, for instance, were filled with examples of desired proposals foregone for want of congressional support. As one presidential advisor said of an initiative he strongly favored but dropped. "We'd love to go after [a provision currently in law], but you can't do that. When we were even thinking of it, people on the committee caught wind of it and really went on the war-path." Another respondent said of a pet project of his, "I've personally advised them that it's not the best thing to do, not because it isn't the right thing to do, but because it's almost certain to bomb."

When an administration does decide to go ahead with a proposal, staffers often shape its provisions by drafting language that will smooth the way on the Hill. Proposals are modified or even dropped altogether because there seems to be little chance of enactment, and pursuing the subject would be both futile and costly in terms of squandered resources.[10] Authoritative accounts of the Carter administration's drafting of their national health insurance proposals, for instance, were filled with references to consultations on the Hill, dropping provisions that had little chance of passage and adding other provisions to attract the support of key members of the House and Senate. The administration's original intention to submit a single comprehensive package went by the boards partly because of anticipated congressional opposition; on the other hand, increased funding for such provisions as maternal and child benefits and expanded Medicaid benefits was added to pick up liberal support. As one particularly astute respondent said of the executive branch drafting process in general, "You'd damned well better consult with the Hill, or you're going to be in deep trouble once your proposal gets up there. If you're smart at all, you make a point of that."

The threat of enactment also sometimes prods bureaucracies into action. Both congressional and bureaucratic sources agreed, for instance, that HEW started an expanded regulation of clinical laboratories after there was a serious attempt to pass new legislation in that area. As a knowledgeable bureaucrat told me, "The fact that the legislation was pending made us take action to straighten out our own house so that we could do it without legislation. There wouldn't have been those kinds of changes without this prod." A Hill source referred to the bill as "a case study of a piece of legislation that didn't go anywhere but accomplished its ends anyway."

Congressional Resources

Why are the people on Capitol Hill important agenda setters? The first resource of Congress is its legal authority. Despite the powerful argument that passage of a statute does not necessarily decide all policy issues, the fact remains that major changes in domestic policy usually require new legislation. As one civil servant told me, "I find it kind of curious that whenever someone wants to

---

[10]See Light's discussion of priority setting in the White House, which argues that highest priority is assigned to bills with the best chance of passage. Light, *The President's Agenda,* op. cit., pp. 161–162.

study policy making, they come and talk to bureaucrats. Actually, public policy is made on the Hill." Congress also has the authority to revise current statute and to fund or cut appropriations. An executive branch political appointee justified his willingness to run a money-losing Amtrak train through an influential senator's state: "It cost two million dollars, but we would rather pay that two million than worry about what he could do to the rest of our appropriations bill. He could take a like amount out of something that you're really interested in."

A second congressional resource is formidable publicity. Legislators hold hearings, introduce bills, and make speeches, all of which can be covered prominently in the press and communicated effectively to other participants. One reason for such publicity is that the Congress, particularly the Senate, is a major breeding ground for presidential candidates. A presidential candidacy not only enhances the publicity advantage, but it also adds other reasons for the member of Congress to affect the agenda. As one astute lobbyist put it before Senator Kennedy's run for the presidency in 1980, "Who knows if Kennedy might be president in a couple of years. That has a tremendous effect. In the politics of this town you can't afford not to hedge your bets with him. You don't want to cross the next president of the United States."

A third congressional resource is blended information. With some notable exceptions, Congress is not the place to find the detailed, technical type of expertise found in the bureaucracy, in the community of academics and consultants, or among the interest groups that are occupied with the detailed impacts of programs and new proposals on the operations of their members. Certainly among senators and representatives themselves, again with some exceptions, "expertise" in the congressional context is really a system in which generalists learn enough about a given subject matter to help other generalists, their colleagues. Even many of their aides exhibit similar characteristics. As one prominent committee staffer said, "I'm so much a staff person, I guess, not a deep thinker. If I were in a university or something, maybe I would have a list of things I'd like done. But here, I'm responding to short-term pressures most of the time, and I'm responding to what you can actually do. I'm a pragmatic sort of person."

Congressional information is not the type of expertise that comes from undertaking a detailed study or being on an operational firing line. Rather, its major characteristic is a *blend* of the substantive and the political, the academic and the pressure group information, the bureaucracy and the constituency. Members and staffers are exposed to an impressive variety of information— studies, administration arguments, leaks, interest group pressures, complaints from the districts, concerns of constituents—and the combination of these various communications is different from the perspectives of others in the system.

One further characteristic of congressional information is its rather free-form quality. This can be disconcerting to those who are not used to it, as one new congressional staffer observed:

> It's interesting, dealing with the Hill. It's very informal. Most of it is oral, most of it is among friends. It's not at all like the executive branch, where I used to be.

> There, you had channels and you were supposed to go through channels. On the Hill, there are no channels. It's who knows whom, which friends you develop.

The result of this set of contacts and communication channels is a body of information that blends the substantive and the political, and that is independent of the information members of Congress might receive from any one source.

The final resource is longevity, which is parallel to the civil servants' advantage and contrary to the short time an administration is in office. One feature of congressional longevity is the seniority of the staffers as well as that of the members. While there is a fair turnover of staffers, it is probably less rapid than in a president's administration, and it does not extend to some senior aides who have been in their positions for years.

Incentives

Why do Hill people engage in agenda-setting activities? The answer lies in legislative goals found to be important in committee and floor deliberations.[11] One goal of a senator or representative is satisfying constituents. Publicity is essential, and one way to get publicity is to push for new policy initiatives. As one respondent put it, "Congress exists to do things. There isn't much mileage in doing nothing." The publicity that follows from advocacy is also useful in the quest for higher office. Senators running for president or House members ambitious to be senators or governors find that agenda-setting activity—advocating policy initiatives and introducing bills; appearing prominently at hearings, on television, or at public gatherings—is a useful way to be taken seriously as an aspirant for higher office.

The goal of satisfying present or future constituents also builds some caution into the initiatives that members advocate. As a journalist observed, "I really think that Congress does reflect public opinion. They are much more representative than they get credit for. If there's a lack of consensus in the public, they will reflect that lack of consensus.[12] If a consensus develops, they will reflect it. But it's not in the nature of the legislative animal to get out there in front. They're quite conservative in that sense, and they don't go out and lead their publics a whole lot." The well-known tendency to duck hot issues or throw them to administrative agencies reflects this caution. As David Price says, issues of high controversy and low salience are particularly unattractive to a politician.[13]

---

[11]See Richard F. Fenno, *Congressmen in Committees* (Boston: Little, Brown, 1973), Chapter 1; and John W. Kingdon, "Models of Legislative Voting," *Journal of Politics* 39 (August 1977): 563–595.

[12]For confirmation, see Gary Orfield, Congressional Power: Congress and Social Change (New York: Harcourt Brace Jovanovich, 1975), pp. 258–263.

[13]David E. Price, "Policy Making in Congressional Committees," *American Political Science Review* 72 (June 1978): 545–574. See also Price's *Who Makes the Laws?* (Cambridge, MA: Schenkman, 1972).

One policy consequence of the desire to satisfy constituents is a geographical distributive element added to most policy considerations on the Hill.[14] Members ask themselves how a given policy change will affect their own districts or their own states, resulting in some attention to the ways proposals will distribute federal largesse. This is not to argue that all policies become distributive when they reach Capitol Hill, but only that a distributive element is generally added there. Senators and representatives will at least ask themselves how a hospital cost containment proposal will affect their own local hospitals or how an Amtrak cutback will affect routes in their states and districts. A cynic referred to congressional interest in distributive patterns as "larding in the pork." This distributive element places a premium on the ability to organize such local constituencies as hospitals, highway interests, and truckers. It affects the orientation of whole policy areas toward one or another part of the country. For instance, several transportation respondents argued that greater concentration of population in urban areas led to increased attention to passenger service, more mass transit funding, and some contribution to movement for deregulation.

A second goal of many members of Congress is enhancing their intra-Washington reputation. Affecting policy agendas on the Hill and downtown demonstrates that one is a figure of some consequence, a "heavyweight" who must be taken seriously. So one tries to carve out a part of the policy turf and become a person to be reckoned with in that area. On occasion, furthermore, it is virtually impossible to distinguish the constituency and the intra-Washington incentives. If a senior senator insists on an Amtrak route through his state or on the use of wooden rather than cement railroad ties because the wooden ones benefit timber interests in his state, he is hustling goodies for his state. But at the same time he is demonstrating his ability to get his way within the Senate. Thus much behavior that seems on the surface to be constituency-related actually may be more involved with intra-Washington prestige and power. The difference in the literature between David Mayhew's model of congressional behavior as motivated by an interest in reelection and Lawrence Dodd's model emphasizing a quest for power may not be amenable to easy resolution because many actions serve both interests at once.[15]

A third goal is to achieve the member's conception of good public policy. Walker found in his study of agenda setting in the United States Senate that a knot of liberal senators was responsible for the lion's share of bill introductions.[16] Senators and representatives may act to affect agendas because they

---

[14]For discussions of such distribution, see R. Douglas Arnold, *Congress and the Bureaucracy* (New Haven: Yale University Press, 1979), Chapter 1; and John A. Ferejohn, *Pork Barrel Politics* (Stanford: Stanford University Press, 1974).

[15]David R. Mayhew, *Congress: The Electoral Connection* (New Haven: Yale University Press. 1974); and Lawrence C. Dodd, "Congress and the Quest for Power," in Dodd and Bruce Oppenheimer, *Congress Reconsidered,* 1st ed. (New York: Praeger, 1977), Chapter 14.

[16]Jack L. Walker, "Setting the Agenda in the U.S. Senate," *British Journal of Political Science* 7 (October 1977): 423–445.

want to affect the shape of public policy; they are ideologues of the left or right, or they simply have an interest in the substance of an issue. This incentive results in the well-recognized tendency for committees of Congress to be populated by members who believe in the programs within the committees' jurisdictions. Highway committees have members and staffs who believe in highway construction; health committees have those with an interest in health issues, either for or against provider interests; agriculture committees consist of farm-area members.

Congressional Staff

Capitol Hill is not simply the elected senators and representatives. A considerable bureaucracy of staffers both serves the members and has its independent place in the congressional agenda-setting process.[17] Some of these aides are on the personal staffs of the members, but those who have the greatest impact on the shape of public policy emerging from Congress are committee staffers[18] and some people in such independent agencies as the Office of Technology Assessment and the Congressional Budget Office. Hill staffers might be quite prominent because of their expertise, but especially because they, unlike the members of Congress, can devote their full attention to one particular substantive policy area.

For all that potential, however, with some significant individual exceptions, congressional staffers are not discussed as frequently in the interviews as members of Congress or the administration, though slightly more frequently than civil servants. They were mentioned as being important in 41 percent of the interviews, and were coded as very important in 2, and somewhat important in 8 of the 23 case studies. Many respondents other than the involved staffers themselves gave examples of staff impact on the congressional agenda. Much of the impetus for food and drug reform, for instance, was laid at the door of Senator Kennedy's committee aide, Larry Horowitz. Staffers of the House Public Works and Transportation Committee were reputed to be prime movers of provisions in highway legislation. Jay Constantine, the head Senate Finance Committee health staffer, had a major hand in many proposals and bills introduced by members of that committee, including the Professional Standards Review Organization legislation, reimbursement reform, fraud and abuse, reorganization of HEW, and health insurance proposals.

Some observers portrayed the congressional staff as highly important in their own right, as reflected in one respondent's comments:

> Most of the time, for both continuing and new programs, an idea will originate with the staff. You have to sell an idea to the staff, and then the staff can gener-

[17]See Michael J. Malbin, *Unelected Representatives* (New York: Basic Books, 1980); and Harrison W. Fox and Susan Webb Hammond, *Congressional Staffs* (New York: The Free Press. 1977).

[18]On committee staffs, see Samuel C. Patterson, "Professional Staffs of Congressional Committees," *Administrative Science Quarterly* 15 (March 1970).

ate support among the congressmen and senators, and then it can get enacted. That happens with maybe 90 percent of the legislation. Sometimes the idea is original with the staff, and sometimes it comes to them from elsewhere.

Other observers were more cautious about attributing power to the staff. Said one:

> Congressional staff people tend to claim credit for something. If something is started, they'll try to say, "It was my idea." Actually, the staff is little more than a conduit. Staff meshes things, fits them together, but really has very little original initiative.

Part of the difference in the impressions of these two observers can be resolved by examining in some greater detail the types of activities staff engage in, and their relationships with their bosses. Senators and House members are simply spread very thin. They serve on several subcommittees, they deal with floor votes, they campaign constantly, and they have their days filled with a myriad of such activities as seeing constituents, holding press interviews, meeting with group representatives, and dealing with executive branch officials. One congressman told me after I asked him several questions about a subcommittee on which he served, "Actually, I don't know about a lot of these things that you're asking me about, if you want to know the truth. If you really want to know what's going on in this subcommittee, you should talk with some staff people and others." If that is an accurate picture for many House members, it is true many times over for most senators, who have many more subcommittee assignments, larger electoral constituencies, and more national attention focused on them. Committee staffers and specialists in staff agencies, by contrast, specialize in one policy area and are not obliged to attend to quite the range of activities that members are. They lead harried lives, to be sure, they have their own deadlines, and their own meetings with lobbyists and pleaders. But they at least focus their attention on a narrower set of substantive concerns.

Thus it is generally up to committee staff to draft legislation, negotiate the details of agreements among the interested parties, arrange for hearing witness lists, and write speeches and briefing materials for the members. In the course of doing these things, staffers sometimes borrow ideas from such sources as academic studies, executive branch reports and proposals, interest group materials, and members' opinions; sometimes they generate ideas of their own. But they are in a position, by virtue of their ready access to important members of Congress, their ability to concentrate all their energies on given subjects, and their straddling of political and technical worlds, to have a considerable impact on the alternatives considered by important people, and even on the agendas of those people.

It is important to remember, however, that staffers do all of these things within the limits that are set by the senators and representatives who hire and can fire them. Even respondents with the highest estimates of staff importance frequently refer to the staff's need to "sell their boss" on an idea. One high-level political appointee described in great detail the negotiations between the administration and a Senate committee on a major piece of transportation legislation as a series of bargains between second-echelon administration officials and committee staff. But in the course of making the point that "it was all done by the staff," he added the significant caveat that "the understanding always was that it would have to be approved by the senators and by the president." As one committee staffer characterized the interaction between staffer and member, "The staffer has an idea. He sells his boss on it, and then he can use his boss to push the idea."

Thus, to return to our distinction between the agenda and the alternatives, the staffers have a marked influence on the alternatives from which the senators and representatives choose, although they cannot control the choice set entirely. Many other participants have access to their bosses, and affect alternatives themselves. Still, staff impact on the alternatives and on the specific provisions of legislative proposals is very great. They have considerable latitude in shaping legislative language and in inserting some proposals and not others. Their impact on the congressional agenda, on the other hand, depends more heavily on the willingness of the members to pursue the staffers' preferred subjects.

Most of the time, the distinction between staffer and member is a bit artificial since they are partners working toward the same ends, each in their own ways.[19] According to many committee staffers, they draft legislative provisions while in frequent contact with the members, to get their ideas and to sense what will fly in the committee when it comes to voting. Thus cooperation between staffer and member is more the order of the day than is conflict. But every staffer can also cite instances in which his or her recommendations were not followed by the members. And there is no doubt on either side about who has the ultimate authority. A powerful committee staffer summarized the relationship between staff and members rather well:

> Staff has to do a good bit. Senators and representatives have a million and one things to do. They're spread far too thin to attend to any of them very thoroughly. They have to rely on staff for a lot. But basically, we're doing what they want us to do. I know that if I weren't doing what my chairman wants me to do, I'd be out on my ass.

CONCLUSION

This chapter has examined the importance and resources of participants on the inside of government. The administration—the president and his political appointees—is central to agenda setting, but has less control over the alternatives that are considered and less control still over implementation. Presidential resources include such legal prerogatives as the veto and the ability to hire and fire, coordination advantages, and the ability to publicize and to appeal to fellow partisans, particularly on the Hill. Career civil servants are not particularly important in agenda setting, relative to other participants, but they have more

[19]See Robert H. Salisbury and Kenneth A. Shepsle, "U.S. Congressman as Enterprise," *Legislative Studies Quarterly* 6 (November 1981): 559–576.

impact on alternatives and yet more on implementation. Their resources include their longevity, their expertise, and the pattern of their relationships with interest groups and with Capitol Hill. Congress is central to both agenda setting and alternative specification, although the members have more impact on the agenda while the staffers concentrate more on the alternatives. Congressional resources include legal authority, publicity, longevity, and a blend of political and technical information.

A Reflection on the Place of Elected Officials

Steeped in the traditions of western democratic thought, we have grown used to accounts of the operation of the American political system that place heavy emphasis on the importance of elected officials. After all, authoritative decisions that bind the governed ought to be made by governors who are held accountable to the people in periodic elections. So we would like to think that governmental institutions are controlled by elected officials. Our elementary and secondary school civics instruction and our college textbooks are filled with the importance of such people as the president and members of Congress.[20] The model of a democratic government controlled by elected officials is not only our normative ideal, but also our dominant picture of empirical reality.

A fair body of scholarship has come to challenge the view that elected officials reign supreme. Many writers have noticed that within government people presumably in authority have trouble seeing their preferences carried into effect. Presidents find they cannot order that something be done and expect it to be done.[21] Members of Congress discover that passage of a law does not guarantee its implementation according to legislative intent.[22] Other scholars portray public policy as the product of nongovernmental actors and processes in which elected officials are either of minor importance or are manipulated by powerful people accountable only to themselves. Obviously, studies that describe the workings of power elites fall into this category,[23] but one need not be a power elite theorist to believe that the power of elected officials is minimal. Interest group theories of politics or studies that suggest the importance of the mass media also describe a political system in which the importance of elected officials is diminished from the democratic ideal.

The research reported in the pages of this book probably will not restore anybody's democratic faith to its pristine state. It really cannot be fairly said

[20]Cronin, *The State of the Presidency,* op. cit., Chapter 3.

[21]Cronin, ibid.; Neustadt, op. cit.; Allison, op. cit.

[22]For two excellent works on implementation, see Robert T. Nakamura and Frank Smallwood. *The Politics of Policy Implementation* (New York: St. Martin's Press. 1980); and Jeffrey L. Pressman and Aaron Wildavsky. *Implementation* (Berkeley: University of California Press, 1973).

[23]For two prominent examples, see C. Wright Mills, *The Power Elite* (New York: Oxford University Press, 1956); and G. William Domhoff, *Who Rules America?* (Englewood Cliffs, NJ: Prentice-Hall, 1967).

that elected officials dominate all of the processes under study. But as we shall argue in Chapter 4, that conclusion obtains primarily because *nobody* dominates these processes. While we cannot say that elected officials dominate other actors, no fair reading of the data presented in this chapter could conclude that elected officials are unimportant. To the extent that anybody is important, it is elected officials and their appointees. The president and the top appointees who make up his administration, for instance, do come as close as anyone can to dominating the agenda-setting process. Key members of Congress and their staffers are also figures very much to be reckoned with. On the other hand, career civil servants seem much less important.

Chapter 3 will show the limits on interest groups and the mass media as agenda agents. Interest groups are very important, but primarily as blocking factors rather than actors who promote agenda items, or as people who get their alternatives considered once the agenda has already been set. Such actors as career bureaucrats and members of interest groups depend on those in elected positions. If the administration or Congress are receptive, these people push their ideas. If not, they shelve their proposals and wait for a different administration or a new mood on the Hill. But in any event, they must persuade elected officials. So we are led by the findings surprisingly (even uncomfortably) close to the textbook maxims about the importance of elections, election results, and elected politicians.

Of course, there may be other phases of policy making in which elected officials are not so prominent. In implementation, for instance, the career bureaucracy could be the location of major action. And as we will argue in the next chapter, generating alternatives may be more the province of participants who are more specialized than elected officials. Indeed, these points make the argument for differentiating among the various policy processes—agenda setting, alternative specification, choice, and implementation—all the more persuasive. Elected officials are also moved about by crises or by the requirements of routine as much as any other participants.[24] But at least with regard to setting discretionary agendas, elected officials loom very large. No one set of actors dominates the process, but elected politicians and their appointees come closer than any other.[25]

[24]Walker distinguishes between required and discretionary items. See Walker, "Setting the Agenda," op. cit., p. 425.

[25]For another statement on the importance of elected officials, see Robert A. Dahl, *Who Governs?* (New Haven: Yale University Press, 1961), Chapter 14 on the mayor in New Haven.

CHAPTER 3

Outside of Government, But Not Just Looking In

Participants without formal government positions include interest groups, researchers, academics, consultants, media, parties and other elections-related actors, and the mass public. As the title of this chapter implies, the line between inside and outside of government is exceedingly difficult to draw. Interest groups constantly lobby and are lobbied by government officials. Certain kinds of researchers have regular and intimate relationships with those in government, sometimes on the payroll as consultants, other times testifying before congressional committees, and often in more informal capacities. People traffic in and out of government, sometimes occupying government positions and at other times being lobbyists, consultants, or just names about town. The communication channels between those inside and those outside of government are extraordinarily open, and ideas and information float about through these channels in the whole issue network of involved people, somewhat independent of their formal positions.[1] Finally, common values, orientations, and world views form bridges, at least to some degree, between those inside and those outside of government.

Yet the distinction between inside and outside retains an important meaning. People in governmental positions have formal authority granted by statute and by the constitution, a status those outside of government do not enjoy. As we have seen, those in the higher governmental reaches—the president and his appointees, and members of Congress—have a formal decision-making authority. Others within government are bound by rules of accountability that do not sim-

---

[1]For a discussion of issue networks, see Hugh Heclo, "Issue Networks and the Executive Establishment," in Anthony King, ed., *The New American Political System* (Washington, D.C.: American Enterprise Institute, 1978), Chapter 3.

ilarly bind people not in governmental employ. These considerations make the distinction between insider and outsider a useful way to divide up the world, even though the distinction is substantially blurred in practice.

INTEREST GROUPS

According to our customary quantitative indicators, there can be little doubt that interest groups loom very large indeed.[2] They were discussed as being very important in fully one-third of the interviews, and somewhat important in an additional 51 percent. This total of 84 percent compares to 94 percent for the administration and 91 percent for members of Congress, thus placing interest groups among the most discussed actors. The case studies tell a similar story. Interest groups were coded as very important in 8 of the 23 cases, and somewhat important in an additional 9.

That first cut at the data masks some interesting finer points. For one thing, interest groups are much more prominent in the transportation than in the health interviews, as Table 3-1 shows.[3] Many respondents attributed the difference to the lesser partisan cast of transportation issues. As one said:

> Transportation is by and large made up of nonpartisan issues. Because of that, they bring into play congeries of special interest groups. You have the industrial

Table 3-1

*Differences Between Health and Transportation
on the Importance of Interest Groups*

Importance	Health	Transportation
Very important	14%	55%
Somewhat important	62	41
Little importance	8	2
None	17	2
Total %	101%	100%
n	133	114

[2]My purpose is not to repeat the findings, theories, and arguments abroad in the interest group literature, nor to draw global conclusions about the degree of pluralism, elitism, or interest group liberalism in the political system at large, but rather to assess the impacts of interest groups on agendas and alternatives. For more general literature on interest groups, see David Truman, *The Governmental Process* (New York: Knopf, 1962); Raymond Bauer, Ithiel Pool, and Lewis Dexter, *American Business and Public Policy* (New York: Atherton, 1964); Mancur Olson, *The Logic of Collective Action* (Cambridge, MA: Harvard University Press, 1965); James Q. Wilson, *Political Organizations* (New York: Basic Books, 1973); and Terry Moe, *The Organization of Interests* (Chicago: University of Chicago Press, 1980).

[3]The case studies exhibit differences in the same direction, but not nearly as pronounced. Interest groups were coded as very or somewhat important in 10 of the 12 transportation cases, and in 7 of the 11 health cases.

interests, the railroads, the Teamsters, rail unions, suppliers, waterway users, construction industry, and then port cities with their own geographical interests, and steel and automobile companies.

A related reason for the difference between health and transportation is the lesser visibility of transportation issues in campaigns for elective office. Said one transportation respondent, "After all, transportation isn't exactly an exciting issue to most people. When the public isn't that involved in it, you have to deal with the vested interests." Generally, then, the lower the partisanship, ideological cast, and campaign visibility of the issues in a policy domain, the greater the importance of interest groups.

Types of Interest Groups

The discussion thus far has treated the Teamsters, the American Medical Association, urban mayors, environmental action groups, Ralph Nader's health group, and the Burlington Northern Railroad as all belonging to the same category. Let us briefly consider the place of each of several different types of interest groups: business and industry, professional, labor, public interest groups, and governmental officials as lobbyists.

When we think of interest groups, we often are thinking of business and industry. In the cases analyzed in this study, business interests are indeed the most often important of the interest groups, particularly in transportation. Business and industry groups are important in 9 of the 12 transportation cases, but in only 2 of the 11 health cases. That difference between the two policy domains is mirrored in the interviews. The power of the modal companies (e.g., railroads, airlines) is discussed as important in 46 percent of the transportation interviews, whereas the power of business is important in 24 percent of the health interviews.

Health has its counterpart to business and industry: the providers of medical care, grouped into such organizations as the American Medical Association (AMA) and the American Hospital Association (AHA). While we coded these groups as professional or practitioner groups rather than business and industry groups, many health respondents still refer to them as "the industry" in medicine. Indeed, such provider groups as the AMA and the AHA are prominently mentioned in fully 64 percent of my interviews, a figure even higher than that for modal companies in transportation, and such lobbies are important in 7 of the 11 case studies.

Organized labor is involved less frequently than the industry or professional groups just reviewed. They were important in the emergence of issues in only 5 of the 23 case studies, with no marked differences between health and transportation. They show up more frequently in the interviews: prominent in 41 percent of the health interviews and in 43 percent of the transportation interviews.

This apparent similarity between health and transportation, however, covers up a fundamental difference in the character of the involvement. Much of the discussion of unions among the transportation respondents concentrates on blocking activity: Teamster opposition to trucking deregulation, railroad labor's opposition to measures designed to increase efficiency, and other union positions intended to preserve the current jobs of their members. Much of the health respondents' discussion, by contrast, centers on labor promotion of national health insurance, particularly on support by the United Auto Workers. Some of this promotion was attributed to union ideology, as reflected by the respondent who said, "I think the UAW really does have a tradition of idealism." But in a more self-interested vein, as medical care costs have increased dramatically over the last couple of decades, fringe benefit costs have loomed larger and larger at the bargaining table, making it harder for union leaders to deliver wage increases to their membership. National health insurance would remove the issue from collective bargaining, which would be particularly advantageous to a union such as the UAW since its health insurance benefits are impressively complete and thus unusually expensive. As one somewhat cynical respondent put it, "Labor wants the American taxpayer to buy them out of their benefit package."

Finally, such groups as consumers and environmentalists, labeled "public interest" groups, sometimes affect policy agendas. They are often discussed in the interviews as counterpoints to the self-interested groups in business, labor, and the professions. According to many respondents, the consensus that used to exist among the participating parties has diminished because of the emergence of these public interest groups on the scene. Highway-building interests used to dominate the highway program more than they do now, for instance, because of the recent and vigorous activity of environmentalists and local antihighway activists. As Hugh Heclo argues, the triangles between bureaucrats, congressional committees, and clienteles that used to dominate policy are no longer as iron as they once were.[4]

Akin to the public interest group is lobbying by governmental officials, particularly representatives of the states and cities. There is often a heavy budgetary impetus to the state and local interest in federal public policy. When mayors found that the privately run mass transit companies in their cities were failing, many cities took over the responsibility, resulting in substantial operating deficits and capital expenditures. Mayors turned to the federal government for relief, lobbying vigorously for a federal mass transit program. Similar entreaties from state officials have resulted in substantial federal programs in highway maintenance and bridge replacement. When health policy makers' attention turns to nationalizing the Medicaid program, one prominent consideration is the budgetary relief such a move would provide to the states.

Types of Interest Group Activity

Obviously, interest group activity is varied. Some of it affects the agenda; other activity affects the alternatives considered by policy makers. Some of it is pos-

[4]Heclo, "Issue Networks," op. cit.

itive, promoting new courses of government action; other activity is negative, seeking to block changes in public policy.

When we say that interest groups are important in agenda setting, we might conclude that they are promoting new agenda items or advocating certain proposals. Actually, much of interest group activity in these processes consists not of positive promotion, but rather of negative blocking. As we noticed in the case of transportation unions, interest groups often seek to preserve prerogatives and benefits they are currently enjoying, blocking initiatives that they believe would reduce those benefits. Thus regulated truckers in combination with the Teamsters put up a strong fight against trucking deregulation. Hints of increasing landing fees for general aviation (not-for-hire aircraft) and of imposing landing restrictions or requiring new equipment for them brought floods of outcry from pilots all over the country. The opposition of medical care providers to health insurance and other new health programs that they believe run counter to their interests is by now legendary. While it is not possible to estimate quantitatively how often interest group activity promotes a potential agenda item and how often it seeks to block consideration of an issue or an alternative, it is clear that a substantial portion of interest group effort is devoted to negative, blocking activities.

Interest group pressure does have positive impact on the government's agenda, and does so with considerable frequency. A group that mobilizes support, writes letters, sends delegations, and stimulates its allies to do the same can get government officials to pay attention to its issues. As one of my respondents described the way subjects rise through his department to the secretary's level due to group pressure, "Generally speaking, the louder they squawk, the higher it gets." Then when I asked him why other groups weren't paid much attention, he replied, "They don't come in very often; they just don't come in."

The interviews contained many examples of items on the governmental agenda because of interest group activity. The pressure by organized labor for national health insurance was one. As one respondent said, "The only driving force for national health insurance right now is the unions. Aside from them, there isn't any force in the public that really pushes for it." And pressure from the bus companies for their share of federal largess along with Amtrak led first to generalized attention to the problems of intercity buses and then to proposals for intermodal terminals that would combine train and bus, intercity and commuter traffic, and for new tax treatment for bus companies. Finally, health legislation is often aimed at particular disorders, partly because of the lobbies for cancer research, kidney dialysis, and other maladies, what several respondents called "the disease of the month club."

Despite these examples, it is still difficult to assign responsibility for the emergence of agenda items solely to interest groups. For one thing, issues generally emerge to a status of serious governmental consideration from a complex of factors, not simply interest group pressure. To return to the examples already discussed, attention to intermodal terminals may have been stimulated by pressure from bus companies, but it also grew out of a generalized sense among policy analysts and involved political decision makers that steps should be taken to encourage a more integrated transportation system. Similarly, attention to national health insurance proposals arises from a complex of factors, not solely organized labor support.

Beyond the complexity of the process, many issues simply do not arise from interest group pressure. Jack Walker argues, for instance, that governmental attention to safety issues is not well understood in terms of an interest group model.[5] As both he and Mark Nadel point out, political scientists who use a pressure group and conflict resolution theory should be surprised by the emergence of a Ralph Nader as an important influence on the governmental agenda.[6] In more general terms, as Mancur Olson argues, interest groups that might promote the provision of collective goods do not readily form in the absence of coercion or of selective benefits to potential members.[7] And as several other scholars point out, even those incentives do not explain the emergence on the American scene of some important political movements, notably consumers, environmentalists, and proponents of alternative energy sources.[8]

Even if an interest group raises an issue, furthermore, it doesn't necessarily control the debate once the issue is raised. Much as we discovered when analyzing the role of the president, a particular actor can sometimes get an issue on the agenda, but then can dominate neither the alternatives considered nor the outcome. Organized labor may have been a primary stimulus to governmental attention to national health insurance, for instance, but once the subject was on the agenda, they could not prevent the serious consideration of catastrophic insurance only, despite their extremely vigorous objections and their promotion of a comprehensive plan.

Indeed, a central interest group activity is attaching one's own alternative to agenda items that others may have made prominent. Lobbies often don't begin the push for legislation or the push for agenda status. But even if they haven't started the ball rolling, once it is rolling they try to insure that their interests are protected in the legislation that emerges. In our terminology, they affect the alternatives considered, even if they haven't affected the agenda. Once talk of national health insurance became serious in the 1970s, for instance, even the American Medical Association introduced a plan of its own, despite its previous bitter opposition. As one source close to AMA thinking put it, "The average physician is not overjoyed with national health insurance. But as a practical

[5]Jack L. Walker, "Setting the Agenda in the U.S. Senate," *British Journal of Political Science* 7 (October 1977): 423–445.

[6]Mark V. Nadel, *The Politics of Consumer Protection* (Indianapolis: Bobbs-Merrill, 1971), Chapters 5 and 7.

[7]Olson, *The Logic of Collective Action,* op. cit.

[8]Jeffrey Berry, *Lobbying for the People* (Princeton: Princeton University Press, 1977); Nadel, *The Politics of Consumer Protection,* op. cit.; Robert Salisbury, "An Exchange Theory of Interest Groups," *Midwest Journal of Political Science* 13 (February 1969): 1–32; and Andrew McFarland, *Public Interest Lobbies* (Washington, D.C.: American Enterprise Institute, 1976).

matter, if it looks like it's coming, we want the best possible bill that we can get." A congressional staffer added, "By adopting one national health insurance plan rather than another, you are either reinforcing the existing system or bringing about very great changes. When that's at stake, everybody with any interest in it leaps in to protect his own turf: the commercial insurance industry, the Blues [Blue Cross and Blue Shield], the hospitals, the practicing doctors, organized labor."

Thus interest groups are central to the processes under scrutiny here, as our first look at the quantitative indicators suggested. But they are important in a variety of ways, not simply as agenda agents. Indeed, the actual creation of policy agenda items by interest groups may be a less frequent activity than blocking agenda items or proposing amendments to or substitutions for proposals already on the agenda.

Group Resources

We needn't dwell at length on the subject of interest group resources since it has been discussed elsewhere.[9] But we should note the resources a group might have in abundance or be lacking, resources that give the group an initial advantage or disadvantage in affecting agendas and alternatives. Impressive political resources do not always guarantee success in achieving the group's goals, nor do deficiencies in resources always spell doom. But the same resources that have been found useful in affecting authoritative governmental decisions are echoed in respondents' discussions of agenda setting and the promotion or blocking of alternatives.

One family of resources involves electoral advantages and disadvantages. Some groups—because of their geographical dispersion in congressional districts throughout the country; their ability to mobilize their members and sympathizers; and their numbers, status, or wealth—are thought to have an ability to affect election outcomes. The hospital lobby is one leading example. When the Carter administration's hospital cost containment proposal was in trouble on Capitol Hill, many respondents attributed that trouble to the characteristics of its opponents, the hospitals. Every congressional district has hospitals and their trustees are pillars of the community. Their administrators and physicians, who are articulate and respected, were mobilized to contact their own legislators not only with opposition but with specific data on the impact the bill would have on their own hospital. One respondent chastized the administration for taking them on as their first major health initiative:

> The whole cost containment thing is a quagmire. I don't know how in the hell the administration got involved with it as their first move. Here you have thousands of hospitals in this country. More than half of them are community hospitals, and you know what that means. There's a lot of community pride wrapped up in them; they've been financed by bake sales. "It's *our* hospital." Others of

[9]For example, see Truman, *The Governmental Process,* op. cit.; and Robert A. Dahl, *Who Governs?* (New Haven: Yale University Press, 1961).

them are proprietary hospitals, owned by politically powerful physicians. The rest of them have some religious affiliation and here they are doing the Lord's work. Why would you want to take them on? Dumb, dumb, dumb.

Governmental officials must also reckon with a group that is in a position to tie up the economy. If the group does so, incomes and livelihoods of large numbers of people are at stake, which can produce politically disastrous consequences. The maritime unions, for instance, can shut down ports throughout the country. While small in numbers of people (Civil servant: "You get more people in the stadium for the Harvard-Yale game."), they are in a critical location for commerce. The rail unions are in an even more critical position, since manufacturing grinds to a halt in a matter of days if parts are not supplied.

Cohesion is another resource that gives a group some advantage in affecting the governmental agenda. Part of a group's stock in trade in affecting all phases of policy making—agendas, decisions, or implementation—is its ability to convince governmental officials that it speaks with one voice and truly represents the preferences of its members. If the group is plagued by internal dissension, its effectiveness is seriously impaired. Thus an early signal that airline deregulation was on the way was the crack in the united front of opposition among the airlines. When one or two carriers came out for deregulation, thus destroying the opposition's cohesion and calling into question the idea that there was such a thing as an "airline position," the stance of the remaining carriers was weakened considerably. The same logic about cohesion internal to a group applies to the cohesion of alliances that are formed across groups.

One cohesion problem involves potential differences between leaders and followers. Interest group leaders find it difficult to argue for their positions if they face opposition from their own ranks. One fascinating example of such potential for division was the elderly and handicapped lobby's push for access to public transportation facilities, including subways and buses. Legislation passed at the urging of the handicapped activists, as interpreted by HEW regulations, called for fully equal access to public transportation. This mandated such changes as elevators in existing subways and wheelchair lifts in all buses. Alarmed by the staggering financial implications of retrofitting existing facilities and purchasing much more expensive new equipment, public transit operators throughout the country fought the regulations. Many of my respondents wondered if the handicapped activists really represented the interests of the handicapped. The activists claimed they did, but others claimed that most handicapped people would prefer door-to-door subsidized taxi or dial-a-ride service, rather than getting themselves to and from public transportation stops and fighting subway crowds.[10] Such service would be far less expensive than the mandated changes, and might also serve the handicapped better. These arguments put the activists on the defensive, tending to their own flanks as they battled for the equal access they regarded as something akin to a civil right.

[10]For a statement of such a position, see Hugh Gallagher's letter to the *New York Times,* 20 May 1980.

This leader-follower problem is a special case of the proposition that organized interests are heard more in politics than unorganized interests. The initial advantage of the organized interests leads to a social class bias in the attention patterns of important people. If they pay attention to organized interests, they perforce pay more attention to those who are relatively well-to-do, and less attention to relatively disadvantaged people. In part, this pattern results from the well-known tendency of middle- and upper-class people to be more active participators in politics than lower-class people.[11] The transportation community's interest in aviation deregulation, for example, probably was fueled by travel habits of businessmen, professionals, and other people who were either relatively wealthy themselves or had expense accounts. Such politically active people would be generally attentive to aviation problems. By contrast, respondents paid scant attention to buses. Of all the variables in my data relating to buses, the largest proportion of transportation respondents discussing buses as important was only 13 percent. As one rather colorfully stated it, "Buses suck hind tit on everything. The buses are sort of out of sight. No opinion leader rides a bus, the way they ride airlines. Busing is a grubby business, and grubby people ride the buses."

Once again, an impressive resource base does not necessarily insure that the group will dominate discussion of issues relevant to its interests, or get its way. The interviews were fairly strewn with examples of supposedly powerful interest groups that had tasted defeat on occasion. The American Medical Association, once enjoying the reputation of standing astride health policy, saw the enactment, over their vigorous objections, of Medicare and then of a series of regulatory programs. The vaunted highway lobby, powerful as it was and still is, saw portions of the interstate system stopped by environmentalists and freeway opponents, and then saw the highway trust fund used in a limited way for mass transit. As Hugh Heclo points out, the powers that used to dominate the iron triangles have found that such countervailing forces as consumers and environmentalists are complicating their lives considerably.[12] The point extends beyond public interest groups as well. Large corporations, for instance, have increasingly been interested in health insurance because of the costs of their fringe benefits, which puts them at odds with the physician-hospital "power elite."

ACADEMICS, RESEARCHERS, AND CONSULTANTS

After interest groups, the collection of academics, researchers, and consultants is the next most important set of nongovernmental actors. One finds their traces

[11]See Sidney Verba and Norman H. Nie, *Participation in America* New York: (Harper and Row, 1972), Chapter 8.

[12]Heclo, "Issue Networks," op. cit.

throughout the policy process. Ideas from academic literature are regularly discussed by Hill staffers, bureaucrats, and lobbyists. Prominent academics are well known by name, and referenced repeatedly in the interviews. Again and again, congressional committees and administrative agencies call on the expertise of researchers and analysts in hearings, meetings, and advisory panels (which one bureaucrat called "outside panels of learned wizards"). Consulting became a booming industry in Washington during the 1970s; some of the resulting studies were done very competently and others were the shoddy work of the so-called "beltway bandits" who hustled federal research contracts. Some consultants are not primarily researchers, but are valued for their political acumen as well as their substantive expertise. Many prominent Washington lawyers, for instance, have included government service in their careers. Current government officials listen to them, and clients seek them out to represent their interests.

Quantitatively, researchers, academics, and consultants are discussed as being very or somewhat important in 66 percent of the interviews, but very important in only 15 percent. They were rated as being very important in 3 of the 23 case studies, and somewhat important in an additional 10 of the 23. There are no major differences in these figures between health and transportation, or from one year to another. These indicators, then, place these people in quite an important position, though not in the top rank occupied by interest groups, the administration, and members of Congress.

Examples of their importance are not hard to uncover. Possibly the most dramatic change in the field of transportation in the 1970s was the movement toward economic deregulation in various modes—air, truck, and rail. As many respondents pointed out, the governmental attention to deregulation was preceded by and depended on a lengthy period in which a substantial scholarly literature on economic regulation was developed and then translated into political action. It really was a case of economic theory's direct impact on a policy agenda. As one respondent summarized the origins:

> In the 1950s and the 1960s the intellectual foundation was laid in academia, and by now it has moved into the political sphere. It is a long, slow process to move from Ph.D. dissertations and academic books to bills that are introduced in Congress, and that work is just now coming to legislative fruition. In an industry like motor carrier, there is no intellectual basis for economic regulation. If you wanted to think of a textbook example of an industry that could be competitive, motor carrier is the one that you would think of.

That academic momentum was carried into the political sphere by such economists as Hendrik Houthakker and Paul MacAvoy, who served at the Council of Economic Advisers and pushed hard for deregulation. The power of the academic literature dramatically affected the Civil Aeronautics Board. The CAB's staff and then members came out early on for a drastic diminution of their own power. As one source pointed out, "You have to remember that this isn't in the best interests of the senior staff [of CAB]. They're sort of talking themselves out of business."[13] Of course, as in nearly all cases of policy change, there were multiple origins of the change and multiple motivations for governmental officials to move with the issue. But the momentum of the academic literature in the case of deregulation was undeniably central.

For a health example, academic literature on the structure of the medical care system has markedly affected the thinking of people in the health policy community. The literature argues that because of the widespread use of open-ended insurance and because the doctor-patient encounter is fundamentally different from a classic producer-consumer encounter, medical care cannot be treated like a market. Insurance pays large bills, so consumers are not themselves directly responsible for the costs. And doctors, not patients, determine the lab tests, lengths of hospitalization, extra office visits, and other things that consumers in many markets would control. As one observer said, "Doctors control both supply and demand, and that screws things up to a fare-thee-well." Some respond to this type of analysis by proposing to make the system more like a market, and others respond with arguments for regulation. But all know and cite by name the leading academicians during their discussions.

Types of Activity

The impacts of academics, researchers, and consultants vary in a number of important ways. For one, academics might well affect the alternatives more than governmental agendas. A close examination of the interviews and the case studies reveals that much of the time the agenda is set by forces and actors outside the researcher-analyst community. Then politicians turn to that community for proposals that would be relevant to their concerns and that might constitute solutions to their problems. The high and escalating cost of medical care, for instance, was the major preoccupation of Washington policy makers during the period of this study. While academics were not responsible for the prominence of that problem on the agenda, they were prominent among the people to whom politicians turned for ideas on how to cope with it. Even transportation deregulation, possibly the item with the greatest academic involvement, has something of this flavor. Because of the temper of the times, politicians found it expedient to promise to "get the government off your back." They then cast about for ways of doing so, and found that academics were ready with deregulation proposals.

The second variation in the importance of academics might be between the short-term and long-term effects. Often, academic work is discussed as if it affects a general climate of ideas which would, in turn, affect policy makers' thinking in the long

---

[13]For an excellent discussion of the importance of academic literature in the deregulation case, see Paul J. Quirk and Martha Derthick, "Congressional Support for Pro-Competition Regulatory Reform," paper for the annual meeting of the American Political Science Association, 1981; and Martha Derthick and Paul J. Quirk, *The Politics of Deregulation* (Washington, D.C.: The Brookings Institution, 1985).

run. Even if some short-term, immediate impact of academic work is not discernible, its long-term impact might be considerable. One researcher described such a process of communication, diffusion, and discussion:

> Writing books gets your ideas into the public eye. Then I get asked to testify. Then I have a lot of informal contacts with staffers on the Hill and in the executive branch. I go to conferences. In addition to writing, I get it out orally because many people don't have time to read. I mail papers to people in academic and in government circles. In academia, there's a network of people, the best researchers, the people that you float things by. In government it's certain positions—head staffers on the major committees, planning and evaluation people in the executive branch.

While the long-term climate of ideas is not the sole province of academics, researchers contribute importantly to its development.

As for the short run, policy makers in government listen to academics most when their analyses and proposals are directly related to problems that are already occupying the officials' attention. For the researcher who wants to have an effect in the short run, there is a premium on knowing what is on the minds of people in government. As one research administrator put it, "We sniffed around, and found out what people wanted us to do." When I said, "That sounds very reactive," the administrator replied, "That's exactly correct, and it's entirely intentional. We are in the social policy research business. We are trying to be reasonably responsive to the social issues in the health area." On occasion, this responsiveness approaches the crass: "One guy had a whole team working on phenomena in the digestive tract. Along came a big new chunk of money for cancer, and he got his team together and said, 'Okay, since cancer of the lower digestive tract is a big deal, let's just move our research down the bowel and deal ourselves in.'"

One nearly sure way for an academic to have a short-run impact is to be in government. Thus some researchers and academics build "inner-outer" careers in which they travel between academia and government, taking leaves of absence from their universities or research organizations to occupy responsible positions in government. Academic work on deregulation in transportation found its way into government in this fashion, partly through the service of prominent economists in such places as the Council of Economic Advisers, the Council on Wage and Price Stability, and the Department of Transportation, and partly through the more gradual infusion of less well-known, younger people throughout the bureaucracy and on the Hill who had some economics training and who were deregulation-oriented. One professor among my respondents referred to academic work proceeding in two waves. First, there was ordinary research by academics—books, scholarly articles, conference papers, and the like. Then there was a set of academics that he called the "political branch, that is plugged into government and into the Washington scene." Some of these may have contributed to the first literature, but all of them are characterized by their contacts in the policy communities of official Washington.

This discussion of the importance of academics and researchers, however, should not be allowed to obscure the instances in which their thinking does not carry the day. In some Washington quarters, there is a distrust of, and even a disdain for, academic work. In other quarters, the value of the work is accepted, but practical people realize that its recommendations cannot always be implemented. The case of catastrophic health insurance illustrates these currents nicely. Nearly every health policy analyst with whom I talked agreed that catastrophic insurance was exactly the wrong plan to enact, reasoning that catastrophic health insurance would create an incentive for providers to furnish the highest-cost medical care, ballooning the nation's total medical bill and diminishing the emphasis placed on areas like primary service delivery. Yet in 1979, fully 92 percent of my health respondents treated the subject of catastrophic insurance as prominent on the governmental agenda, a dramatic jump from 33 percent only the previous year. When I asked why, in view of this near-unanimous opinion of the best analysts, one respondent replied, "The time comes when the politicians take over, and theorists or health economists or whoever they might be take second place." Another broadened the point beyond catastrophic to national health insurance proposals more generally:

I've never gotten very carried away with his plan or her plan and the details of it, if you want to know the truth. Everybody can cost out their plan, draw up its detailed provisions, make the thing a nice integrated whole, and really do a beautiful job of devising their plans. But when you get right down to it, you get there in the Finance Committee and [Chairman Russell] Long sits there and he says, "Well, let's cut this thing off," and then he says, "Okay, well, that's okay to leave in," and then they go off to lunch and come up with a statement of understanding and that's what the agreement is going to be. By the time you get it through committees, floors of two bodies, and conference, the bill is going to be written by those kinds of processes and not by this elaborate staffing that goes into it ahead of time.

THE MEDIA

Media are often portrayed as powerful agenda setters. Mass media clearly do affect the public opinion agenda. As other scholars have discovered, the mass public's attention to governmental issues tracks rather closely on media coverage of those issues.[14] If energy is receiving a lot of press play, for instance, people will cite energy prominently among their candidates for the "most important problem" facing the country. The same potential for media importance

[14]See Arthur H. Miller, Edie N. Goldenberg, and Lutz Erbring, "Type-Set Politics: Impact of Newspapers on Public Confidence," *American Political Science Review* 73 (March 1979): 67–84; Erbring, Goldenberg, and Miller, "Front-Page News and Real-World Cues: A New Look at Agenda-Setting by the Media," *American Journal of Political Science* 24 (February 1980): 16–49; and G. Ray Funkhouser, "The Issues of the Sixties: An Exploratory Study in the Dynamics of Public Opinion," *Public Opinion Quarterly* 37 (Spring 1973): 62–75.

could apply to the governmental agenda as well. As I argued in *Congressmen's Voting Decisions,* media attention to an issue affects legislators' attention, partly because members follow mass media like other people, and partly because media affect their constituents.[15]

Despite good reasons for believing that media should have a substantial impact on the governmental agenda, our standard indicators turn out to be disappointing. Mass media were discussed as being important in only 26 percent of the interviews, far fewer than interest groups (84 percent) or researchers (66 percent). It was quite common for me to ask my standard question about what problems my respondent and others were occupied with, and to engage in a half hour of conversation before the media would be introduced, even obliquely. Media were very important in only 4 percent of the interviews. The picture with the case studies is no better. Media are somewhat important in 4 of the 23 cases, and never very important. There are no differences between health and transportation in either interviews or cases. One can find examples of media importance—the *Washington Post* ran a continuing series on the battle over waterway user charges that probably added some significant impetus to the movement to impose a charge—but such examples are fairly rare.

Much more common is the instance of quite an intensive period of sensational coverage, with the policy community riding serenely above the media storm. Active policy makers often express their disdain for media sensationalism. One health respondent, for example, ridiculed the "public fuss" over issues like saccharin and Medicaid fraud, while more fundamental issues having to do with the economic or political structure of medical care were left relatively neglected. He complained, "Deformed gnomes make quite an impression in front of the television cameras." Despite tremendous media attention, the subject of saccharin was totally ignored by 86 percent of my health respondents in 1977, the high point of its media attention during the four years; it was discussed as a somewhat important subject in only 6 percent of the interviews in that year. Similarly, the issue of Medicare and Medicaid fraud and abuse was treated as a somewhat important problem by only 15 percent of my respondents in 1978, its high point of media exposure, and completely ignored by 76 percent. Congress did pass legislation on both of these subjects, which consumed some of the health committee and agency time. Thus the subjects were "on the agenda" in some sense,[16] but they were simply not regarded as truly significant issues. They were more like short-term annoyances, even to active participants, than subjects of major importance.

One reason for the media's less-than-anticipated effect on the policy agenda is the press's tendency to cover a story prominently for a short period of time

[15]John W. Kingdon, *Congressmen's Voting Decisions,* 2nd ed. (New York: Harper and Row, 1981), Chapters 8 and 12.

[16]In Walker's terms, they were not chosen problems, but they did require some sort of action anyway. See Walker, "Setting the Agenda," op. cit.

and then turn to the next story, diluting its impact.[17] As one bureaucrat put it, "People read about a given subject only so long and then they get tired of it. So the media have to keep moving along to something new. They don't have the staying power that's necessary." Several journalists agreed. Said one, "The press has the world's shortest attention span. We don't stick to a story for long enough to educate anybody. We move from one crisis to the next."

The media report what is going on in government, by and large, rather than having an independent effect *on* governmental agendas. As one prominent committee staffer said, "The media has some importance, but it's slight. Either media people are reporting what we're already doing, or they're reporting something that we're already aware of." A prominent reporter agreed: "I think media are largely responsive to the issues that are being aired, and media don't affect what's aired a lot." The media's tendency to give prominence to the most newsworthy or dramatic story actually diminishes their impact on governmental policy agendas because such stories tend to come toward the end of a policy-making process, rather than at the beginning. For instance, the media may cover a carefully staged and dramatic congressional hearing that look weeks to prepare or that was prompted by some event beyond the control of either media or Congress. In either case, the agenda was set much earlier and by processes not much affected by the media.[18]

Even though media have much less effect on governmental policy agendas than we had anticipated, they may be important in some interesting ways and under some circumstances. First, media act as a communicator within a policy community.[19] Various people scattered both inside and outside of government, dealing with similar problems day in and day out, sometimes communicate with each other in surprisingly indirect ways. They are all busy people and their paths may not cross frequently in the normal course of events, but they do all read newspapers. So one way to bring an idea to the attention of someone else, even someone who is a fellow specialist, is to be covered in the pages of the major papers. A high-level bureaucrat told me, for instance, that a concern of theirs had not made it to the White House level until it appeared in the *Washington Post,* whereupon the president and the secretary discussed it the very same day. This use of the media even occurs within one institution. One analyst in a staff agency of Congress said:

[17]For a discussion of just such dynamics, see Anthony Downs, "Up and Down with Ecology—The 'Issue-Attention Cycle,'" *The Public Interest* 28 (Summer 1972): 38–50. For a useful amendment, which stresses the greater staying power of specialized media over mass media, see Barbara J. Nelson, *Making an Issue of Child Abuse* (Chicago: University of Chicago Press, 1984), Chapter 4.

[18]Walker's data on safety legislation shows exactly this pattern. See Walker, "Setting the Agenda," op. cit.; see also Funkhouser, "The Issues of the Sixties," op. cit.

[19]See Bernard C. Cohen, *The Press and Foreign Policy* (Princeton: Princeton University Press, 1963), pp. 39–45.

> Congressmen and senators read the mass media. The big problem on the Hill is
> the oversupply of information. They have no way of dealing with it. So they
> don't, mostly. We can write reports and papers and they don't read it. But if the
> *Times* or *Post* picks up our report and does a story on it, they do read that, and it
> gets their attention.

Some of this communication within policy communities takes place through media that are more specialized than the daily newspapers.[20] In health, for instance, many people follow such publications as the McGraw-Hill newsletter and the *New England Journal of Medicine;* in transportation, various trade publications are regularly read; and those in both areas read the *National Journal.* Such specialized publications do not figure very prominently in the interviews or case studies. They were prominent in only 10 percent of the interviews, and were important in only 2 of the 23 case studies. Nevertheless, they probably are more important as communicating devices than these data indicate.

A second way media affects the agenda is by magnifying movements that have already started elsewhere, as opposed to originating those movements. They pick up an idea that originated in the bureaucracy or in Congress, or a movement that began in some segment of the society, and they accelerate its development and magnify its impact. As one journalist put it, "Media can help shape an issue and help structure it, but they can't create an issue." The well-known Washington practice of leaking is an example. Sometimes active participants in a bureaucratic process want to enlarge a conflict beyond the confines of usual channels. If they appear to be losing a battle, one way to turn the tide is to leak information to the press that would be embarrassing to their opponents. Because the smell of dramatic conflict is in the air, media are only too glad to oblige. To the extent that expansion of a conflict is a central feature of agenda setting, then media play a part.[21]

Third, to the extent that public opinion affects some of the participants, media might have an indirect effect. If the media affect public opinion agendas, as there is reason to think they do,[22] then the attention of such participants as members of Congress to public opinion might well imply media importance. One congressional staffer, for instance, told me that his boss paid more attention to Medicaid fraud and abuse than he might have in 1977 because the issue was repeatedly exposed in the newspapers and on television, and people from

[20]Nelson, *Making an Issue of Child Abuse,* op. cit.

[21]On the subject of expansion of conflict, see Roger Cobb and Charles Elder, *Participation in American Politics* (Boston: Allyn and Bacon, 1972), pp. 50–52. I may have been more impressed with the agenda-setting potential of media in my study of congressmen's voting decisions than in this study since I was dealing then largely with generalists, the sort of population to whom specialists might want to expand a conflict. But specialists are too involved and too tied into their knowledge and orientation to be affected by media as much as generalists might be.

[22]See the two articles by Erbring, Goldenberg, and Miller, "Type-Set Politics" and "Front-Page News," op. cit.; and Funkhouser, "The Issues of the Sixties," op. cit.

his district were beginning to ask what he intended to do about the problem. We will return to the impact of public opinion on government policy agendas later in this chapter.

Finally, the importance of the media may vary from one type of participant to another. Insiders, those who already are key government decision makers or who have easy access to those decision makers, might have less need for media coverage than outsiders, those who have less access and hence need to go to some lengths to gain the attention of important government officials.[23] As one of the outsiders put it, "If there is a strong organized interest in keeping the status quo, you have to overcome it somehow. Your only hope is to go public." But an insider portrayed a very different situation, as well as summarizing the point well:

> Mass media coverage is not critical. It is one of your vehicles. Here, in a position like this one, you use what you have. We have alternatives of leverage on the system, and we don't have to use the media very much. The media will follow us because what we do makes news. If we get a proposal sold to the White House and it goes to the Hill, then that's news. So I don't think the media adds much. If I weren't here, though, I would worry about it. If I didn't have the levers I have, the media would be very important to me, and I would use it as much as I could.

ELECTIONS-RELATED PARTICIPANTS

Because they produce the officials who make many important decisions in government, elections may affect policy agendas. Also, people in and around government may interpret election results as mandates for one or another policy direction, or at least as hints of the electorate's preferences. The 1980 election of Ronald Reagan and the shift in Senate control to the Republicans, for instance, was widely interpreted as a shift to the right in American politics, rightly or wrongly. Politicians also make many promises during campaigns, and parties take positions in platforms. These commitments could conceivably form an agenda for them once in office.

Despite their potential, however, elections, campaigns, and political parties are not particularly prominent, either in the interviews or in the case studies. They are neither among the least important sources, nor among the most important. Elections were mentioned as important in 30 percent of the interviews, and were important in 7 of the 23 case studies. When we combine mentions of elections, parties, and campaigns, it turns out that respondents discussed at least one of the three as being important in 58 percent of the interviews.

[23]This point is similar to Goldenberg's argument that resource-poor groups need media to gain access to government more than groups that are richer in political resources. See Edie N. Goldenberg, *Making the Papers* (Lexington, MA: D.C. Heath, 1975), p. 1. See also Michael Lipsky, "Protest as a Political Resource," *American Political Science Review* 62 (December 1968): 1144–1158.

Despite this middle-rank frequency of discussion in interviews, elections still have some powerful indirect effects on governmental policy agendas. We noticed in Chapter 2 that the president and the appointed officials in his administration were very prominent features in the agenda-setting landscape. A change of administration would change agendas, alternatives, and approaches to policy problems all over town. The administration would advocate some programs and, even more important, would not advocate others. The proponents of alternatives that had been bypassed by the administration would quietly shelve their advocacy until a more propitious time. The only rivals for the administration as influences on agenda setting were members of Congress, again elected officials. Indeed, a new and different class of legislators, as appeared in 1965, is capable of changing agendas all over town. As a result, advocates of programs that find a sympathetic ear with the new members seize the opportunity to push their proposals through the legislative maze. Thus elections take on great importance, not because there is any kind of mandate from the public to move in one direction rather than another, but simply because the cast of characters in positions of authority can change.[24]

Campaigners

One part of elections—campaigns and campaign promises—might affect governmental policy agendas. As a part of attracting groups and individuals during a campaign, presidential candidates promise action on many policy fronts. Once in office, it is possible that these promises rather directly affect the agendas of new administrations, partly because presidents and their close aides believe in their stated policy goals and want to see them advanced. But there is also at least an implicit exchange involved—support for the candidate in return for action on the promises. Politicians may feel constrained to deliver on their part of the bargain, and supporters attempt to hold them to their promises.

In quantitative terms, campaigns leave important but not overwhelming traces in the data. They are discussed as important in 29 percent of the interviews, and they are important in 4 of the 23 case studies. But the impact of campaigns is uneven across policy domains. Health evidences much more attention to campaigns than does transportation. Fully 44 percent of the health interviews contain prominent discussion of campaigns, compared to only 11 percent of transportation interviews. Similarly, all four case studies in which campaigns were important are health cases. As one transportation journalist said in 1976, "I haven't even seen any candidates mentioning transportation. It's just not one of those kinds of issues." Health, on the other hand, is of intense interest to large segments of the population. It universally affects people right where they live, literally; its costs affect fringe benefits throughout the

[24]This observation fits rather nicely with the research that suggests government policy agendas change with party realignments. See Benjamin Ginsberg, "Elections and Public Policy," *American Political Science Review* 70 (March 1976): 41–49; Barbara Deckard Sinclair, "Party Realignment and the Transformation of the Political Agenda," *American Political Science Review* 71 (September 1977): 940–953; and David Brady, "Congressional Party Realignment and Transformations of Public Policy in Three Realignment Eras," *American Journal of Political Science* 26 (May 1982): 333–360.

land; and articles on the latest cure or the latest disease are prominently displayed in even the smallest-circulation newspapers.

The coalition that is built during a campaign is clearly important to politicians while in office. As they look forward to the next election, they are acutely aware that they must maintain their supporting coalition as intact as possible. Campaign promises do not affect the agenda simply because they were made. Rather, they are important because some significant part of the politician's electoral coalition remembers the promise and attempts to hold him to it, even accusing him of welshing and threatening desertion in the next campaign if he does not deliver. In the end, the mass public's awareness of the campaign issues is not as critical to politicians as the satisfaction of the activist leaders that promises have been kept.

The progress of the national health insurance proposals in the Carter administration is the leading example. In Chapter 1, we recounted the story of Carter's campaign support from the United Automobile Workers, his negotiations with labor and Senator Kennedy on national health insurance, and the UAW's subsequent unhappiness over the administration's slow pace in health insurance and other issues. The threat of a Kennedy-labor challenge to Carter in 1980 entered the picture as a prominent part of the coalition politics that would hold the administration on course.

Contrast this story to the proposals for an integrated transportation trust fund. The idea was to abolish separate highway and airport trust funds, merging them into one system, possibly combined with general revenues, to facilitate the setting of priorities and allocating resources among various transportation modes. Carter did propose actions during the campaign that would lead in that direction, but a campaign promise to that effect was never discussed in my interviews. When the idea was mentioned, it was referred to as Transportation Secretary Brock Adams's idea, but not in the context of a campaign pledge. One reason for the contrast is that there was a constituency holding the administration to its promise in the national health insurance case, but none in this case. In fact, the major interests in transportation, including both the highway interests and the mass transit people, would be against it.

Thus there is nothing automatic about campaign pledges finding their way into public policy. For a campaign promise to gain policy agenda status, it must be accompanied by something else—perhaps a firm presidential commitment, or a constituency that pushes the idea and tries to hold the president to his promise. But in the absence of these considerations, campaign promises by parties or by candidates will not by themselves produce a high standing on the subsequent agenda.[25]

Political Parties

Political parties might affect policy agendas through the content of their platforms, the impact of their leadership in Congress and more generally in the

[25]For a discussion that argues as I have here, see Paul C. Light, *The President's Agenda* (Baltimore: Johns Hopkins University Press. 1982), pp. 96–100.

country, the claim they might have on their adherents, and the ideologies they represent. Much as in the case of campaign promises, a party platform might form the core of an agenda for a subsequent administration of that party.

Quantitatively, political parties and partisan factors show up about as frequently as elections and the other campaign factors we have been discussing. Parties are discussed as being important in 29 percent of the interviews, and they are important in 7 of the 23 case studies. As we found in the case of campaigning, there are important differences between health and transportation, health being the more partisan of the two. Fully 38 percent of the health interviews contained a prominent mention of parties or partisanship, compared to 18 percent of the transportation interviews, and 5 of the 7 case studies in which parties were important were in health. As one political appointee in the transportation field told me, "Transportation is not partisan really. There are conflicts between highway people and the mass transit people, between the rural and urban areas, and so forth. But there is not a conflict between Republicans and Democrats." Even allowing for some exaggeration, it would be quite unusual to find such a statement in a social service area like health.

As with the case of campaigning, parties affect the agenda more than they affect the detailed alternatives considered by policy makers. My examination of the 1976 party platforms, for instance, revealed a grab bag of mostly very vague concerns, ranging from the Republicans' clarion call for a "comprehensive approach" to mental health problems to the Democrats' fearless championing of a "healthy" transportation system. While differences between the two platforms are obvious, and while the agendas of the two parties are different and reasonably clear, the party positions could not possibly constitute a serious guide to policy making once the party is in power.[26] Rather, the platform is one of many forums in which advocates for policy change attempt to gain a hearing. As one astute lobbyist told me, "The platform is important in a *pro forma* way. We'll get a plank in the Democratic platform, and that will be nice because the party then will be on record and we can point to that. But it's not too important." Thus the parties might affect agendas, but the origins of the detailed alternatives seriously considered by policy makers largely lie elsewhere.

Which party's members are elected to public office, however, is a matter of considerable moment, for there are substantial differences between the two parties' agendas. Comments in the interviews on the subject of party differences roughly parallel the findings of a wealth of previous studies in political science.[27] The Democrats are portrayed as more interventionist, more willing to spend on domestic (particularly social) programs, and more willing to use gov-

[26]For a parallel finding, see Hugh Heclo, *Modern Social Politics in Britain and Sweden* (New Haven: Yale University Press, 1974), p. 295.

[27]Among others, see Julius Turner, *Party and Constituency,* revised by Edward Schneier (Baltimore: Johns Hopkins Press, 1970), Chapter 3; Aage R. Clausen, *How Congressmen Decide* (New York: St. Martin's Press, 1973), Chapter 5; Douglas A. Hibbs, "Political Parties and Macroeconomic Policy," *American Political Science Review* 71 (December 1977): 1467–1487; and John W. Kingdon, *Candidates for Office* (New York: Random House, 1968), Chapter 3.

ernment to regulate the private sector than the Republicans. Some respondents referred to the differences in the coalitions supporting the two parties, with labor prominent among the Democrats and business groups among the Republicans. Others spoke of ideological differences between Democrats and Republicans, particularly in the health area, with Democrats more inclined to greater spending and government regulation.

PUBLIC OPINION

Governmental officials may make some rather general judgments about the state of public opinion that affect their policy agendas. At least they might be thinking of a rather vague mood in the country—the state of public tolerance for new taxes, for example. At most, there might be instances in which they feel the public at large virtually directs them to pursue a course of action.

In our standard quantitative indicators, general public opinion is treated as important in 57 percent of the interviews, and as important in 6 of the 23 case studies. There are no major differences between health and transportation, and no major variations by type of respondent (e.g., whether the respondent is on the Hill, downtown, or outside of government). Thus public opinion seems to be approximately as important as the factors related to elections that we just discussed: neither insignificant by any means, nor among the most prominent in the total array of sources, but just about in the middle.

Public opinion can have either positive or negative effects. It might thrust some items onto the governmental agenda because the vast number of people interested in the issue would make it popular for vote-seeking politicians. For example, passenger service is much more visible to the public than freight, which is one reason aviation deregulation came along before trucking and rail deregulation. As one prominent participant in the battles said, "People actually pay for tickets, and they can see the effects of deregulation every time they pay. But if you're talking about the effects of deregulation on the price of a can of dog food, the public doesn't see that because it doesn't make the difference of more than a cent or two in the price of the dog food. Trucking is different from airlines because you don't see the benefits on the grocery shelves."

The negative public opinion effects—the constraints imposed on government rather than the positive forces prompting government action—are probably more noticeable. Public opinion may sometimes direct government *to* do something, but it more often constrains government *from* doing something.[28] Health officials know, for instance, that the nation's bill for medical care could be lowered considerably by a change in such health habits as smoking, drinking, and reckless driving. But they feel keenly the limits on government action in this area, as one told me:

[28]On public opinion boundaries, see Kingdon, *Congressmen's Voting Decisions,* op. cit., Chapter 12. On opinion dikes, see V. O. Key, *Public Opinion and American Democracy* (New York: Knopf, 1961), p. 552.

As a taxpayer and a citizen, I don't want my life to be regulated all that much. I don't want the government to be telling me that I can't smoke or drink, or that I can't drive more than 40 miles an hour, all in the interests of the general health of the country. If I want to smoke and shorten my life in the process, in full knowledge of the facts, that's my business. There's a limit to public acceptance.

The short life of the seat belt interlock was testimony to the limits of public acceptance, as citizens rose up in wrath at fastening seat belts for grocery bags, and Congress repealed the requirement in months.

Of course, there are also severe limits on the ability of general public opinion to affect policy formation. Many important spheres, for one thing, are nearly invisible to the general public. The intricacies of health manpower legislation or the effects of rail deregulation may be known to the sectors of the public most directly affected and interested, but these issues never cause so much as a ripple in the average person's pond. In other cases, a majority of the mass public may favor one priority, but a smaller number of people with different preferences of greater intensity may affect government priorities more.[29] And developments may take place in government quite independent of general public opinion. Between 1976 and 1978, for example, the proportion in the polls of people who favored national health insurance versus those favoring private insurance stayed roughly stable, but the issue really heated up in government. We will develop a theory later in this book to account for such a dramatic rise on the governmental health agenda, but the point to make at this juncture is that the change had little to do with some dramatic shift in popular preferences.

Mass public opinion affects the agenda more than the alternatives. Governmental officials may pay attention to a set of subjects partly because those subjects are on the minds of a fairly large number of ordinary people. But it would be difficult to claim that the general public defines, to the same extent, the alternatives that are considered in government. Public opinion may set limits on the possibilities and may affect an agenda of subjects in a general way, but the general public opinion is rarely well enough formed to directly affect an involved debate among policy specialists over which alternatives should be seriously considered. As one staffer on the Hill discussed health issues in general:

Pressure from the public is very diffuse. Congressmen get letters asking for national health insurance, without any notion of which kind or anything. They get vague concern from the public about costs, but no real guidance about what to do. So they get this diffuse pressure, and they search around for ways to get a handle on it.

Indeed, it is likely, even with regard to agenda setting, that governmental officials and other activists affect the agenda in the mass public more than the other way around. As one particularly thoughtful journalist said of national health insurance, "The argument you hear around town in some quarters is that

[29]For an excellent discussion of the concept of intensity, see Robert A. Dahl, *A Preface to Demo cratic Theory* (Chicago: University of Chicago Press, 1956), Chapter 4.

people really want national health insurance. I'm inclined to think that it goes the other way, actually. Well-known politicians make an issue, and 'the people' come aboard." A well-known advocate of national health insurance agreed: "People often talk in terms of the public clamor, but in my experience, the public clamor follows the activities of a circle of experts, rather than the other way around." As we noticed when we were discussing the mass media, the agenda of items the public thinks is the most important is strongly affected by media content. To the extent that media are reporting the activities of political leaders, which we also noticed happened frequently, the public opinion agenda is being affected by the governmental agenda.

Thus models of agenda setting that rely on some form of translation of public preferences into government seem incomplete. For instance, some authors discuss ways items are taken from a public agenda and placed on a governmental agenda.[30] Quite often, items on a governmental agenda never were on a public agenda, or they were on a public agenda in a form so inchoate as to have only minimal impact on governmental officials.[31] People like presidents, senators, and cabinet secretaries have their own goals, their own proposals, their own agendas. These officials may attempt to mobilize the public in support of their objectives, but on many occasions they will choose not to. When they do mobilize expanded publics, furthermore, it may be more in pursuit of passage than for agenda setting. Presidents sometimes set the agenda, for instance, then mobilize the public to pass their legislative proposals.[32]

CONCLUSION

This chapter has examined the importance of various participants outside of government. Interest groups are among the most important. Because they are often concerned with protecting current benefits and prerogatives, they affect the governmental agenda more by blocking potential items than by promoting them. Rather than structuring a governmental agenda, interest groups often try to insert their preferred alternatives into a discussion once the agenda is already set by some other process or participant. Groups with electoral clout, the ability to affect the economy, cohesion, and organization have better initial resources

---

[30]For instance, see Roger Cobb and Charles Elder, *Participation in American Politics* (Boston: Allyn and Bacon, 1972), Chapter 7; and Robert Eyestone, *From Social Issues to Public Policy* (New York: Wiley, 1978).

[31]For example, Nelson says that child abuse was on the Children's Bureau agenda *before* it made a public opinion agenda. See Nelson, *Making an Issue of Child Abuse,* op. cit., Chapter 3.

[32]Van der Eijk and Kok, after a most interesting review of the relationship between public and governmental agendas which largely employs a basic "public input and government output" model, end by questioning the assumption that the public affects governments, rather than the other way around. See C. van der Eijk and W. J. P. Kok, "Nondecisions Reconsidered," *Acta Politica* 10 (July 1975): 277–301.

than those lacking in such respects. But even groups with excellent initial resources do not always carry the day.

Academics, researchers, and consultants affect the alternatives more than the agenda, and affect long-term directions more than short-term outcomes. Mass media turn out to be less important than anticipated. They seem to report events more than influence governmental agendas. But media's indirect impacts include affecting public opinion, which affects politicians, and magnifying events as opposed to originating them. Specialized media, followed by those particularly involved in a given policy area, serve to communicate within policy communities, and thus may have more impact on agendas and alternatives than mass media.

Elections-related participants and public opinion both affect governmental agendas more than the alternatives. Elections result in changes of administration and congressional turnover, both of which have powerful effects on agendas. But campaign promises and party platforms are not generally a very detailed guide to public policy. They set general themes, thus affecting agendas, but are not specific enough to feed much into the debate over alternatives. But the politicians' perceptions of a "national mood" do affect agendas. Public opinion acts more as a constraint on what is possible than as a promoter of a particular item.

Visible and Hidden Clusters of Participants

There is a fair body of writing that concentrates on each of the various participants separately. Thus one author portrays the president as central to an understanding of agenda setting and develops an executive-led model. Another scholar, possibly reacting to the first, argues that initiative often comes from Congress, that policy is legislative-led. Yet another maintains that ideas have their origins in professional communities composed of researchers, bureaucrats, and other specialists, some of them with vested interests and others relatively disinterested. Then another will concentrate on party realignment and other elections-related phenomena, tracing the effects of partisan and electoral change on public policy agendas. A preoccupation with the fit between public opinion and government policy becomes a representation model. A final writer will concentrate on the effects of the mass media. Each of these accounts of agenda setting grasps a part of reality; none are unimportant, but all are incomplete.

Actually, there are two general groupings of the participants: a visible cluster of actors and a hidden cluster. These clusters are not absolutely different from one another, but they are distinct enough to be meaningful. The visible cluster—those participants who receive a lot of press and public attention—includes the president and his high-level appointees, prominent members of Congress, the media, and such elections-related actors as political parties and campaigns. The relatively hidden cluster includes such specialists as academics and researchers, career bureaucrats, congressional staffers, and administration appointees below the top level. Interest groups travel between the two clusters, with some of their activities very public and others hardly visible at all.

One way to clarify the roles of the various participants is to return to our distinction between the agenda and the alternatives. We repeatedly found in Chapters 2 and 3 that agenda setting is affected by the visible cluster of participants, while the generation of alternatives occurs more in the hidden cluster. The administration, probably the most prominent visible actor, is a powerful agenda setter. When a president and his top appointees decide to place a high priority on a given item, agendas are set all over town. Members of Congress, bureaucrats, and lobbyists all pay attention to that priority item. Conversely, by virtue of such an administration decision, other subjects that could be prominent agenda items in different administrations are put on the shelf for the time being. This blocking of issues is at least as important an agenda-setting effect as positively promoting an item. Despite the administration's power in agenda setting, however, we also discovered that they do not necessarily control the alternatives among which authoritative choices might be made.

Prominent members of Congress can also affect a public policy agenda. A key Senate committee chairman, for instance, can move an item into prominence by scheduling hearings or markup sessions dealing with that subject. We found a similar pattern with other relatively visible actors. Mass media, elections, parties, campaigns, and changes in mass public opinion or national mood were all found to affect the agenda more than the alternatives.

The less visible actors, on the other hand, were repeatedly described as affecting the alternatives but not the agenda. The work of researchers of various descriptions, for instance, might well feed into the design of alternative proposals, but would only rarely be responsible for altering officials' attention to one subject rather than another. Career civil servants are more frequently generators of alternatives than agenda setters. The same goes for lower-visibility appointed people—congressional staffers, White House staff, and political appointees in departments and bureaus below the very top appointees. The process of generating alternatives is less visible than the agenda-setting process.

Obviously, these distinctions are tendencies; they are not iron-clad absolutes. Presidents do sometimes wade into the details of proposals, for instance, and a scientific discovery by a previously obscure researcher might affect a public policy agenda. Some actors, particularly interest groups and members of Congress, are involved in both agenda setting and alternative specification. But even with those actors, the distinction between visible and hidden activities is useful. If legislators want to affect agendas, for instance, they "go public" with hearings, speeches, and bill introductions. As they affect alternatives, however, they meet with staffers, lobbyists, and experts outside of government to hear views, air options, and eventually devise proposals. Similarly, interest groups are often involved with the alternatives: drafting proposals, attaching their solutions to problems already on an agenda, bending a preexisting debate in their direction if they can, and, particularly, trying to block proposals they regard as antithetical to their interests. When they try to affect agendas, however, they depend heavily on the visible activities and actors: persuading a congressional committee chairman to schedule hearings, for instance, or getting their point of view aired in a speech by a high administration official.

Why does agenda setting tend to be identified with a visible cluster of activities and actors, and alternative specification with a hidden cluster? The answer lies in the resources that are needed to perform each task and the incentives that draw people to each task. To generate alternatives, some degree of expertise and willingness to concern oneself with minute details is required. As we will see in Chapter 6, much of the discussion in policy communities of specialists is highly technical, specialized, and detailed. One cannot draft credible proposals without such attention. This fact makes a party platform or a campaign statement, for instance, not the best forum for presenting a thoroughly worked-out proposal. What the platform or the campaign can do to contribute to a policy agenda, however, is bring attention to a general subject, leaving the detailed alternatives to be worked through in other contexts.

The incentives in the visible arena are quite different. Senators and representatives are not known for being shrinking violets. Publicity gives them a boost, in terms of their reelection and in terms of any ambitions for higher office they might harbor. It is a very rare member of Congress who delves deeply into policy detail. Rather, the member is more likely to set the general direction and leave details to the staffers, who then consult with bureaucrats, interest group representatives, researchers, and other specialists. Similarly, presidents are involved in the highly public arena from the beginning. The broad-brush approach of such actors—presidents, cabinet secretaries, prominent members of Congress, parties, and media—is much better suited to agenda setting than to the generation of policy alternatives. The appeals in the visible cluster would be made to such desiderata as the potential for public support, electoral consequences of doing one thing rather than another, and incentives for political career advancement, rather than things like the technical quality of a proposal. Due to their authoritative governmental positions, elected officials also have several constitutional and legal prerogatives that enhance their ability to affect agendas.

So the visible participants try to affect agendas, and then they turn to specialists in the less visible policy community like bureaucrats, staffers, researchers, and interest groups for the alternatives from which an authoritative choice can be made.

CHAPTER 4

Processes: Origins, Rationality, Incrementalism, and Garbage Cans

We turn now from participants, the subjects of Chapters 2 and 3, to processes. First, we consider three common approaches: tracing the origins of initiatives; comprehensive, rational decision making; and incrementalism. Each of these is familiar, and each does describe *parts* of policy formation. We discuss the contributions of each approach to our understanding, but also note the limitations of each. A later part of this chapter then sketches a set of concepts that gives us a more comprehensive understanding, and subsequent chapters fill out that sketch.

ORIGINS

A concentration on the origins of initiatives does not make for very complete theory about agenda setting or alternative specification. I reach that conclusion for three reasons: (1) ideas can come from anywhere; (2) tracing origins involves one in an infinite regress; and (3) nobody leads anybody else.[1]

Ideas Can Come from Anywhere

Even a brief examination of public policy case studies would lead a researcher to despair of ever finding a given source of initiative that seems to be important across several cases. One case shows that one source is important; the next case shows something different. Public policy is not one single actor's brainchild. Across case

---

[1]For a general discussion of related problems, see George D. Greenberg, Jeffrey A. Miller, Lawrence B. Mohr, and Bruce C. Vladek, "Developing Public Policy Theory," *American Political Science Review* 71 (December 1977): 1532–1543.

studies, the proximate origin of the policy change varies from one case to the next. Even within a case study, it is often difficult to pinpoint who was responsible for movement. Ideas come from anywhere, actually, and the critical factor that explains the prominence of an item on the agenda is not its source, but instead the climate in government or the receptivity to ideas of a given type, regardless of source.

A brief look at several health initiatives illustrates the generalization that the proximate origins—the sources of initiative close in time to enactment—vary a great deal from one case to the next. First, the initiative for Health Maintenance Organizations was the brainchild of Paul Ellwood, the head of a group in Minneapolis called InterStudy, as we noticed in Chapter 1. Second, the Professional Standards Review Organization (PSRO) program was enacted in 1972 at the initiative of Senator Wallace Bennett (R-Utah), the ranking Republican on the Finance Committee. PSROs were to be physician organizations in each locality designed to monitor the hospital care that Medicare and Medicaid patients were receiving, to dampen unnecessary utilization, and to assure quality. Third, health planning started in two separate tracks, on the Hill and downtown. Several programs that dealt in one way or another with facilities planning—including Hill-Burton, Regional Medical Programs, and Comprehensive Health Planning—were all coming up for renewal at roughly the same time. Staffers on the Hill and people in the executive branch independently had the idea of combining the programs and adding provisions for planning organizations in each locality (which came to be called Health Systems Agencies). Our fourth case, a federal blood policy, was confined to the career civil service. To cut down on hepatitis in the blood used for transfusions, an HEW task force, using threats of government regulation and legislative proposals, pressured the blood banks and other interested organizations into voluntarily cutting down on the use of paid blood donors. Finally, the federal reimbursement for kidney dialysis depended in the first instance on the development of a technological advance, the shunt that would allow patients with end-stage renal disease to be hooked up to a dialysis machine.

Clearly, these cases are distinguished by the extraordinary variety of origins. Sometimes it's the administration or the Hill; at other times, it's civil servants, an outside analyst, the scientific community, or a lobby. Many times, there are several origins at once. At other times, a single proximate source of the idea can be quite readily identified. But nobody has a monopoly on ideas. They come from a plethora of different sources. Thus the key to understanding policy change is not where the idea came from but what made it take hold and grow. It *is* critical that an idea starts somewhere, and that it becomes diffused in the community of people who deal with a given policy domain, a process we discuss in Chapter 6. But as to the origins, as one Hill staffer put it, "Ideas come from anywhere."

Infinite Regress

We have discovered that as we move from one case to another, we have difficulty discerning a pattern to the origins. It is also true that within a given case, when we try to track down the origins of an idea or proposal, we become involved in an infinite regress. An idea doesn't start with the proximate source. It has a history. When one starts to trace the history of a proposal or concern back through time, there is no logical place to stop the process. As one respondent sagely pointed out, "This is not like a river. There is no point of origin."

Another look at case studies illustrates the problem. Serious proposals for national health insurance, for instance, go back in the United States at least to Teddy Roosevelt, and those really serious about tracing origins could go back to Bismarck and possibly beyond. One author traces recognition of the need for health planning far beyond recent efforts, to the 1927 Committee on the Costs of Medical Care.[2] HMOs did not start fresh in the mind of Paul Ellwood, but rather had a considerable history preceding the events of the Nixon administration HMO initiative. Similarly, there was quite a bit of experience with peer review by physicians prior to Senator Wallace Bennett's PSRO proposal. As one respondent summarized the problem, "You'll always find that things have their start somewhere else. People don't sit down and think up whole new approaches in a flash of insight. They borrow from somewhere else."

Because of the problem of infinite regress, the ultimate origin of an idea, concern, or proposal cannot be specified. Even if it could be, it would be difficult to determine whether an event at an earlier point in time was more important than an event at a later point. Indeed, "importance" would turn out to be tricky to define. So tracing origins turns out to be futile.

Nobody Leads Anybody Else

I originally designed this research to track the movement of items from one category of respondents to another in the policy community. If career civil servants were leaders over the others in the community, for instance, they might talk about a given subject in 1977, and it would take until 1978 or 1979 before others discussed it prominently in the interviews. Strictly in the sense of the early appearance of items in their interviews, then, some people might be called leaders.

It turns out that there are no leaders, at least not consistently across many possible subjects. Taking each public policy item in my data that changed during the four years, I noted the respondents who had discussed the subject at the low point in the four years, before it had become prominent in the interviews. I then added these frequencies across all variables. If one category of respondents was consistently talking about subjects before others, it should have higher scores. But as Table 4-1 shows, no category of respondents exhibits that sort of prescience. If one examines the percentages of respondents in each category who treat subjects as very or somewhat important at the *low* points in the curves, before the subjects caught on with respondents as a whole, the figures are quite uniform across categories. The exceptions to the uniformities are those with very small numbers of interviews, making conclusions about their ability to anticipate issues quite shaky. Nearly all of the time, the percentage in

---

[2]See Carol McCarthy, "Planning for Health Care," in Steven Jonas, ed., *Health Care Delivery in the United States* (New York: Springer Publishing Co., 1977), p. 352.

Discussion When Subjects Are Not Prominent*

	Congressional staff	Congressional agency	White House appointees	White House civil servants	Departmental appointees	Departmental civil servants	Interest groups	Journalists	Researchers, Academics Consultants	Total
Health										
Very or somewhat prominent	19%	13%	15%	31%	17%	15%	11%	15%	18%	16%
Little prominence or no mention	81	87	85	69	83	85	89	85	82	84
Total %	100%	100%	100%	100%	100%	100%	100%	100%	100%	100%
n	77	31	13	13	24	123	64	52	96	493
Transportation										
Very or somewhat prominent	17%	17%	23%	21%	4%	18%	13%	12%	20%	16%
Little prominence or no mention	83	83	77	79	96	82	87	88	80	84
Total %	100%	100%	100%	100%	100%	100%	100%	100%	100%	100%
n	132	59	13	24	24	176	137	52	94	711
Combined										
Very or somewhat prominent	18%	16%	19%	24%	10%	17%	12%	13%	20%	16%
Little prominence or no mention	82	84	81	76	90	83	88	87	80	84
Total %	100%	100%	100%	100%	100%	100%	100%	100%	100%	100%
n	209	90	26	37	48	299	201	104	190	1204

*To explain the method by which the figures are derived, I first defined a "change," as in the Appendix. For all changes, I determined a low point and a high point in the curve. For instance, catastrophic insurance was mentioned by 14 percent of my respondents in 1977 as being very or somewhat prominent, and by 92 percent in 1979. I then noted which respondents were among the 14 percent—were they Hill staffers, lobbyists, civil servants, or whom? I did the same things for all changes, excluding some that duplicated others. I then added across all the changes. Thus we have a measure of the degree to which a given category of respondents such as congressional staff or lobbyists discusses a subject seriously, before other categories of respondents do so. Among health congressional staffers, for instance, 19 percent of their interviews include a very or somewhat prominent discussion of these subjects at the low points in their curves, while 81 percent of congressional staff interviews neglected those subjects, again at the low points.

Table 4-2

Discussion When Subjects Are Prominent*

	Congressional staff	Congressional agency	White House appointees	White House civil servants	Departmental appointees	Departmental civil servants	Interest groups	Journalists	Researchers, Academics Consultants	Total
Health										
Very or somewhat prominent	65%	57%	69%	75%	82%	48%	60%	58%	69%	61%
Little prominence or no mention	35	43	31	25	18	52	40	42	31	39
Total %	100%	100%	100%	100%	100%	100%	100%	100%	100%	100%
n	40	14	13	4	17	95	53	43	80	359
Transportation										
Very or somewhat prominent	51%	50%	0	83%	33%	56%	58%	74%	75%	61%
Little prominence or no mention	49	50	0	17	67	44	42	26	25	39
Total %	100%	100%	0	100%	100%	100%	100%	100%	100%	100%
n	84	18	0	24	42	108	132	54	138	600
Combined										
Very or somewhat prominent	56%	53%	69%	82%	47%	52%	59%	67%	73%	61%
Little prominence or no mention	44	47	31	18	53	48	41	33	27	39
Total %	100%	100%	100%	100%	100%	100%	100%	100%	100%	100%
n	124	32	13	28	59	203	185	97	218	959

*The procedure is the same as described in the footnote to Table 4-1, except that these figures are for the *high* point in the curves. Here, we see if certain categories are disproportionately represented among respondents who rated a subject as prominent, during the year that it was hot.

each category of respondents is within five percentage points of the aggregate for them all.

I did the same sort of analysis for the *high* points in the curves, with roughly parallel results, as indicated in Table 4-2. In this instance, there is slightly more variation, although (again) many of the unusual categories have perilously low numbers on which to base calculations. In the main, however, attention to problems is fairly even across categories of participants at the points of most attention to a subject, as it was at the points of least attention.

Thus topics do not seem to move around in these policy communities from one type of participant to another with any regular pattern. No category of participant consistently discusses subjects ahead of others, and no category participates disproportionately when the subject is hot. When subjects hit the agenda, they seem to hit all participants roughly equally. Whole communities are affected simultaneously across the board.

Combinations and the Fertile Soil

The more that case studies and the place of various actors in processes of policy formation are examined, the more one concludes that attempting to pinpoint a single origin is futile. Instead, a complex *combination* of factors is generally responsible for the movement of a given item into agenda prominence. Even when we were considering the president himself, probably the most important single actor in the system, we were impressed by multiple causation. We set forth examples in which it appeared at first that the president was very powerful in setting the agenda, only to discover on some reflection that the agenda was set through a confluence of factors, including but not limited to presidential initiative.

If the president himself is only one among many, surely other actors are even less able to influence public policy single-handedly. It would be tempting to say that HMOs came to the fore because of Paul Ellwood, but the concentration on Ellwood as its proximate source would miss the importance of other factors—the administration's interest, the previous experience with prepaid group practice, the general national concern about medical care costs—that all came together at once. The same could be said for nearly every other case.

For a number of reasons, a combination of sources is virtually always responsible. One reason is the general fragmentation of the system. The founders deliberately designed a constitutional system to be fragmented, incapable of being dominated by any one actor. They succeeded. Thus a combination of people is required to bring an idea to policy fruition. In our discussion of the difference between the agenda and the alternatives, we also noticed that a variety of resources is needed. Some actors bring to the policy process their political popularity; others, their expertise. Some bring their pragmatic sense of the possible; others, their ability to attract attention.

Finally, nobody really controls the information system. It is tempting to say that the congressional staff controls the flow of information to their bosses, or that higher-level executive branch appointees depend on their civil service subordinates for expertise, ideas, and information. When we reach these conclusions, we seem to operate with an implicit hierarchical notion that information must flow up and down through channels, to and from superiors and subordinates. That approach misses the extraordinary looseness of the information system. Ideas, rumors, bits of information, studies, lobbyists' pleadings—all of these float around the system without any hard-and-fast communication channels. Subordinates cannot control that flow of information because their bosses have many others from whom they hear—lobbies, academics, media, each other, and their own experience and ideas. The same argument about the inability to control information flow can be applied to everybody, not just subordinates. No source monopolizes the flow of information and ideas.

The prominent feature of the processes under study here is the *joint* effect of several factors coming together at once. As one respondent put his experience with an important piece of legislation, "I'm sure that each of three or four people would gladly tell you that they originated it. The truth probably is that it sort of developed in that group of people." Said another, about a different issue, "I guess that each of us could claim credit, but actually, it came out of the agreement among us." In such cases, it's much less interesting *where* an idea got started than *that* it did.

Thus, the critical thing to understand is not where the seed comes from, but what makes the soil fertile. As one of my respondents eloquently stated the point:

> I can trace the paths of ideas. But my personal theory is that people plant seeds every day. There are a lot of ideas around, and there is no lacking for ideas. The real question is, which of these ideas will catch hold? When you plant a seed, you need rain, soil, and luck.

A major reason that health policy makers became very interested in the subject of the implications of sophisticated technology, for instance, is that they were preoccupied with cost and saw such technological advances as renal dialysis, CAT scanners, and heart bypass surgery as major contributors to cost inflation. Their concern with costs was the fertile soil that made it possible for the seed of concern over technology transfer to flourish. Or the academic thinking about deregulation in transportation took root in the fertile soil of a national mood that politicians perceived as being fed up with big government. Seeds come from many places. Why they germinate, grow, and flourish is much more interesting than their origins.

COMPREHENSIVE, RATIONAL DECISION MAKING

We need only have a brief word about how rational or comprehensive these processes appear because critiques of such models are already amply developed in earlier literature.[3] If policy makers were operating according to a rational, compre-

[3]For example, see James G. March and Herbert A. Simon, *Organizations* (New York: Wiley, 1958), Chapter 6; Charles E. Lindblom, "The Science of Muddling Through," *Public Administration Review* 14 (Spring 1959) 79–88; and Aaron Wildavsky, *The Politics of the Budgetary Process,* 3rd ed. (Boston: Little Brown, 1979), Chapters 2 and 5.

hensive model, they would first define their goals rather clearly and set the levels of achievement of those goals that would satisfy them. Then they would canvass many (ideally, all) alternatives that might achieve these goals. They would compare the alternatives systematically, assessing their costs and benefits, and then they would choose the alternatives that would achieve their goals at the least cost.

For various reasons already developed by other writers, such a model does not very accurately describe reality. The ability of human beings to process information is more limited than such a comprehensive approach would prescribe.[4] We are unable to canvass many alternatives, keep them simultaneously in our heads, and compare them systematically. We also do not usually clarify our goals; indeed, this is often counterproductive because constructing a political coalition involves persuading people to agree on a specific proposal when they might not agree on a set of goals to be achieved.[5] It could be that some individual actors in the process are fairly rational a fair amount of the time, but when many actors are involved and they drift in and out of the process, the kind of rationality that might characterize a unitary decision-making structure becomes elusive.

The case studies in this research also don't have the flavor of a rational, comprehensive approach to problem solving. Often, the participants are not solving problems at all. They have not specified their goals very precisely and have not identified their problems with great care. They often seem to push for given proposals, developing information about the problems they are supposedly solving along the way as a means of justifying their position. The case studies have something of a loose, messy quality to them, not the tight, orderly process that a rational approach specifies. Often, a somewhat accidental confluence of factors seems to loom rather large in the descriptions.

Another conception of orderly process is that policy proceeds in stages. Events, for example, proceed from agenda setting, through decision, to implementation. We also might believe that people recognize problems first and then seek solutions to them.[6] As we will argue presently, neat stages do not describe these processes well.[7] While there are indeed different processes, they do not necessarily follow one another through time in any regular pattern. Instead, several streams develop independently; they are logically coequal, and none necessarily precedes the others chronologically. Then, the separate streams become coupled at critical junctures, rather than following from one another.

[4]March and Simon, ibid.

[5]Lindblom, "The Science of Muddling Through," op. cit.

[6]For two other conceptions of stages, see Roger Cobb, Jennie-Keith Ross, and Marc Howard Ross, "Agenda Building as a Comparative Political Process," *American Political Science Review* 70 (March 1976): 127; and Barbara J. Nelson, *Making an Issue of Child Abuse* (Chicago: University of Chicago Press, 1984), Chapter 2.

[7]Cobb and Elder agree. See Roger W. Cobb and Charles D. Elder, "Communications and Public Policy," in Dan Nimmo and Keith Sanders, eds., *Handbook of Political Communications* (Beverly Hills: Sage, 1981), p. 394.

It may be that some parts of the process approximate a rational decision-making model more closely than others. Paul Light argues, for instance, that there are occasions in priority setting in the White House when people do sit down with a fairly full set of alternatives and compare them systematically, assessing their substantive and political costs and benefits.[8] It is also not fair to say that the processes are irrational: They may be just about as orderly as human beings can make them, under the circumstances. Still and all, a rational-comprehensive model does not describe very well the processes under investigation in this book, taken as a whole.

INCREMENTALISM

Partly in response to writings which imply that a rational-comprehensive model either is or should be used in governmental policy making, Charles Lindblom and others developed their description and defense of an incremental approach.[9] Instead of beginning consideration of each program or issue afresh, decision makers take what they are currently doing as given, and make small, incremental, marginal adjustments in that current behavior. By taking that tack, they need not canvass formidable numbers of far-reaching changes, they need not spend inordinate time defining their goals, and the comparisons they make between the current state of affairs and the small adjustments to be made in current behavior are entirely manageable. The result is that policy changes very gradually, in small steps.

Such a model describes many political and governmental processes. Aaron Wildavsky argues that the budgetary process works this way.[10] All participants assume that agencies have a base budget to work from. People rarely examine an entire budget from scratch because they are overwhelmed with information if they try, and they proceed instead to add or subtract small increments to or from the base.

There are also notable instances of incrementalism at work in my interviews. If a program has basically settled down into a stable pattern, for instance, few questions are raised about it, there is little controversy surrounding it, and whatever changes that do occur are modest. There are changes, but they proceed gradually, piece by piece. For instance, federal highway funds were traditionally spent only for new

[8]For example, see Paul C. Light, *The President's Agenda* (Baltimore: Johns Hopkins University Press, 1982), Chapter 6.

[9]Lindblom, "The Science of Muddling Through," op. cit.; Wildavsky, *Politics of the Budgetary Process,* op. cit. For alternative perspectives, see Amitai Etzioni, "Mixed Scanning," *Public Administration Review* 27 (December 1967): 385–392; and Paul R. Schulman, "Nonincremental Policy Making," *American Political Science Review* 69 (December 1975): 1354–1370.

[10]Wildavsky, ibid., Chapter 2; and Otto A. Davis, M. A. H. Dempster, and Aaron Wildavsky, "A Theory of the Budgetary Process," *American Political Science Review* 60 (September 1966): 529–547. See also several articles that modify or criticize an incremental model, including Peter B. Natchez and Irvin C. Bupp, "Policy and Priority in the Budgetary Process," *American Political Science Review* 67 (September 1973): 951–963; John Wanat, "Bases of Budgetary Incrementalism," *American Political Science Review* 68 (September 1974): 1221–1228; and John F. Padgett, "Bounded Rationality in Budgetary Research," *American Political Science Review* 74 (June 1980): 354–372.

construction. As road surfaces deteriorated, however, the need for maintenance became obvious to everyone. The federal government gradually got into the maintenance business, not by suddenly declaring that they would do so but by gradually defining more and more maintenance activities as construction: replacement, then rehabilitation, then resurfacing, then bridge repair. But "they didn't really come out and call it maintenance," in the words of one lobbyist. By the late 1970s, when I asked whether the federal government actually was financing maintenance, one congressional staffer replied, "I think we crossed that watershed a year or two ago."

Incrementalism is also treated in the interviews, not as a description of the way the world is but as a strategy that one might use to manipulate outcomes. People are sometimes reluctant to take big steps. Apprehensive about being unable to calculate the political fallout, politicians shy away from grand departures. Apprehensive about not fully understanding the unanticipated consequences that might ensue, specialists also avoid significant changes. Both worry about budgetary implications of massive new programs. Given this natural caution, those who advocate major changes find they often must push for one small part at a time in order to move in their preferred direction. Thus respondents often talked about getting to national health insurance in bits and pieces, starting with Medicare and Medicaid in the 1960s, and gradually expanding. One could expand by population groupings, for instance, so that the next step after the elderly and the poor might be maternal and child benefits, bringing young people into coverage. One respondent labeled this a "kiddie-in-the-door" approach. Another way to expand would be to enact catastrophic coverage for the entire population and gradually reduce the deductible over the years. Another would be to finance given procedures, gradually adding to the list. When Congress enacted the program for renal dialysis and kidney transplants, for instance, a congressional staffer called it national health insurance one organ at a time.

As good a description as incrementalism is of some parts of the processes under scrutiny in this book, and as good a strategy as it might be under some circumstances, an incremental or gradualism model does not describe agenda change particularly well. If agendas changed incrementally, a gradual heightening of interest in a subject over the course of years would be apparent. In my interview data, for instance, a subject may be mentioned by 5 percent more respondents each year, for a total change of 20 percent spread over the four years. But interest does not gradually build in this fashion. Instead of incremental agenda change, a subject rather suddenly "hits," "catches on," or "takes off." After decades of thinking about the problem, a sudden flurry of interest in waterway user charges produces a program within two years. Serious discussion of catastrophic health insurance jumps from 33 percent of my respondents in one year to 92 percent the next year. One extremely well-informed health respondent said at the time, "If you had asked me three months ago, I would have said that nothing was going to happen. Something really has come along to move national health insurance onto the front burner." Said another, when I reminded him that he had predicted a year earlier that it would be ten years before there would be any movement, "Actually, I would still have said that three or four weeks ago." The same comments were made about the deregulation movement in transportation. Respondents referred to the changes in ICC interpretations that al-

Table 4-3

Size of Changes*

Size of change, in %	Number of health variables exhibiting change	Number of transportation variables exhibiting change	Total
60%+	4	6	10
50–59%	2	6	8
40–49%	5	12	17
30–39%	9	12	21
20–29%	9	10	19
n	29	46	75

*I included all variables for policy subjects for which there had been some change over the four years (see Appendix for operational definitions). There were 29 such health variables, and 46 in transportation. I then noted for each included variable the magnitude of the largest difference across the four years. If a given item rose from 23 percent of my health respondents discussing it as very or somewhat prominent in 1976 to 63 percent in 1978, for instance, there would be a 40 percent difference. The cell entries in the table, then, are the numbers of variables that fall into the categories on the left. Four of the 29 health variables, for instance, show their largest change over the four years to be 60 percent or higher; 10 of the 46 transportation variables show a change of between 20 and 29 percent.

lowed much greater flexibility in pricing, entry, and abandonment as "unbelievable," "revolutionary," and "utterly without precedent clear back into the previous century." Even a casual glance at the quantitative indicators presented throughout this book, including the charts in the Chapter 1 case studies, reveals a lot of sudden spikes upward, rather than gradual, incremental changes.

Nor are selected case studies isolated instances. I analyzed all changes in my data, and found that there were as many nonincremental as incremental changes. Table 4-3 shows that pattern. If incremental changes dominated this picture, one would see the changes clustered disproportionately at the low end, in the twenties and thirties. Remember that a change of 40 percent, for instance, is really quite substantial: it means going from, say, 30 percent to 70 percent of my respondents. Of course, conclusions in this area turn on how one defines "incremental." I have resisted the temptation to set an arbitrary definition at, for example, 35 percent change. Instead, I present the whole array in Table 4-3, and let the reader make his or her own interpretation. However one sets an exact level, an incremental model does not very completely describe these data since the variables are fairly evenly distributed across the categories. At least it can be said that there are many clearly nonincremental changes.

But do these changes take place over all four waves of my interviews, or do the subjects suddenly shift from one year to an adjacent year? Table 4-4 presents the data in Table 4-3, but broken down by the number of years it took to traverse the largest change. Once again, the variables spread rather evenly across the categories. The changes do not tend disproportionately to take place gradually over all four waves of interviews; indeed, somewhat more of them shift over one year.

Table 4-4

Size of Changes, by Years*

	Health			
Size of change	Over 1 year	Over 2 years	Over 3 years	Total
60%+	0	3	1	4
50–59%	1	1	0	2
40–49%	1	1	3	5
30–39%	5	2	2	9
20–29%	3	1	5	9
Totals	10	8	11	29

	Transportation			
Size of change	Over 1 year	Over 2 years	Over 3 years	Total
60%+	3	1	2	6
50–59%	1	2	3	6
40–49%	3	6	3	12
30–39%	5	5	2	12
20–29%	5	5	0	10
Totals	17	19	10	46

*The procedure here is the same as in Table 4-3, except that I have also noticed here the number of years the change took. If there was a 53 percent rise between 1976 and 1977, for instance, that goes in the "one year" column; a 34 percent drop between 1976 and 1979 goes in the "three year" column. There is some under reporting of the sharpness of change. If a variable went from 12 percent in 1976, to 14 percent in 1977, to 46 percent in 1978, for instance, it is dutifully recorded as a 34 percent change over two years, even though there was clearly a sharp rise in one of the two.

If we were to call a change nonincremental if *either* it is 40 percent or higher *or* it takes place over one year, 53 of the 75 variables (71 percent) would be classified as nonincremental changes. The reader can invent other definitions to suit his or her taste. But again, even by quite a variety of reasonable definitions, many instances of sharp, substantial, sudden changes are evident in these data. It might be fair to describe some changes as incremental, but not all or even a majority of them.

To return to our distinction between the agenda and the alternatives, agenda change appears quite discontinuous and nonincremental. But incrementalism might still characterize the generation of alternatives. As policy makers consider the alternatives from which they will choose, they repair to ideas and approaches with which they are already familiar. The Nixon administration picked up on prepaid group practice, an arrangement with an extensive previous track record, for its Health Maintenance Organization initiative. The concept of waterway user charges depended heavily on the financing of other modes by user charges, and on an extensive history of waterway proposals. The proposals are often quite familiar and have been floating around in circles of cognoscenti for some time. But the agenda is capable of changing quite abruptly—with the election of a new administration, a crisis like the collapse of the Penn Central, or a variety of other things that we are detailing in this book.

In fact, incremental processes are discussed quite often in the interviews. They were prominent in 62 percent of the interviews, and in 14 of the 23 case studies. But this discussion often refers to either the development of proposals or alternatives or to the enactment of changes in small increments, rather than to agenda change. One respondent in the aviation area described interest in higher landing fees in peak traffic periods as a way of creating an incentive for some traffic to flow in the less busy times of the day or week:

> The idea has been around for some time. But as a policy issue, it goes up and down. Sometimes OMB might be interested in it and then they drop it. Sometimes the environmental quality people get interested in it and then drop it. Lately, there has been no great pressure to do anything about it, but we are continuing to look at it as an alternative to investment in capital projects.

In this description, an old alternative—known to specialists, and discussed and refined at length by analysts—pops up on and disappears from policy agendas. The content of the idea is quite stable; its appearance on the agenda is not. Similarly, actual enactments into law might be quite small, gradual, and incremental. Another transportation respondent described small steps taken over many years toward greater coherence and integration in transportation planning: "These things proceed in small, incremental steps. Something is enacted, everybody concludes that it's not so bad, and that gets people ready for the next bite." So the agenda might be quite volatile, but the alternatives policy makers consider and the actual proposals they are prepared to enact might represent much less dramatic changes.[11]

Thus incrementalism is important, particularly in understanding the development of alternatives and proposals. We will return to the developmental process that takes place in communities of specialists in Chapter 6. But agendas exhibit a good deal of nonincremental change.

THE FEDERAL GOVERNMENT AND GARBAGE CANS

To this point in our journey through the labyrinth of policy formation, we have come across many important and interesting partial answers to our central questions: how the agenda is set, how the alternatives for choice are specified, and why these processes work as they do. By now, we know a lot about the participants who are important and about the conditions under which they are important, and we have explored the potential of some notions that might be used to contribute to our understanding. But the answers have been partial, and our understanding has been in bits and pieces. This section starts the process of as-

[11]For an account of the cumulative effect of incremental changes, see Hugh Heclo, *Modern Social Politics in Britain and Sweden* (New Haven: Yale University Press, 1974), especially pp. 304–322.

sembling pieces into the whole. We provide here an overview of the theory we develop in subsequent chapters, a kind of skeleton that is fleshed out in the chapters to follow.

Our point of departure is a model developed by Michael Cohen, James March, and Johan Olsen which, in a masterpiece of indelicate language, they called a "garbage can model of organizational choice."[12] What I have observed in my research seems similar in many of its major contours to the essential logic of their model. I will add several features of my own to their argument and will alter their model in some major respects to fit the phenomena under study here, which is why their model is our point of departure rather than our finish line. I begin by describing their concepts and then I will show how those ideas can be changed to suit our purposes.

The Garbage Can Model

Cohen, March, and Olsen set about to understand organizations that they called "organized anarchies." Their empirical referent for such organizations, it pains and embarrasses an academic to admit, is universities. Organized anarchies have three general properties: problematic preferences, unclear technology, and fluid participation. As to preferences, people characteristically do not define their preferences very precisely, much as political actors often fail to (or refuse to) define their goals. Yet, as Lindblom argues, people act in the absence of clearly defined goals; indeed, action is often facilitated by fuzzing over what one is trying to accomplish.[13] When participants do define their preferences with a modicum of precision, they conflict. So the preferences are inconsistent, both between individuals and even within a given individual. Thus, as Cohen et al. put it, the organization is "a loose collection of ideas [rather than] a coherent structure; it discovers preferences through action more than it acts on the basis of preferences."[14] This is not like a small business, for instance, in which everyone agrees that the firm must turn a profit.

Second, as to unclear technology, an organized anarchy's members do not understand the organization's processes very well. They may know their own jobs, and the organization as a whole may get along rather well, but its members have only fragmentary and rudimentary understandings of why they are doing what they are doing and how their jobs fit into a more general picture of the organization. They operate a lot by trial and error, by learning from experience, and by pragmatic invention in crises. Third, participants drift in and out of decision making, so the boundaries of such an organization are rather fluid. The time and effort members of the organization devote to different subjects vary; even within a given subject their involvement varies from one time to another. Who shows up for or is invited to a given critical meeting, and their degree of activity at the meeting, for instance, turn out to make a tremendous difference. Despite these characteristics, such organiza-

---

[12]Michael Cohen, James March, and Johan Olsen, "A Garbage Can Model of Organizational Choice," *Administrative Science Quarterly* 17 (March 1972): 1–25.

[13]Lindblom, "The Science of Muddling Through," op. cit.

[14]Cohen, March, and Olsen, "A Garbage Can Model," op. cit., p. 1.

tions do function: They make decisions, adapt, and survive, at least after a fashion and sometimes quite well.

On the face of it, this looks a lot like the federal government. People do disagree about what they want government to accomplish, and often are obliged to act before they have the luxury of defining their preferences precisely. They often don't know how to accomplish what they want to accomplish, even if they can define their goals. If they want to eliminate poverty, for instance, the technology to do so is quite elusive; it's not like making widgets. People also don't necessarily understand the organization of which they are a part: The left hand doesn't know what the right hand is doing. Participation is definitely fluid. Even within a relatively hierarchical bureaucracy, some people take on an importance that is not commensurate with their formal role, and others are impotent despite considerable powers on paper. Both the legislature and the executive branch are in the act, further clouding organizational boundaries. And various categories of people outside of government also drift in and out of decision making. Participation changes from one decision to another and one time to the next. Turnover of personnel adds to the fluidity. Thus a description of the federal government as an organized anarchy is not far wide of the mark.

Running through such organizations or decision structures are four separate streams: problems, solutions, participants, and choice opportunities. Each of the streams has a life of its own, largely unrelated to the others. Thus people generate and debate solutions because they have some self-interest in doing so (e.g., keeping their job or expanding their unit), not because the solutions are generated in response to a problem or in anticipation of a particular upcoming choice. Or participants drift in and out of decision making, carrying their pet problems and solutions with them, but not necessarily because their participation was dictated by the problem, solution, or choice at hand. As Cohen, March, and Olsen say, this kind of organization "is a collection of choices looking for problems, issues and feelings looking for decision situations in which they might be aired, solutions looking for issues to which they might be the answer, and decision makers looking for work."[15]

As a choice opportunity (e.g., the selection of a dean) floats by in the organization (e.g., a university), various participants, each with their own resources, become involved. Various problems (e.g., maintaining scholarly quality, curriculum improvement, affirmative action) are introduced into the choice, and various solutions (e.g., inside candidates for a deanship, outside candidates, expanding the unit, abolishing the unit) may be considered. A choice opportunity thus is "a garbage can into which various kinds of problems and solutions are dumped by participants as they are generated. The mix of garbage in a single can depends on the mix of cans available, on the labels attached to the alternative cans, on what garbage is currently being produced, and on the speed with which garbage is collected and removed from the scene."[16]

[15]Ibid., p. 2.

[16]Ibid.

The outcomes, then, are a function of the mix of garbage (problems, solutions, participants, and the participants' resources) in the can and how it is processed. Who is invited to or shows up for a meeting (i.e., who the participants are) affects the outcome dramatically. Which solutions are ready for airing and which problems are on people's minds are critical. The various streams are coupled in these choice contexts. When a given solution is proposed, it may be regarded by the participants as irrelevant to the problem and is thus discarded. Or even more likely, the participants have fixed on a course of action and cast about for a problem to which it is the solution, discarding problems that don't seem to fit. The solutions and problems that come to the fore might change from one meeting to the next, as given participants attend or fail to attend.

Sometimes, problems are actually resolved. At least as often, problems drift away from the choice at hand to another garbage can, not being resolved in the current round at least. Or important problems are ignored altogether, possibly because there is no available solution for them. At any rate, the logical structure of such a model is (1) the flow of fairly separate streams through the system, and (2) outcomes heavily dependent on the coupling of the streams—couplings of solutions to problems; interactions among participants; the fortuitous or purposeful absence of solutions, problems, or participants—in the choices (the garbage cans) that must be made.

Note that this picture is quite unlike various models we discussed earlier. It certainly does not look like comprehensive, rational decision making. People do not set about to solve problems here. More often, solutions search for problems. People work on problems only when a particular combination of problem, solution, and participants in a choice situation makes it possible. Nor do they go through a prescribed logical routine: defining the problem, canvassing the possible solutions, evaluating the alternatives in terms of their ability to solve the problem at the least cost. Rather, solutions and problems have equal status as separate streams in the system, and the popularity of a given solution at a given point in time often affects the problems that come up for consideration. Nor is change produced by such a process necessarily incremental. It can be, but a coupling of streams in a decision context can also produce quite an abrupt change, as a new combination previously untried comes into play.

A Revised Model

We now adapt this general line of thought to understand agenda setting in the federal government. In this adaptation, we will bend the ideas to suit our purposes and add features of our own where it seems appropriate. The streams described here also differ from those in the Cohen-March-Olsen model. But the general logic is similar. The federal government is seen as an organized anarchy. We will find our emphasis being placed more on the "organized" than on the "anarchy," as we discover structures and patterns in the processes. But the properties of problematic preferences, unclear technology, and fluid participation are in evidence. Separate streams run through the organization, each with a life of its own. These streams are coupled at critical junctures, and that coupling produces the greatest agenda change.

As I have observed them, there are three families of processes in federal government agenda setting: problems, policies, and politics. People recognize problems, they generate proposals for public policy changes, and they engage in such political activities as election campaigns and pressure group lobbying. In theory, each of the participants discussed in Chapters 2 and 3 could be involved in each of these processes. Members of Congress could both run for reelection and formulate proposals, for instance, and interest groups could both push for recognition of pet problems and for adoption of their solutions or proposals. In practice, while many participants do cut across the three process streams, there is also some specialization. Academics and researchers, for example, are more involved in generating policy proposals than in the electioneering or pressure activities that we label "political," and political parties are more involved in the political stream than in the detailed work of formulating proposals. Conceptually, however, any actor can be involved in any stream, and some of them actually are involved in several. In other words, we distinguish between participants and processes.

The three major process streams in the federal government are (1) problem recognition, (2) the formation and refining of policy proposals, and (3) politics. First, various problems come to capture the attention of people in and around government. In the health area, for instance, people could be worried about the cost of medical care and, within that problem, about the subproblems of cost to the government, cost to insurers, and cost to consumers. Or they could concentrate on the access to medical care, health habits in the population, biomedical research frontiers, or the latest epidemic. So we need to understand how and why one set of problems rather than another comes to occupy officials' attention; we will focus on that stream in Chapter 5.

Second, there is a policy community of specialists—bureaucrats, people in the planning and evaluation and in the budget offices, Hill staffers, academics, interest groups, researchers—which concentrates on generating proposals. They each have their pet ideas or axes to grind; they float their ideas up and the ideas bubble around in these policy communities. In a selection process, some ideas or proposals are taken seriously and others are discarded. These phenomena, akin to the garbage can model's stream of solutions, are discussed in Chapter 6.

Third, the political stream is composed of things like swings of national mood, vagaries of public opinion, election results, changes of administration, shifts in partisan or ideological distributions in Congress, and interest group pressure campaigns. Events in this stream occur independently of the streams of problems and proposals. Thus politicians discern a new mood among their constituents; election results bring a new administration to power; or an influx of new and different legislators changes the complexion of Capitol Hill. We concentrate on the political stream in Chapter 7.

Each of the actors and processes can operate either as an impetus or as a constraint. As an impetus, an interest group or a president can push for the inclusion of a given item on a governmental agenda, or the recognition of a problem or the development of a solution can prompt higher agenda status for a given item. But people in and around government also find themselves coming up against a series of constraints. If the costs of paying attention are too high, otherwise worthy items are prevented from becoming prominent. Thus the problems stream can push some items higher on the agenda, but it can also retard the upward movement of others, particularly through the budget constraint. Other items are not considered because there is a lot of public opposition, either from the general public or from activists of various descriptions. If an unacceptable political cost would have to be paid, the item is shunted aside. So the political forces we describe in Chapter 7 can operate either as an impetus or as a constraint.

These three streams of processes develop and operate largely independently of one another. Solutions are developed whether or not they respond to a problem. The political stream may change suddenly whether or not the policy community is ready or the problems facing the country have changed. The economy may go sour, affecting the budget constraint, which imposes a burden on both politicians and policy specialists that was not of their own making. The streams are not absolutely independent, however. The criteria for selecting ideas in the policy stream, for instance, are affected by specialists' anticipation of what the political or budgetary constraints might be. Or election outcomes in the political stream might be affected by the public's perception of the problems facing the country, connecting (to a degree) the political and problems streams. Despite these hints of connection, the streams still are largely separate from one another, largely governed by different forces, different considerations, and different styles.

Once we understand these streams taken separately, the key to understanding agenda and policy change is their coupling. The separate streams come together at critical times. A problem is recognized, a solution is available, the political climate makes the time right for change, and the constraints do not prohibit action. Advocates develop their proposals and then wait for problems to come along to which they can attach their solutions, or for a development in the political stream like a change of administration that makes their proposals more likely to be adopted. In Chapter 8 I label an opportunity for pushing one's proposals a "policy window"—open for a short time, when the conditions to push a given subject higher on the policy agenda are right. But the window is open for only a while, and then it closes. Enabling legislation comes up for renewal, for instance, and many potential changes in the program can be proposed only in the context of the renewal consideration. Or an unanticipated influx of new members of Congress makes action on certain items possible, but those legislators might not last beyond their first two-year term. Thus an item suddenly gets hot. Something is done about it, or nothing, but in either case, policy makers soon turn their attention to something else. So opportunities pass, and if policy entrepreneurs who were trying to couple a solution to the hot problem or the propitious political situation miss the chance, they must wait for the next opportunity. Chapter 8 discusses these policy windows and the coupling of the streams that takes place when they open.

This chapter has only sketched out the line of argument that we pursue in the remainder of the book. We turn now to a series of chapters that paint the more complete picture. The next three chapters consider each of the process streams in their turn. Chapter 8 then discusses the coupling of the streams that takes place when a policy window opens. Chapter 9 wraps up the argument of the book, and presents some reflections on the structure of the processes and the implications of our findings. Chapter 10, written for the second edition, adds new case studies and further reflections.

CHAPTER 5

Problems

At any time, important people in and around government could attend to a long list of problems. People in transportation, for instance, could conceivably be examining the costs of regulation, infrastructure deterioration, automobile safety issues, production of a new supersonic airplane, the potential collapse of rail service in one or another section of the country, deficiencies in commuter movement, and the costs and shortages of energy. Obviously, they pay attention to some potential problems and ignore others. This chapter considers how problems capture the attention of these people. Sometimes their attention is affected by a more or less systematic indicator of a problem. At other times, a dramatic event seizes their attention, or feedback from the operation of existing programs suggests that not all is well. But problems are also not entirely self-evident. How people define something as a problem is worth some consideration.

INDICATORS

Fairly often, problems come to the attention of governmental decision makers not through some sort of political pressure or perceptual slight of hand but because some more or less systematic indicator simply shows that there is a problem out there. Such indicators abound in the political world because both governmental and nongovernmental agencies routinely monitor various activities and events: highway deaths, disease rates, immunization rates, consumer prices, commuter and intercity ridership, costs of entitlement programs, infant mortality rates, and many others. For example, administrators of health manpower programs monitor the number of physicians being produced by medical schools, by specialty and by location of employment. They use such figures to assess the degree of shortage or oversupply, and can recommend adjustments in manpower policy to remedy problems.

One of the most common of the routine monitoring activities is following the patterns of federal expenditures and budgetary impacts. People in government know when their budgets are rising or falling, and problems directly affect them through the budget process. One reason that medical care costs dominated the health interviews was that the numbers simply spoke to these people. When I asked one health respondent why cost containment was high on the agenda, his instant reply was, "It is on the agenda of Washington policy makers because it deserves to be. When you start to take a look at HEW, the increasing costs of Medicare and Medicaid just hit you over the head with a two-by-four."

In addition to routine monitoring, studies are often conducted on a particular problem at a given point in time, either by a government agency or by nongovernmental researchers or academics. Such studies may also suggest a problem that might need governmental attention. A survey of the population, for instance, estimates the proportion of households without any health insurance, or with minimal health insurance. Or a statute mandates a study by the Department of Transportation of the problems of the railroad industry, the causes of those problems, and the options that might be considered to remedy them. When I asked one respondent why the studies showing that people could promote their own health by changing their habits (exercising, eating a balanced diet, not smoking) had become so popular in health policy circles, his semi-baffled reply was, "Well, it just makes a lot of sense, I guess. An intelligent idea catches on every once in a while."

Such indicators or studies are not used primarily to determine whether or not a given problem exists; such determination is a matter of interpretation, a subject to which we return momentarily. Rather, decision makers and those close to them use the indicators in two major ways: to assess the magnitude of a problem and to become aware of changes in the problem. At some level, for instance, everyone agrees that some people in the population do not have adequate health insurance. A study of the proportion of the households that have no insurance and that have insurance of various descriptions helps to establish the magnitude of the problem that everyone intuitively knows exists in some form. There will still be disputes about the adequacy of the insurance coverage, whether this is a problem, and, if a problem, whether it is a problem that government should address, but at least some such indicator can establish the magnitude of the condition. Or even if everybody agrees according to personal experience and intuition that highways and bridges need repair, some kind of systematic engineering study still is useful in estimating the magnitude of the deterioration.

Important people in and around government also look for changes in such indicators. A steady state is viewed as less problematic than changing figures. For example, transportation respondents' discussion of the financial problems of the railroads in general, and of Conrail in particular, rose sharply between 1977 and 1978, as Figure 5-1 shows. In 1977, very optimistic talk about

Figure 5-1

Discussion of Rail Financial Problems and Conrail Deficit

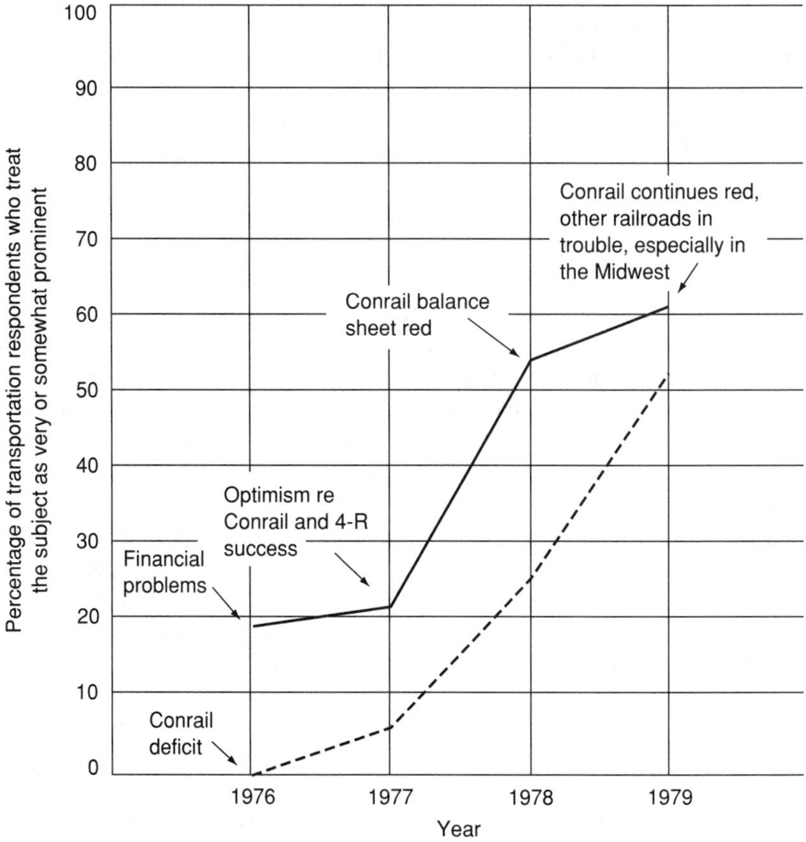

Conrail's financial viability was heard, but that evaporated by 1978 with the announcement of Conrail's deficit and its requests for much larger than anticipated infusions of federal support. Several midwestern railroads showed signs during roughly the same period of serious financial trouble, reminiscent in some people's eyes of the Penn Central collapse. One respondent, interviewed in June 1978, dramatized the abruptness of the shift:

> Up until April of this year everybody thought that Conrail was going along pretty well. We knew that it would take a little more money, but there was a confidence around it. This great experiment in keeping railroads in the private sector would work. There has really been an incredible switch over the period of just a couple of months. There has been an amazing turnabout. Now people are anticipating having to face the possibility that Conrail will not make it.

Policy makers consider a change in an indicator to be a change in the state of a system; this they define as a problem. The actual change in the indicator, however, gets exaggerated in the body politic, as people believe the change is symbolic of something larger and find that the new figures do not conform to their previous experience. Thus indicator change can have exaggerated effects on policy agendas.

Pervasive, Necessary, and Powerful Indicators

Reference to some types of more or less objective indicators of problems is widespread in the interviews. Fifty-two percent of the interviews included prominent discussion of such indicators. They were even more central in the case studies, important in 19 of the 23 cases. There are no major differences between health and transportation. When we think of things that drive items into greater prominence, we are often prone to think of pressure campaigns or dramatic events that bring problems to the attention of important people. These things are important, as this book demonstrates, but people often pay attention to a problem rather straightforwardly because there actually is a demonstrable problem that needs their attention.

Demonstrating that there is indeed a problem to which one's solution can be attached is a very real preoccupation of participants in the policy process. It becomes a major part of the policy debate we will describe in Chapter 6. Constructing an indicator and getting others to agree to its worth become major preoccupations of those pressing for policy change. The need for such indicators can make people grasp for indicators with serious deficiencies. As one respondent summarized the need for indicators, particularly quantitative measures, "It helps for a problem to be countable. You can count beds, you can survey their vacancy rates, and that sort of thing."[1] The countable problem sometimes acquires a power of its own that is unmatched by problems that are less countable. Mass transit people become fixed on ridership, and find it much more difficult and less rewarding to concentrate on such "softer" areas as quality of service. The Professional Standards Review program becomes evaluated according to its impact on utilization and cost control, rather than its impact on the quality of care that Medicare and Medicaid patients receive.

The indicator itself is very powerful. Concern over Amtrak's budget rose over my four years of interviewing, from only 14 percent of my transportation respondents discussing it prominently in 1976 to 65 percent in 1979. This increased concern reflected quite straightforwardly the inability of Amtrak to turn the profitability corner. Even Secretary of Transportation Brock Adams, a longtime supporter of Amtrak while in Congress, toward the end of his tenure in office proposed a 43 percent cut in Amtrak mileage. Many observers laid his change at the door of the powerful budgetary figures. As one put it, "Traditionally, Adams was one of those who supported Amtrak against the department. Now he gets in here as secretary, and he comes face to face with the reality of a half a billion dollar deficit for an organization that is running a

[1]This is analogous to quantifying workload. See John W. Kingdon, "A House Appropriations Subcommittee: Influences on Budgetary Decisions," *Southwestern Social Science Quarterly* 47 (June 1966): 68–78.

bunch of empty trains. He still has a desire to be constructive, but that doesn't mean that he's just going to let Amtrak go on as they have been doing." One congressional staffer summarized the point nicely: "As I have observed these things over the years, Congress is impotent in the face of facts in many cases."

Interpretation of the Indicators

Indicators are not simply a straightforward recognition of the facts. Precisely because indicators have such powerful implications, the methodology by which the facts are gathered and the interpretations that are placed on these facts become prominent items for heated debate. For instance, a lively debate always surrounds the question of whether truckers are paying their share of highway construction and maintenance. Studies of fair shares are actually extremely complicated cost allocation problems that turn strikingly on the assumptions the researcher makes about marginal costs. If you assume that highways are basically for passenger vehicles, then trucks are responsible only for the wear and tear above the passenger level; but if you assume that highways are freight-ways, then truckers would be obliged to assume a much higher fraction of costs. The question is where between these assumptions is the right balance. Debates become even more complicated, delving into such areas as whether miles or ton-miles traveled is the appropriate measure, and whether truck weight or weight per axle is appropriate.

Similar problems of interpretation are evident in the health area. Infant mortality, for instance, is widely taken to be an index of a nation's health. Yet it turns out that the relatively poor performance of the United States on that index is due to the pregnancy rate among teenagers. As one respondent said, "If you take only women over 19, we have the best rate in the world. The reason that the rate is so bad is that young women are getting pregnant long before they should, then they get no care, their nutrition is terrible, and so forth." Uncritical use of the overall indicator misses such subtlety. Even something as seemingly straightforward as the cost of medical care turns out to be difficult to define as a problem. Consider the hue and cry over the fact that medical care had passed 8 percent of GNP in 1976. As one respondent mused, "People say that medical care is consuming more and more of GNP. So it is. But is it too much? If 8 percent of GNP is too much, then why is it, compared to what we spend on, say, automobiles each year? Why shouldn't it be 10 percent? There's no obvious answer as to why the cost we're currently incurring is too high." Thus the data do not speak for themselves. Interpretations of the data transform them from statements of conditions to statements of policy problems. We return to such translation shortly.

FOCUSING EVENTS, CRISES, AND SYMBOLS

Problems are often not self-evident by the indicators. They need a little push to get the attention of people in and around government. That push is sometimes provided by a focusing event like a crisis or disaster that comes along to call attention to the problem, a powerful symbol that catches on, or the personal experience of a policy maker.

Events of this sort are discussed with some frequency in the interviews, although not overwhelmingly. Thirty-five percent of the interviews included a prominent mention of crises, disasters, or other such events, and they were important in 7 of the 23 case studies. But there is a dramatic difference between health and transportation. Fully 63 percent of the transportation interviews included prominent discussion of crises, compared to only 11 percent of health interviews. Similarly none of the health case studies had crisis coded as important at all; but they were very important in half of the transportation case studies. Airplane crashes stimulate concern about air safety; the wreck of the Penn Central prompts government action on railroad finances; bridge collapses focus attention on highway infrastructure deterioration. Consider the following observations of transportation respondents:

> The whole process is crisis. This system responds to crisis. It's the only thing that it does respond to. That's what politics is all about. In the American system, you have to get hit on the side of the head before you do something.

> An issue becomes a burning issue when it reaches crisis proportions. Until there's a crisis, it's just one of many issues. Governmental policy always has been, and always will be, a function of crisis.

> You have to fall out of bed before you get any help.

> The whole legislative process is putting out brush fires, not building a good fire department.

There are rather few comparable health examples. So when we speak of crises and disasters, such references apply almost exclusively to transportation, and very little to health.

Why such a striking difference? One explanation might be the greater public visibility of health. Health is universal, affecting all of us. News of the latest disease and cure appears prominently in the printed and broadcast media, while transportation news is relegated to the business pages. Marcus Welby and Trapper John perform their miracles of healing before our eyes each week, but we do not view a gripping television drama about a railroad traffic manager. Somehow, open-heart surgery means more to most of us than the Alton, Illinois, Lock and Dam 26. Health is naturally on our agendas more of the time. To make an item from a less visible arena move up on a governmental agenda, something must happen, and that something often is a real crisis—the sort of thing government decision makers cannot ignore. Conditions must deteriorate to crisis proportions before the subject achieves enough visibility to become an active agenda item. So as a general proposition, the more visible the policy domain, the less important are crisis and disaster.

Another explanation for the difference between health and transportation involves the structure of the two domains. Crises may be more aggregated in transportation than in health. The basic unit in health is a patient-provider exchange. When something goes wrong, it doesn't show up as a major crisis. If there is to be a crisis-style impact, it must occur in a series of minute changes, patient by patient, and eventually build to a problem of major proportions, or the individual cases must be aggregated into a study or statistic that proves to be compelling. But in transportation, something that goes wrong is often already preaggregated. An airplane goes down, killing hundreds of people at once rather than killing one patient at a time. The Penn Central collapses, and such a substantial failure has an immediate impact on the entire economy of a region. The health analogy would be the collapse of Blue Cross, a possibility but not as likely an occurrence. One can extend the same logic about aggregation to differences within policy domains, as we will see presently.

Variations on the Focusing Event

Sometimes crises come along that simply bowl over everything standing in the way of prominence on the agenda. Many respondents treated the collapse of the Penn Central railroad that way. As one put it, "It was a threat to the economy of the nation as a whole. It was horrendous and unthinkable to allow service to stop." Such events demand some sort of action so clearly that even inaction is a decision. On the other hand, potential agenda items sometimes languish in the background for lack of a crisis that would push them forward.

But focusing events are not always so straightforward. A couple of variations on the theme are the personal experiences of policy makers and the impact of powerful symbols. Sometimes, subjects become prominent agenda items partly because important policy makers have personal experiences that bring the subject to their attention. Biomedical research, for instance, has such an advantage. Members of Congress and other important people all have had brushes with health disorders, either themselves or among their families or friends. As one respondent said, lobbyists for biomedical research "know the disease of the day, they know which congressman's mother died of which disease and which one's wife has which disease, and they play on it." Patterns of attention to the various transportation modes, for another example, are probably affected by policy makers' personal travel. As one respondent said of aviation, "To policy makers, air travel is very visible. They travel by air a lot themselves, and they do it for pleasure as well as for business. Because they travel by air a lot, they are very quick to pick up anomalies." By contrast, they do not see much of buses, and a social class bias in attention results. One respondent puckishly twitted his fellow transportation policy specialists:

> Buses are used by poor people, and poor people have no clout. A funny thing happened to me a while ago. I went to a conference, and I went on the bus. I got to the conference with all these transportation experts, and as soon as I told them I had come on the bus, they all gathered around me, they asked what happened to me, and how it was riding on the bus.

Despite the credence many people place in personal experiences as forces affecting the agenda, they do not turn out to be very important in our quantitative indicators. Personal experiences were important in only 13 percent of the interviews, slightly more important in health than in transportation. We coded them as very important in none of the 23 case studies, and as somewhat important in three, all of them in health. Health is thus a bit more apt to reflect the personal experiences of policy makers, probably because it affects them more than their transportation from one place to another. In sum, personal experiences of policy makers are occasionally important, but they are not among the major influences on agenda status. They act more as reinforcements for something else, or as factors that might heighten a problem at the margins, rather than as prime movers.

Another variation on the focusing event is the emergence and diffusion of a powerful symbol.[2] A subject is on the minds of important people anyway, and a symbol comes along to focus their attention. The contributions of technology to the cost of medical care, for instance, became part of the *lingua franca* of health policy people during the 1970s. As they were discussing the problem, they would often refer to the spreading use of the CAT scanner as their shorthand for the proliferation of an expensive technology whose payoff and appropriate uses had not yet been fully determined. They might refer to "the CAT scanner problem," for example, in the midst of a longer discussion. Indeed, during 1976 and 1977, at the height of such talk among my respondents, nearly a third of the health interviews included a mention of CAT scanners by name, without any prompting from me. The Washington METRO became something of a symbol for very high-cost fixed rail transit systems, and was mentioned in at least a passing way in nearly a third of my interviews with transportation respondents.

There can be symbols for political events and policy proposals as well as for problems. The passage of Proposition 13 in California, for example, became symbolic of a perceived restiveness among taxpayers, a shift in public opinion. Politicians had felt something like a taxpayer revolt coming for some time, but Proposition 13 became their shorthand way of referring to it. They would refer in an offhand way to a "Proposition 13 mentality" or a "Proposition 13 atmosphere," meaning a severe public opinion constraint on government spending, higher taxation, and new, expensive programs. Indeed, the symbol diffused very rapidly, probably because it captured the mood rather convincingly, at least as politicians saw it. Proposition 13's passage came in the midst of my 1978 interviews. It was discussed by name as being important in only 2 of the 26 interviews taken before its passage. But 15 of the 38 postpassage interviews (39 percent) contained a spontaneous, nonprompted mention of Proposition 13 by name, quite a remarkable diffusion of a symbol among policy elites over a short period of time.

In general, such a symbol acts (much as personal experiences) as reinforcement for something already taking place and as something that rather powerfully focuses attention, rather than as a prime mover in agenda setting. Symbols catch on and have important focusing effects because they capture in a nutshell

[2]A central discussion of symbols and politics is Murray Edelman, *The Symbolic Uses of Politics* (Urbana: University of Illinois Press, 1967). A more recent treatment is Charles D. Elder and Roger W. Cobb, *The Political Uses of Symbols* (New York: Longman, 1983).

some sort of reality that people already sense in a vaguer, more diffuse way. As one respondent said, "Behind every cliché there is some truth."

How Focusing Events Need Accompaniment

Crises, disasters, symbols, and other focusing events only rarely carry a subject to policy agenda prominence by themselves. They need to be accompanied by something else. We have already made the point, first, that they reinforce some preexisting perception of a problem, focus attention on a problem that was already "in the back of people's minds." One transportation respondent, commenting on the high cost of urban mass transit projects, said, "The Proposition 13 syndrome simply emphasizes some things that have been coming along for some time now. There has already been a lot of questioning by people other than the standard reactionaries about whether the public investment in urban mass transit is not already excessive." Or as another informant very astutely observed of the impact of Lock and Dam 26 on the movement toward waterway user charges, "A fortuitous catalyst was thrown into an existing environment."

Second, sometimes a disaster or crisis serves as an early warning; attention is called to something that could be considered a problem if subsequent consideration really establishes that there was a widespread condition that needs attention. Bridge deterioration is an excellent case in point. In 1967, the Silver Bridge across the Ohio River between Ohio and West Virginia collapsed, killing several dozen people. Such an event could be an isolated fluke or it could be an indication of a more widespread problem. If it is an isolated incident, then a general policy response may not be warranted. But as one respondent summarized the progress of the issue:

> In 1967, a bridge fell into the Ohio River without any advance warning. That led Congress to establish a program for bridge inspection. That program and the studies that have come from it led to the conclusion that there were something like 80,000 deficient bridges. Once that fact became known, Congress started a separate program for bridges. It's a nice example of the progress of an issue. First the problem comes to their attention. Then you have to quantify the problem to see how widespread it is. Then that quantifying leads to a program.

Even if the Federal Highway Administration estimate of 80,000 was inflated, there was a problem that would be hard for politicians with bridges in their districts to ignore. But in general, a disaster by itself is not enough to create a definition of a policy problem. The disaster acts as an early warning, but then needs to be combined with more solid indication that the problem is widespread.

Third, these focusing events can affect problem definition in combination with other similar events. If one bridge collapse, one aviation accident, or one railroad bankruptcy isn't sufficient to create a sense of a general problem, then several of them occurring close together might be. Awareness of a problem sometimes comes only with the second crisis, not the first, because the second cannot be dismissed as an isolated fluke, as the first could. Attention to the subject of energy among transportation specialists illustrates this phenomenon rather nicely. After the 1973 Arab oil embargo, there was a flurry of interest in energy, and some substantial government action as well, such as the automobile fleet economy standards. But as Figure 5-2 shows, by the mid- to late-1970s, important people in the transportation policy-making community were not discussing the subject a great deal. Policy makers maintained in 1979 (in retrospect) that energy was high on their agendas before 1979, but their actual interview responses indicated otherwise. They simply were not paying very serious attention to the subject from 1976 through 1978. As one said in 1976, "Energy was an issue two years ago, but it is no longer an issue because there are no lines in front of gas stations. The prominence of that issue is tied directly to the length of the lines in front of gas stations."

Then came the gas lines in the spring of 1979. The indicators of attention jumped abruptly, as Figure 5-2 shows. As one respondent said in response to my very first question about the major problems with which he was occupied,

Figure 5-2

Discussion of Supply, Cost, and Transportation of Energy

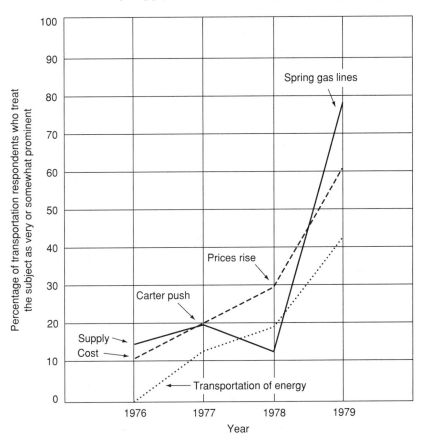

"If I said anything other than energy, I bet you'd be very surprised." His own discussions during the previous three years had relegated energy to a very minor position on the list of subjects vying for his attention. Many respondents treated this second shortage differently from the first. As one put it, "I can't see it just going away as a policy concern. It did in 1973, but then it came back again, and after a couple of times I think people will start to conclude it's a problem that's not just going to go away." As another respondent succinctly summarized the point, "Even a mule pays attention to you when you hit it a second time across the head."

The aggregation of disasters has a similar effect. We argued earlier that the greater reference to crisis in transportation than in health may be due to the greater aggregation of the disasters. The same happens *within* such a domain as transportation. Consider the difference between highway and aviation safety. Attention to aviation safety is brought about quite directly by crashes. All of the prominent spontaneous mentions of airplane accidents in my interviews over all four years were in 1979, following hard on the heels of the DC-10 crash in Chicago and the midair collision over San Diego. Yet there are far more highway deaths, both per passenger mile and in total. As one journalist stated the importance of aggregation:

> There are 50,000 to 60,000 people killed in transportation every year. But it's not a crisis issue; it's not very visible. Most of it is on highways, and it goes on all the time, an accident here and an accident there. There's no one big catastrophe. Transportation safety would get a lot more action than it does if there were some kind of big highway disaster. In aviation, I think it's fair to say that all the advances in aviation safety have come as a result of a crash. But that's not possible in highway safety.

Some aggregation of highway deaths prompts government attention. Someone does count them up, for instance, and when they reach some magic threshold (e.g., 50,000 per year) then it can be called a crisis. Aggregated disasters do have noticeable public policy impacts. The air traffic control system was developed in response to a midair crash over the Grand Canyon. The San Diego crash led to greater Federal Aviation Administration (FAA) control over general aviation. Indeed, in a somewhat cynical but possibly realistic interpretation, some aviation observers alleged that FAA invented a new measure of a "near-miss report" when there weren't enough actual accidents to justify increases in safety expenditures.

FEEDBACK

In the normal course of events, governmental officials receive feedback about the operation of existing programs. They monitor expenditures, have experience with administering programs, evaluate and oversee implementation, and receive complaints. This feedback often brings problems to their attention: programs that are not working as planned, implementation that does not square with their interpretation of the legislative mandate, new problems that have arisen as a result of a program's enactment, or unanticipated consequences that must be remedied. We coded feedback from the operation of existing programs as important in 18 of the 23 case studies. It was also discussed prominently in 26 percent of the interviews.

Sometimes, the feedback comes to officials in the form of rather systematic monitoring and evaluation studies. For instance, transportation officials monitor the performance of Amtrak and of urban mass transit systems by regularly following such indicators as ridership, load factors, on-time performance, inflation in construction costs, and operating deficits. And health officials regularly collect data on rates of various types of surgery, incidences of various diseases, hospital utilization and lengths of stay, and manpower distributions by geographical location and by specialty.

Quite often, feedback comes to governmental officials more informally. For one thing, complaints and casework lead to awareness of problems. As John Johannes points out, citizens' complaints to their legislators and requests for congressional intervention in the bureaucracy to straighten out their individual problems lead members of Congress into oversight activities in which they might not have otherwise engaged.[3] As a result, they become more acutely aware of problems that are more general than the individuals' complaints. Travelers and state highway officials complain about deteriorating road surfaces and the lack of funds at the state level to repair them. Businessmen complain about regulation, leading to a more generalized concern with the heavy hand of government.

Quite apart from feedback from the public, bureaucrats themselves become aware of problems through the day-to-day administration of a program. Said one respondent, "Bureaucrats who are administering the program find that it just doesn't work and must be fixed." For instance, the Food and Drug Administration (FDA) found the Delaney amendment's absolute prohibition on any carcinogenic substance, no matter how weak a carcinogen or how much an accumulation of the substance is necessary to produce an effect, most difficult to administer in a case like saccharin. Indeed, speculation was rife about town that the FDA announced their partial ban on saccharin partly to raise the policy question of statutory rigidity. Of course, bureaucrats also have some interest in preventing feedback from reaching policy makers, especially if that feedback might reflect negatively on their stewardship or might raise serious questions about whether their program should be continued. Still, one of civil servants' most important contributions to the agenda, to the extent that they affect the agenda, is their awareness of problems that comes from their experience in administering a program.

Content of Feedback Messages

We have discussed the channels of feedback—systematic monitoring, complaints and casework, and bureaucratic experience. But what information that

[3]John R. Johannes, "Casework as a Technique of U.S. Congressional Oversight of the Executive," *Legislative Studies Quarterly* 4 (August 1979): 325–352.

flows through these channels is interpreted as a problem? The first category of problem is implementation that does not square with legislative or higher administrative intent. Some of that lack of fit seems inevitable. Said one observer, "The process of writing regulations is terribly important. It is a quasi-legislative function, and it is totally hidden from public view."

Either by design or not, implementers sometimes interpret legislative or higher administrative mandates in a way that the authors subsequently argue was not their intent. Interstate Commerce Commission (ICC) interpretation of the deregulation provisions of the 1975 rail act was widely cited by critics as a case in point. The act allowed the ICC to give railroads somewhat greater flexibility in setting rates and abandoning unprofitable lines, except in certain specified circumstances, such as a railroad's domination of a given market. According to critics, the ICC interpreted market dominance so broadly that the possibility for substantial deregulation was effectively throttled. This storm of criticism quickly reached legislators and administration officials. Indeed, nearly half of my transportation respondents in 1979 spontaneously discussed implementation of the rail act as a prominent agenda item. The feedback then contributed both to further legislation and to new, more deregulation-minded Carter appointments to the ICC. It is not clear in such a case where "blame" might lie. It could easily be the fault of Congress for not defining its intent precisely in a conflictual situation—"tossing the hot potato to an agency," as one respondent put it. But the feedback process eventually resulted in further change.

Another type of information that indicates a problem is a failure to meet stated goals. If the administrators of a program have themselves set targets that they then do not meet, various overseers wonder if there is a problem to which they should devote some attention. Many transportation respondents pointed to Amtrak as their example. Amtrak projected many trends in ridership and deficit reduction that, as the years went on, did not pan out according to projection. Even if it were no fault of Amtrak management, the failure to meet targets left their critics outraged and even their supporters edgy. Said one sympathetic congressional staffer in 1977, "Amtrak is getting to the point where they have been in business for six years, Congress has invested one and a half billion dollars in it, and every year they say, 'Wait until next year.' Amtrak is forever promising that they will turn the corner next year." Of course, such experiences create an incentive for administrators to avoid setting their targets too precisely whenever they can, and a countervailing incentive for critics and evaluators to establish such goals as precisely as possible.

Another obvious type of feedback is the cost of the program. Sometimes programs come to be so costly that policy makers rethink future initiatives, and may even cut back the existing programs to save money. As one transportation respondent said in 1979, "While Conrail is not a bottomless pit, it is a much deeper pit than anyone thought three or four years ago." This burgeoning cost resulted in Conrail cutbacks and in further moves to deregulate railroads, to give them greater capital through the reduction of unprofitable operations. It also shelved for the time being any serious talk of nationalization or of further heavy subsidies. Similarly, the rapid rise in the cost of Medicare led health policy makers first to adopt a series of regulatory programs (Professional Standards Review Organization, Health Systems Agencies, etc.), then to consider reimbursement reform, then to propose various cost containment schemes either on their own or as a part of national health insurance proposals, and then eventually to shelve national health insurance for the time being.

Finally, unanticipated consequences of a public policy come to the attention of decision makers. Negative consequences that are anticipated create enough problems. But consequences that have some major impacts and that are not anticipated create a sharper sense that something is amiss and should be examined. When interstate highway construction was being considered, for instance, few involved people anticipated many of the side consequences that ensued: deterioration of the railroads due to truck competition for freight, dislocation and unplanned sprawl in urban areas,[4] and sharply rising maintenance costs that imposed tremendous burdens on state governments. Few health policy makers anticipated the raft of regulatory programs that would ensue from the enactment of Medicare and Medicaid. Occasionally, the unanticipated consequences are positive. The 55 mile per hour speed limit, enacted for fuel-saving reasons, resulted in greater highway safety which, in turn, became a powerful argument for keeping the lower speed limit. Even for the best plans laid by the smartest people, some unanticipated consequences seem to be inevitable.[5]

WHY PROBLEMS FADE

Why do issues drop from agenda prominence? Sometimes people in government feel they have solved a problem. The interstate highway system was built, for instance, which did result in easier movement of automobiles and trucks from city to city. And Medicare's passage did result in the payment of large portions of elderly people's medical bills. Not all problems are solved by such enactments, of course, and new problems are spawned in the course of implementing such initiatives. But in the process of concentrating on these new problems, we should not lose sight of the fact that government programs sometimes actually do accomplish fair portions of their objectives.

Even if it is questionable whether governmental officials have solved a problem, they sometimes feel that they have addressed it by passing legislation or making an administrative decision. If they have, they turn their attention elsewhere, and then that subject drops from their agendas. The waterway user charge became virtually invisible in my interviews, for instance, one short year

[4]For an account of impacts on urban areas, see Alan Altshuler, "Changing Patterns of Policy," *Public Policy* 25 (Spring 1977): 176; and Donald Haider, *When Governments Come to Washington* (New York: Free Press, 1974), p. 154.

[5]For a discussion of unanticipated consequences, see Aaron Wildavsky, *Speaking Truth to Power* (Boston: Little, Brown, 1979), pp. 69–71.

after it was passed. To strategists pressing for a fuller solution, such a result may be more distressing than no passage at all. Said one health staffer:

> People told me before I came here, and it's absolutely true, that Congress legislates something, and then there's a great tendency to say that has solved the problem. That means that they don't pay attention to it after that. You might sometimes prefer *not* to have legislation, because then it keeps attention focused on the problem.

Other problems, even though not solved or addressed by the federal government, fade from view. Malpractice was a major agenda item in the early 1970s, for instance, due to doctor strikes and large legal settlements. By the time of my interviewing, however, it had faded almost completely from view, largely because sufficient state action made the more extreme consequences less frequent. And the Concorde landings occupied a lot of Department of Transportation time, but faded from view as people became used to the noise and other disadvantages of the landings around Dulles and Kennedy airports.

A corollary of addressing a problem is that growth inevitably levels off. Jack Walker shows that Congress ran through all the safety legislation they could think of—auto, mining, occupational—and stopped when they had simply played out the string.[6] It's also possible for programs to grow until there is negative feedback, as there was with occupational safety regulation. And sometimes expansion levels off just because it is not sustainable. As one respondent pointed out, if biomedical research expenditures had continued to grow at the 1960s rate, "By 1985 you would have an astonishing proportion of the gross national product going into biomedical research. You could not have kept up a continuation of that growth."

Failure to solve or even address a problem, as well as success, may result in its demise as a prominent agenda item. It takes time, effort, mobilization of many actors, and the expenditure of political resources to keep an item prominent on the agenda. If it appears, even after a short time, that the subject will not result in legislation or another form of authoritative decision, participants quickly cease to invest in it. As one respondent aptly put it, "Congress is easily fatigued. It gets to a point after a while, after everybody's been hassling them and it doesn't look like anything will pass, that they say, 'Go away, don't bother me.'" In fact, such exhaustion is true of the problems that are addressed as well. One heavily involved congressional staffer said in 1976 after the passage of the railroad act, "Right now, we are all exhausted over railroad reorganization, and we don't have a lot of energy left to start something new." In either case, addressing or not addressing the problem, the subject fades: people figure either they solved it, or they did the best they could and the issue must lie fallow for a time until they make another try.

If Anthony Downs is right, problems often fade from public view because a short period of awareness and optimism gives way to a realization of the finan-

[6]Jack L. Walker, "Setting the Agenda in the U.S. Senate," *British Journal of Political Science* 7 (October 1977): 423–445.

cial and social costs of action.[7] As people become impressed with the sacrifices, dislocations, and costs to be borne, they lose their enthusiasm for addressing the problem. For example, ecology runs afoul of the realization that mobility by automobile, jobs, or the convenience of abundant energy might be affected.

Respondents occasionally even portrayed the rise and fall of interest in an issue or idea as faddish. A subject gets attention when it is novel. When it is no longer novel, people's attention may turn away from the subject even though it may still be valid or important, largely because it is boring. There was no solution, the idea still may be potentially useful, but the fad has passed. Said one respondent:

> In Washington, the world of ideas is like the world of fashion. Ideas don't last for more than four or five years. They catch on, they become very popular, and because of that, they burn themselves out in a burst of growth, and others take their place. It's like a hula hoop craze. How do you start a hula hoop craze? I can't answer that. There's this guy in New York who goes around clothing animals. He's been doing it for years and years, and every few years, he gets into the media again. Someday, his idea will catch on, and we'll all be diapering our horses.

BUDGETS: A SPECIAL PROBLEM

The budget constitutes a particular kind of problem that deserves a section of its own. Money makes the world go around, as the saying goes. Even if it does not quite do that much, the budget is a central part of governmental activity. Programs, agencies, and professional careers wax and wane according to their budget share. A budget pinch very directly affects both bureaucrats and legislators since the programs in which they have a personal career stake are affected. Budgetary considerations sometimes force items higher on the governmental agenda, acting as a promoter. At other times, budgets act as constraints, holding some items low on (or even off) the agenda because the item would cost more than decision makers are willing to contemplate.

Budgetary considerations certainly loom large in the data generated for this study. In the interviews, budgets were important in 70 percent of the interviews, and in 15 of the 23 case studies. They are slightly more prominent in health than in transportation[8] for two reasons. First, federal government expenditures for health are simply much higher. When the highway program was

---

[7]Anthony Downs, "Up and Down with Ecology—The 'Issue-Attention Cycle,'" *The Public Interest* 28 (Summer 1972): 38–50.

[8]The figures are as follows: 74 percent of the health interviews rated budgetary considerations as very or somewhat important, compared to 64 percent of the transportation interviews; 9 of the 11 health case studies showed budgets very or somewhat important, compared to 6 of the 12 transportation studies. In the highest year for budgetary concern, 1978, fully 94 percent of health interviews included a very or somewhat prominent discussion of budgets, compared to 81 percent for transportation.

costing about $6 billion, Medicare and Medicaid cost $40 billion. Not only is the magnitude vastly different, but the rate of inflation in medical care, including in government programs, is also much more marked. Within two years of the passage of Medicare, policy makers were astonished by the steep rise in the cost. Sometimes the budget constraint can be so severe that it virtually paralyzes people. As one health respondent despaired of any action, "Nothing is on the front burner. Everyone is just stymied. They are sitting there looking at the costs rising, watching the red meter shooting up."

Let us distinguish between the budget as a constraint, which obliges important people to reduce the cost of proposals or to ignore some options altogether because of a perceived prohibitive cost, and the budget as a promoter, which pushes some items higher on a governmental agenda. An excellent example of the budget as a promoter is the concern over the costs of medical care. During the period of my interviewing, cost was clearly the number one problem on the minds of health respondents. As one put it, "The word 'preoccupation' is too mild. It is an obsession. It just pervades everything. The cost consideration has found its way into every program." When asked whether governmental policy makers were concerned about cost to government itself or to such other entities as private insurers or individuals, their overwhelming response was that the federal budget itself prompted the high ranking of this problem ahead of many others. As one analyst said, "The estimates are that health expenditures in the federal budget will double every five years. The budgetary pressures are just unbelievable." In the process of worrying about cost, other problems, such as access to or the quality of medical care, were shunted aside. As one former bureaucrat rather wistfully phrased it, "We had this big reform agenda in the Public Health Service, but couldn't get any money for it because of Medicare and Medicaid. It was as if we were tossing leaves into a stream, and the leaves were just floating away, carried along by this tremendously strong current that is Medicare and Medicaid."

Probably the foremost concern about budgets, however, is as a constraint. Budgetary considerations prevent policy makers and those close to them from seriously contemplating some alternatives, initiatives, or proposals, or at least oblige them to revise their proposals to reduce estimated expenditures. Some options are ignored altogether. Transportation planners, for instance, came to the point of ruling out future federal expenditures on large-scale fixed rail subway systems because of the high cost of San Francisco's BART and Washington's METRO. In the health area, long-term care was not prominently discussed in my interviews, despite the demographics pointing to increased need for it. The highest proportion of respondents discussing any item related to long-term care was only 13 percent. When asked why such an obvious problem was not prominent on the agenda, most respondents immediately concentrated on the budget constraint. Said one, "Here's the chain of logic: The problem is the care isn't adequate. The solution is to spend money. Do we have money? No. Zip, to the back burner."

So some potential agenda items never make it to agenda status because they do not pass the hurdle of the budget constraint. Other items that do achieve some prominence on the agenda are affected greatly by budgetary considerations. Proposals for national health insurance during the late 1970s constitute a nice example. As advocates of various plans plied their wares during 1977 through 1979, they all came face to face with the fact—and it was treated as a simple fact—that the federal budget could not accommodate a comprehensive plan, what one opponent called a "lust to dust" plan. As a congressional staffer summarized it, "You're faced immediately with this fierce budget constraint. That's a very, very significant factor. I can't stress it too strongly." So everybody jockeyed to see how much of their plans they could get off the budget. Even advocates of comprehensive insurance proposed mandated private coverage as a substantial part of their package. Others cut back on coverage or benefits, retreating from a completely comprehensive plan. One respondent summarized the operation of the budget constraint very nicely:

> Ever since I've been dealing with these things, it's been my impression that the single overriding issue is the impact on the federal budget. You can take all the analysts and get them in a room, and they'll talk and talk and talk, but when you get into a serious discussion with the president or with a committee chairman, the first thing they begin with is, "I think we can spend x dollars." And x dollars is what you come up with. That happened with welfare reform. I would guess that if you asked anybody proposing welfare reform, "Why five billion," they'd say, "That's what we can buy right now." They'd probably say it's the wrong thing to do too, but that's what we can buy.

In times of severe budget constraint, inexpensive programs come to the fore. They are of three general types. First, some of them attempt to regulate, to control the rise in costs. The alarming rise in Medicare and Medicaid expenditures, for instance, led to several regulatory programs and proposals. Health planning legislation was designed to retard the growth of capital expenditures on the assumption that some of the rise in medical care costs was due to a surplus of beds and to an increase in the availability of high-technology care. The Professional Standards Review Organization program, an attempt to regulate unnecessary utilization, came on line. Fraud and abuse legislation was passed, and hospital cost containment was proposed. These programs, as implemented, enjoyed varying degrees of success, but our main purpose is understanding why attention turned to them in the first place. They became agenda items because they had two virtues during a time of budgetary pressure: They cost little on their own terms, and they held some promise for controlling rising costs.

The second type of inexpensive program is not directly regulatory, but policy makers become convinced that it will save money. Health Maintenance Organizations took off, for instance, partly due to the argument that their introduction would provide competition for traditional fee-for-service medical practice, saving money over the long run both for consumers and for government. Health policy makers turned increasingly during the 1970s to the promotion of good health habits because it was a good idea, but also because keeping people well would keep them out of the medical care system, thus saving money. The percentage of my health interviews including a prominent mention of prevention rose from 13 percent in 1976 to 42 percent in 1979. On the transportation side, rail deregulation was spurred along by the argument that the federal government had come to a turning point: Either it would be obliged to sink more and more subsidy into entities like Conrail, or government should deregulate, allowing railroads to make it or fail in the marketplace.

Third, at a time when no large-expenditure initiatives (such as national health insurance or fancy subway systems) are possible, attention turns to initiatives that cost little, even if they would not necessarily contribute to actual cost savings. In Chapters 6 and 8, we will describe the activities of policy entrepreneurs in some detail. Suffice it to say here that they are engaged in a restless search for something to propose. If they cannot propose large-ticket items, they will search for proposals that are less expensive. In health, for instance, attention might turn to FDA reform or clinical laboratories, and in transportation, to such low-capital improvements as bus lanes, van pooling, traffic management, and pedestrian malls. One health respondent, while discussing current interest in child health, put this search for inexpensive items during a time of tight budgets very well: "With kids' stuff in general, kids are cheap. You can do what you have to do with kids in the medical area without spending a lot of money because, basically, kids are well. So if you're looking for something to do in health and you don't want it to cost a lot, do kids."

The budget constraint is related more generally to the state of the economy. Constraint is not entirely due to the shape of the larger economy, but when the economy is not growing rapidly, when government revenues fall off and various entitlement expenditures rise, the budget constraint becomes severe. When the economy is growing, on the other hand, more slack resources are available to government for innovation. One reason for government expansion in the 1960s, for instance, was the relatively robust economy. Officials' preoccupation with national economic conditions affects agendas indirectly as well. When President Carter was concerned about inflation, for instance, he was unusually receptive to proposals that could be tied to that particular battle. His continued interest in hospital cost containment, far past the time that the proposal had any realistic chance on the Hill, was due in large part to his desire to point to some initiatives he had taken in the general fight against inflation, rather than to any dynamic in the health area itself.

Some of the budget constraint is perceptual. There are objective facts about such things as the state of revenues or the financial obligations of entitlements, but the budget constraint is also subject to interpretation. Some policy makers can find a deficit of a given size as tolerable, for instance, while others would find it outrageous. The budget constraint can be cited as an argument against a proposal that one does not favor on other grounds, and can be side-stepped for proposals that one does favor, by underestimating their cost or ignoring their long-range cost altogether. Even with a hard-headed estimate of cost, governmental officials still have at their disposal, at least conceptually if not politically, the option of raising revenue for programs that they favor strongly. As one budget official said, "There's always room in the budget if you are willing to raise taxes or if you are willing to cut other programs. The budget constraint isn't so much there, as it is a question of how you handle the budgetary implications."

Usually, budgets form a real constraint: Policy makers anticipate costs and revenues, and if necessary trim back initiatives to make them fiscally manageable. There may be disagreements over the realism of the estimates, but at least they try. Occasionally, however, if they find the circumstances sufficiently compelling, policy makers simply ignore the budget. The program to finance kidney dialysis, for instance, was added as a rider on the floor of the Senate, apparently without any thought to the costs that would ensue. Politicians found that the moral inequity created by having this dramatic life-giving therapy available to some but not to all was simply intolerable. The program burgeoned within two or three years into a billion-dollar expenditure. One knowledgeable respondent claimed, "Those who voted for it had no idea of the cost that would ensue. Even if they had known of the cost, it wouldn't have made any difference."

Finally, these comments about budgetary constraints can apply in many respects to slack resources in general. We have argued that the availability of money makes possible governmental innovation that would be impossible in times of severe budgetary constraint. As one respondent said, "When you're looking at a large deficit that you have to make up somehow, you don't have very many new ideas." The same argument can be applied to the availability of resources other than money. Tight times lead people to be conservative, to protect what they have, and to avoid big changes. Slack resources free up organizations. They have more room for experimentation and more resources to sink into the production of innovations. For instance, problems involving inadequate quality in clinical laboratories and unnecessary lab tests had been known for some time. Congress got moving on bills regulating clinical laboratories in the mid-to late-1970s when a Robert Wood Johnson Foundation fellow came onto the staff of the Senate health subcommittee, and the head of the minority staff saw this as an opportunity to do something about clinical labs. The available slack in the form of a new and unassigned staffer enabled the subcommittee, then the House subcommittee, and finally the HEW bureaucracy responding to the legislative pressure to make substantial changes in their regulatory procedures.

PROBLEM DEFINITION

There is a difference between a condition and a problem.[9] We put up with all manner of conditions every day: bad weather, unavoidable and untreatable illnesses, pestilence, poverty, fanaticism. As one lobbyist said, "If you have only four fingers on one hand, that's not a problem; that's a situation." Conditions become defined as problems when we come to believe that we should do something about them.[10] Problems are not simply the conditions or external events

---

[9]I would like to thank James Q. Wilson for highlighting this point for me.

[10]Wildavsky says, "A difficulty is a problem only if something can be done about it." See Wildavsky, *Speaking Truth to Power,* op. cit., p. 42. In my usage, a condition is a problem when people want to change the condition, not necessarily when they actually have a solution. I would like to thank Herbert Jacob for calling to my attention some problems that stay prominent on agendas without solutions attached (e.g., crime in the streets).

themselves; there is also a perceptual, interpretive element. As one respondent replied, when I asked him why a new initiative on smoking should come from HEW at the time that it did:

> I don't know. I don't know if there is any answer to that kind of question, even in the abstract. People just finally decide that they have to do it. That sort of thing has happened with a lot of social problems. We live with these social problems for a while, and then we finally decide that if we're serious about them we should do it. The problem doesn't have to get any worse or any better. It doesn't have to be some major change in the problem. Take poverty. Poverty didn't get any worse. Lyndon Johnson just decided to undertake this war on poverty. Why one moment seems better than another I don't know.

There are great political stakes in problem definition. Some are helped and others are hurt, depending on how problems get defined. If things are going basically your way, for instance, you want to convince others that there are no problems out there. One respondent associated with freight shippers told me that all of the recent legislative and implementation changes "have gone the way that the shippers would like them to go. Basically, we don't have a lot of problems with what's been happening." But when less comfortable changes come your way, as Robert Walters points out, you attempt to define the problem in such a way as to place the burden of adjustment elsewhere, and to avoid changing your own pattern.[11] The automobile companies, for instance, defined their market share problem in the 1970s as unfair foreign competition and repressive government regulation. If others agree on their definition of the problem, adjustments must be made elsewhere, particularly by the federal government. But their problem could as easily have been defined as plush union contracts, poor quality control, and inept management decision making (e.g., decisions to produce large cars). Auto manufacturers preferred not to define problems in these ways, however, because the burden of doing something about them would then rest on their own shoulders. Thus problem definition and struggles over definition turn out to have important consequences.

How do conditions come to be defined as problems? Values, comparisons, and categories contribute to the translation.

The Place of Values in Problem Definition

The values one brings to an observation play a substantial role in problem definition. A mismatch between the observed conditions and one's conception of an ideal state becomes a problem. Conservatives and liberals might agree that there is a given income distribution in the population, for instance, and might even agree that some people are poor by any classification. But those who believe in using government to address poverty would define the presence of poor people as a problem; those who do not believe in using government for such

---

[11]Robert S. Walters, "The Steel Crisis in America," in H. K. Jacobson and D. Sidjanski, eds., *The Emerging International Economic Order* (Beverly Hills: Sage, 1982), pp. 101–128.

purposes would define poverty as a condition. That tendency is accentuated if one adds the phrase, "appropriate for governmental action." Some conservatives might grant that poverty is a problem, but not a problem "appropriate for governmental action."

One prominent set of arguments in health policy—over whether or not access to medical care is a right—revolves quite nicely around such ideological factors. If one sees access as a right, then government presumably should guarantee that right. If some people do not have access to medical care, that condition is defined as a problem, and particularly as a problem appropriate for governmental action. On the other hand, if one views medical care as something that might be nice to have, but not as a right, then differences in access are defined as a condition rather than a problem. To the extent that a definition of medical care as a right becomes diffused both in the population and among specialists in health policy, the pressure for such government action as comprehensive national health insurance becomes much greater.

Comparisons and Problem Definition

Problems sometimes involve comparisons. If one is not achieving what others are achieving, and if one believes in equality, then the relative disadvantage constitutes a problem. If Alexis de Tocqueville's belief that Americans place a particular emphasis on equality was right, then unfavorable comparison creates many problems in the United States. Thus the fact that some receive high-quality medical care and others do not would be regarded as a problem because of the comparisons involved. Sometimes people make these comparisons across nations. It can often be a powerful argument that the French have high-speed trains or the Canadians have national health insurance. The Soviet launch of the first Sputnik set off a dramatic chain of initiatives—including aerospace initiatives but extending far and wide into research, development, and education— designed to catch up. The mere fact of being behind in "the greatest country on earth" is enough to constitute a problem for some people.

Categories

The first cut at analyzing anything is to place it in its proper category. People will see a problem quite differently if it is put into one category rather than another. Thus much of the struggle over problem definition centers on the categories that will be used and the ways they will be used. You may not be able to judge a problem by its category, but its category structures people's perceptions of the problem in many important respects.

For example, one of my respondents attributed the passage of a waterway user charge partly to a change in categories. As he put it, "Navigation always used to be considered a part of water resources policy. It is only recently that it has come to be thought of as transportation." This change had an important effect. If waterways are categorized as water resources, then such navigation projects as locks and dams, canals, and dredging would be compared to such projects as reclamation and irrigation. But if waterways are viewed as corridors of transport, then a barge's use of locks and dredged channels without paying any user fee is unfair when compared to the fuel taxes paid by users that finance highway construction and maintenance, the ticket tax on airline travel that finances airport construction, and the railroads' own expenditures for right-of-way construction and maintenance.

A second and most interesting example of the importance of categories is the transportation of the handicapped. During the 1970s, handicapped activists agitated for and eventually won statutory language and regulatory interpretations which mandated retrofitting of existing subway systems for elevators and other devices that would make public transit accessible. Transit operators and even many handicapped people themselves argued that the handicapped could be transported more cheaply and more conveniently around urban areas with dial-a-ride service or in subsidized taxis. The issue turned on how one classified the problem. If it was defined as a civil rights issue, then equal access to subways was called for because separate is not equal. On the other hand, if it was a transportation issue, then equal access was not necessary and other solutions were appropriate. The category into which the issue was placed made a tremendous difference.

Old categories and old means of classifying subjects into those categories tend to persist. But what of changed circumstances? In the face of changed needs or new problems, government's first instinct is to preserve the old categories as long as possible. A change in categories represents a threat to somebody's interests, and politicians like to put off that day of reckoning as long as they can. Thus it had been the accepted theory that the federal highway program would help construct highways, but the states and localities would be responsible for maintaining them once constructed. As the 1960s and 1970s wore on, it became clear to most knowledgeable people that the states simply could not or would not keep pace with the maintenance requirements. Yet if the federal government simply agreed to pay for maintenance, the expense would be enormous, and the distinction between a local responsibility (e.g., a rural county road) and a federal responsibility (e.g., an interstate highway) would be increasingly difficult to draw. The burden of adjustment, to return to a previously discussed concept, would be placed on the federal government. So the first step was to define some maintenance activities as construction. The federal government might not pay for filling potholes, but it would treat reconstruction the same as new construction. Resurfacing, spreading a whole new sheet of asphalt on an existing road, would be called construction and paid for by the federal government. Thus one congressional committee staffer said that the distinction between construction and maintenance "still is the theory, but the definition of what constitutes construction has been altered over the years. There are some things that are being included now that once were considered maintenance."

Eventually, the fit between the categories and reality becomes so weak that new categories emerge. The number of cases that do not fit the old categories increases so dramatically that people must use new categories simply to make themselves understood. To return to the previous example, at least some people admit that the federal government is indeed financing highway maintenance. But during the 1960s and 1970s, other modes of transportation were deteriorating, including railroad rights-of-way, and locks and dams. Eventually, transportation people began to think in terms of "transportation infrastructure deterioration," rather than of the separate deterioration of each of the modes' infrastructures. The emergence of that category has important implications for the way people see problems. They make explicit connections between the experiences of the railroads and highways, arguing that if we defer maintenance on highways and bridges as the railroads did on rights-of-way, we will be in a similar mess. The new category also creates the sense that there is a much more massive problem than if people were seeing each of the pieces separately. That in turn argues for the devotion of more resources to rebuilding.

The emergence of a new category is a signal public policy event. When people start thinking of transportation or energy, for instance, instead of their separate components classified into other categories, entirely new definitions of problems and conceptualizations of solutions come into play. In important respects, the categories define our ways of looking at the problems.

CONCLUSION

This chapter has considered how governmental officials fix their attention on one problem rather than another. Various mechanisms—indicators, focusing events, and feedback—bring problems to their attention. They use indicators to assess both the magnitude of and the change in a problem. Their interpretation of indicators turns out to be a process more complicated than a straightforward assessment of the facts. Focusing events, including disasters, crises, personal experience, and symbols, are important, but need accompaniment in the form of preexisting perceptions which they reinforce, firmer indicators, or combinations with other such events. Feedback gives information on current performance that may not square with legislative or higher administrative intent, indicates a failure to meet stated goals, or suggests unanticipated consequences. Just as a problem can rise on an agenda, it can also fade from view. Government may address the problem, may even solve it after a fashion. If there is a failure to address the problem, the result may be frustration and a turn to something more tractable. Problems may also fade simply because their growth rate levels off, because people become used to the condition, or because attention is faddish.

Budgets constitute a special kind of problem. Sometimes budgetary conditions act as an impetus to the emergence of a set of concerns or proposals into prominence. More often, the budget acts as a constraint, dampening enthusiasm for expensive proposals or for attending to problems whose solution would be expensive. The presence of slack resources in the economy makes the budget constraint less severe. In general, slack resources make innovations possible.

Once again, the budget constraint is not necessarily obvious on its face, but is subject to a variety of interpretations.

In general, not every condition is seen as a problem. For a condition to be a problem, people must become convinced that something should be done to change it. People in and around government make that translation by evaluating conditions in the light of their values, by comparisons between people or between the United States and other countries, and by classifying conditions into one category or another.

The Importance of Problem Recognition

Sometimes, the recognition of a pressing problem is sufficient to gain a subject a prominent place on the policy agenda. The collapse of the Penn Central Railroad, for example, was reason enough for government to pay attention to the imminent cessation of service and its resultant economic dislocation, and to take action. But just as often, problem recognition is not sufficient by itself to place an item on the agenda. Problems abound out there in the government's environment, and officials pay serious attention to only a fraction of them.

Nor is solving a problem the only reason government enacts a solution. Several considerations independent of problem solving prompt government to act. Politicians cast about for ways to make their mark. Bureaucrats propose initiatives designed to help them keep their jobs or expand their turf. Prevailing values change, resulting in new problem definition. Simple interest group pressure or other expressions of preferences may gain issue prominence, independent of a problem being solved. There are many reasons for agenda status, apart from the straightforward impulse to identify problems and solve them.

National health insurance quite nicely illustrates this attention to solutions before problems. Its advocates argue that there are a number of problems in the health care system that national health insurance is supposed to address, including gaps in private insurance coverage, lowered access to medical care for those who have inadequate coverage, heavy financial burdens on some parts of the population, and an inability on the part of government or anyone else to control rapidly rising costs. While all of these problems might have existed in some sense during most of the years of my interviewing, most of my health respondents did not emphasize them. Rather, they seemed to share one congressional staffer's sense that the problems are not particularly pressing:

> The bulk of the working people have reasonably good coverage right now. Low-income people are covered by Medicaid, even though they might not be covered as well as they could be. The aged and disabled are covered under Medicare. So actually, there is quite a bit of coverage out there. Medicare was easy to make the case for, because there really were a lot of people out there who didn't have coverage, who weren't getting the right kind of health care, and who really needed it too. This national health insurance issue is not like Medicare at all.

Yet between 1978 and 1979, there was a dramatic increase in the proportion of my respondents who said that there was in fact a need or constituency for national health insurance. In 1978, only 3 percent of them prominently discussed that possibility; in 1979, 42 percent of them did. It is extremely unlikely that the problems became that much more serious in one year's time. What happened was that Senator Russell Long started pushing a bill in the Finance Committee, and the Carter administration produced their proposal. The prominence of these proposals on the agenda affected the prominence of the problems which the proposals were supposed to solve. The events brought to the fore all of the problems and needs that "everybody knew were out there all along."

It does seem true, however, that linking a proposal to a problem that is perceived as real and important does enhance that proposal's prospects for moving up on the agenda. While the emergence of a widespread feeling that a problem exists out there may not always be responsible for prompting attention to a subject, people in and around government still must be convinced somewhere along the line that they are addressing a real problem. One would not consider national health insurance, for example, unless one were convinced that it would address real problems. Or as one respondent said of moves to control rising hospital costs, "Of course, the indicators of cost are used in the argument. You wouldn't start a cost containment program if the indicators were going down. You'd be laughed out of court."

Focusing attention on one problem rather than another is often no accident. Activists invest considerable time and energy in their efforts to bring problems to public and governmental attention. We will reserve most of our discussion of policy entrepreneurs—those willing to make investments of their resources in return for future policies of which they approve—for Chapters 6 and 8. But here, it is important to recognize that they affect attention to problems. They highlight indicators, for instance, by press releases, hearing testimony, speeches, and other devices. They try to bring problems into the personal experiences of important people by giving them a first-hand look. A Seattle pediatrician, Abe Bergman, highlighted the problem of flammable children's clothes by inviting Senator Warren Magnuson to view horrible burn cases in the hospital. These entrepreneurs make a point of generating feedback in the form of letters, visits to decision makers, and protest activity. They also push for one kind of problem definition rather than another.

Getting people to see new problems, or to see old problems in one way rather than another, is a major conceptual and political accomplishment. Once a particular problem comes to capture the attention of important people, some whole classes of approaches come into favor and others fall from grace. If the cost of medical care is seen as "the" problem, for instance, attention to more costly initiatives is dampened, and all present and proposed activities are scrutinized according to their contribution to cost. Or if the efficiency of the economy becomes "the" national problem rather than inequality of income, then the enactment of more ambitious welfare and regulatory programs becomes less likely than moves toward deregulation and spending cuts. The process of fixing attention on one problem rather than another is a central part of agenda setting.

CHAPTER 6

The Policy Primeval Soup

*I took [the draft bill] into the Senator—I was an eager young
fellow at the time—and we engaged in pleasantries. After
about twenty minutes, he indicated that I should leave. I said
to him, "But Senator, don't you want to ask me any questions
about this, discuss the policy implications or anything?" "No,"
he said, "I'll just introduce it tomorrow." "But Senator," I said,
"aren't you even going to read the bill?" "No," he said, "I'll just
introduce it tomorrow." Then he said, "Let me tell you something. We'll introduce this tomorrow, but it will take twenty to
twenty-five years for it to be brought into being. If it takes that
long, there's not much point in my looking at the bill now, is
there?"*

—a respondent who had worked with collaborators for
more than a year on a landmark bill

Picture a community of specialists: researchers, congressional staffers, people
in planning and evaluation offices and in budget offices, academics, interest
group analysts. Ideas float around in such communities. Specialists have their
conceptions, their vague notions of future directions, and their more specific
proposals. They try out their ideas on others by going to lunch, circulating papers, publishing articles, holding hearings, presenting testimony, and drafting
and pushing legislative proposals. The process often does take years, as the
quotation above illustrates, and may be endless.

Generating alternatives and proposals in this community resembles a
process of biological natural selection.[1] Much as molecules floated around in
what biologists call the "primeval soup" before life came into being, so ideas

---

[1]Robert Axelrod's work is a brilliant combination of biological natural selection and social science
mathematical models. See his "The Emergence of Cooperation Among Egoists," *American Political Science Review* 75 (June 1981): 306–318; his *The Evolution of Cooperation* (New York: Basic Books,
1984); and his article coauthored with William Hamilton, "The Evolution of Cooperation," *Science* 211
(27 March 1981): 1390–1396. For another application of evolution in social sciences, see Richard Nelson
and Sidney Winter, *An Evolutionary Theory of Economic Change* (Cambridge: Belknap Press of Howard
University Press, 1982).

float around in these communities.[2] Many ideas are possible, much as many molecules would be possible. Ideas become prominent and then fade. There is a long process of "softening up": ideas are floated, bills introduced, speeches made; proposals are drafted, then amended in response to reaction and floated again. Ideas confront one another (much as molecules bumped into one another) and combine with one another in various ways. The "soup" changes not only through the appearance of wholly new elements, but even more by the recombination of previously existing elements. While many ideas float around in this policy primeval soup, the ones that last, as in a natural selection system, meet some criteria. Some ideas survive and prosper; some proposals are taken more seriously than others.

This chapter describes the policy primeval soup and the selection process. We begin by describing the policy communities; then we consider how ideas float around, and how the community of specialists and the public is "softened up." We present various criteria for survival of an idea, analyzing how some ideas become more prominent than others. Finally, the presence of an available alternative is portrayed as another important factor that makes it likely a subject will achieve lasting high agenda status.

POLICY COMMUNITIES

Policy communities are composed of specialists in a given policy area—health, housing, environmental protection, criminal justice, to name a few. In any one of these policy areas, specialists are scattered both through and outside of government. Some of them are on committee staffs in Congress, or in such congressional staff agencies as the Congressional Budget Office or the Office of Technology Assessment. Others work downtown, in places like planning and evaluation offices and budget offices. Still others are academics, consultants, or analysts for interest groups. But they have in common their concern with one area of policy problems.

They also have in common their interactions with each other. People in the health community know each other's ideas, proposals, and research, and often know each other very well personally. As an unobtrusive indicator of these interactions, I asked respondents to name others to whom I should speak. The same names would rather quickly surface as I went from one person to the next, suggesting that the circle of specialists was fairly small and fairly intimate. More than once, an interview was interrupted by a telephone call from someone who was also on my list of respondents.

This community of specialists hums along on its own, independent of such political events as changes of administration and pressure from legislators' constituencies. These specialists are affected by and react to the political

---

[2]For an excellent discussion of evolution and its various implications, see Richard Dawkins, *The Selfish Gene* (New York: Oxford University Press, 1976). His description of the primeval soup is on p. 16. The word "primordial" could also be used, but I have chosen to follow Dawkin's usage. Another discussion is in L. E. Orgel, *The Origins of Life* (London: Chapman and Hall, 1973).

events, to be sure. But the forces that drive the political stream and the forces that drive the policy stream are quite different: each has a life of its own, independent of the other. As one astute journalist observed: "There are a lot of technicians in medical policy, and that world follows a separate track from the political. Welfare reform is an example of that. The formulation of the Nixon administration proposals came out of that community of welfare professionals, and it has lived on in that community as well."

Fragmentation

From one policy area to another, the relevant communities of specialists vary tremendously in the degree of fragmentation. Some communities are extremely closed and tightly knit. Others are more diverse and fragmented. Health and transportation provide an instructive contrast because health is far less fragmented. The health community does have diverse elements, including biomedical researchers, manpower specialists, health insurance advocates, and budget makers. But most health specialists deal with problems related to making people healthy and paying for their medical care, and there is a fair amount of interaction among the admittedly diverse elements. One health analyst perhaps overstated the point by saying, "Everybody knows everybody. This system is very inbred." During my years of interviewing, the interaction was even formalized in a tradition called the Health Staff Seminar, funded primarily from foundation grants, which brought together health specialists working in government from all over town to hear presentations, think about common problems, and meet one another in a quasi-social context. In the process, they exchanged information, developed more common ways of looking at problems, and cultivated their informal contacts in the health network.

The transportation community is much more fragmented, partly because it is divided into the different modes. I would ask a congressional committee staffer, for instance, about the major problems in transportation, and he would reply, "We're railroads here." Or it might be urban mass transit, or highways, or aviation. It was not unknown for health respondents to say at the beginning that they were only going to deal with biomedical, or manpower, or Medicare, but such a disclaimer was far more common in transportation. The technologies involved in the modes are different from one another, the industries and interest groups tend not to cut across modes, and the jurisdictions of both the administrative agencies and the congressional committees are defined by mode. Thus there are communities of specialists in rail, highways, aviation, urban transit, and waterways, but very few people are concerned with issues that involve two or more of these modes.

Nor is modal fragmentation in the transportation community the only kind. There is also a division between those involved in regulation and those involved in federal grants programs. Both the Interstate Commerce Commission and the Federal Highway Administration deal with truckers, for instance, but the regulatory and grants worlds are completely different. Then there is the freight world versus the passenger world. There may be other dimensions of fragmentation as well.

A few structures in transportation bridge these various sources of fragmentation. The Department of Transportation does act as an umbrella under which various modes must gather. For the most part, the Department is only a collection of the separate fiefdoms, but some degree of cross-modal planning and competition does take place that would not occur in the absence of the Department. The Office of the Secretary examines the work of the various modal administrations, coordinates approaches to the White House and the Hill, and introduces some modicum of communication across the modes. As one observer put it, "You couldn't have them together in the same department for too long before it became obvious that these things related to each other. You could see right away that highways were related to mass transit, for instance." Such a bridging departmental structure might encourage at least some people to think of such proposals as intermodal passenger terminals that would accommodate train, bus, and commuter traffic; multimodal freight transportation through containerization; or even multimodal trust fund arrangements in which user charges from various modes would be brought together into a single fund with allocations considered tradeoffs among the modes. There are limits to the efficacy of such a structure knitting together an inherently fragmented system, but at least some integration has taken place.

Consequences of Fragmentation

The first consequence of system fragmentation is policy fragmentation. The left hand knows not what the right hand is doing, with the result that the left hand sometimes does something that profoundly affects the right hand, without anyone ever seeing the implications. Transportation respondents often cited the beginning of the interstate highway program as their case in point. Basically, the debates at the beginning swirled around highway issues themselves—how the financing would be arranged, trust fund versus general revenues, the extent of the system, and the location of the highways. Yet the construction of the system, in addition to reaping all of the benefits of convenient long-haul passenger and freight transportation, also created tremendous problems for the railroads and for urban areas. The railroads found themselves extremely hard pressed by long-haul trucking competition, which was one major factor (among several) leading to the deterioration of railroad service. Urban areas experienced considerable dislocation as multilane highways were built: new land-use patterns, the spread of both residences and industry from the central city, and the leveling of whole neighborhoods to make room for highways. One might find after diligent searching that somebody, somewhere had anticipated these consequences. But according to several respondents, such consequences received only scant attention at the time, due quite directly to the fragmentation of the transportation policy community.

Second, a more closely knit community generates common outlooks, orientations, and ways of thinking. These common features, a result of the relatively tight integration of the community, in turn strengthen that integration. As people have a common language, they can better communicate with one another. A fascinating example occurred in my health interviews. As I asked people in health what the major problems were, respondent after respondent referred to what one of them called "the big three": cost, access, and quality. They often started with the cost of medical care to consumers, insurers, and government. But they would also discuss gaps in access to medical care, and the quality of care that people receive. Over and over, health respondents discussed these concepts in general terms, and used exactly the same three labels to refer to them. It could be that this magic triumvirate was first mentioned in some by-now-ancient commission report, or that it has come to be a common paradigm in public health instruction around the country. But even for people not socialized in these circles, the triumvirate had entered *lingua franca* in the trade.

Nothing like this common paradigm emerged in transportation. There could in principle be such a paradigm, as respondents might classify the world into passenger versus freight, regulation versus finance, interstate versus commuter, or air versus surface. Indeed, each of these classification schemes would be entirely recognizable among transportation specialists, entirely commonsensical, and implicitly used every day. But the striking feature in the interviews was that health respondents spontaneously produced an explicitly common paradigm, using exactly the same terminology, whereas transportation respondents did not. Such a paradigm not only indicates an integrated community, but it also enhances the integration.

Finally, fragmentation begets instability. There have been previous hints of greater stability in health than in transportation: Crisis events were far more important in transportation; similarly, fewer health than transportation variables exhibited change over the four years (Table 4-3). Let us now observe directly the agenda stability in the two domains.

Table 6-1 shows the intercorrelations among groupings of variables across the four years in health and in transportation. Substantively, a high correlation between two years means there was a high degree of stability within the groupings. The cost of health care, for instance, was prominently discussed each year, so that the values for cost remained high across the four years. On the other hand, mental health was mentioned quite infrequently in each of the four years. But with both cost and mental health, there was a high stability—cost remained prominent in the interviews, mental health remained low—and the values did not fluctuate much from one year to another. For the regulation grouping in transportation, by contrast, the highest-valued variable jumped abruptly between 1978 and 1979. If there were many such changes, the correlations from one year to the next would drop, indicating less stability.

Note in Table 6-1 that the correlations for health are noticeably higher than for transportation. The highest transportation figure is lower than the lowest health figure, and the mean correlation is much higher for health than for transportation. This indicates that the agenda changed from one year to another a good bit more within transportation than within health. Between 1978 and 1979 in transportation, for instance, the correlation is quite low indeed, due to the rapid take-off of the deregulation and energy-related variables and the sharp decline in others (including highways and waterways).

I believe that agenda stability is due to what we might call "structural anchors to the agenda." Transportation, with its greater fragmentation, fewer

Table 6-1

Correlations Among High-Valued Variables Across Year*

	Health (N = 17)		
	1976	1977	1978
1977	.81		
1978	.83	.93	
1979	.83	.83	.86
	Mean correlation for health = .85		

	Transportation (N = 20)		
	1976	1977	1978
1977	.79		
1978	.66	.72	
1979	.60	.59	.39
	Mean correlation for transportation = .63		

*I first defined a "grouping" of variables. All of the variables related to the cost of medical care, for instance, would constitute a cost grouping within the health domain. I then noted the variable within the grouping that had the highest value (the highest percentage coded "very" or "somewhat" important) for each year. In the health cost grouping, for instance, the highest-valued variable in 1976 was 83 percent, in 1977, 81 percent, in 1978, 82 percent, and in 1979, 71 percent. Thus there was not a great deal of change within the health cost grouping over the four years, with cost always being very prominent. But for the "transportation regulation" grouping, the comparable values were 43, 44, 45, and 83, indicating an abrupt change upward in 1979. There were 17 such groupings for health, and 20 for transportation.

I then made up a data matrix in which the four variables were the four years (1976–1979), and the cases within each variable were the groupings. Thus the values for the cost grouping within the health domain would be 83, 81, 82, 71 (the percentage values for that grouping ranged across the four years or four variables). I entered analogous values for each of the 17 health and each of the 20 transportation groupings. I could then correlate the values among the years. A high correlation would show that there was high stability from one year to another, whereas a low correlation would show that the values flopped around a good bit from one year to another.

agreed-upon paradigms, and greater susceptibility to crisis, is simply less completely structured. That relative lack of structure leaves the agenda free to shift from one time to another in a more volatile fashion. In the more tightly knit health community, with its greater sharing of paradigm, there is less chance for the health agenda to shift abruptly. The fragmentation of a policy system affects the stability of the agenda within that system.

COMMUNITIES AND THE SOUP

Within the policy communities we have just described, many, many ideas are considered at some stage and in some way. Many people have proposals they would like to see considered seriously, alternatives they would like to see become part of the set from which choices are eventually made. They try out their ideas on others in the policy community. Some proposals are rather rapidly discarded as being somehow kooky; others are taken more seriously and survive, perhaps in some altered form. But in the policy primeval soup, quite a wide range of ideas is possible and is considered to some extent. The range at this stage is considerably more inclusive than the set of alternatives that is actually weighed during a shorter period of final decision making. Many, many things are possible here.

To deal with the deteriorating condition of the railroads, for instance, many ideas and proposals have floated among those who make policy or are close to policy makers in the rail area. Over the past decade or two, these ideas have included complete nationalization, nationalization of the roadbed only, regional nationalization, subsidies for equipment or operating expenses, loan guarantees, greater freedom from regulation to allow railroads to abandon unprofitable operations and gain greater pricing flexibility, merger reform, government-operated passenger service, a free marketplace that lets economically sick railroads go under, and even a proposed pneumatic tube to suck passengers in capsules from Washington to New York. To deal with rising medical care costs, health specialists have contemplated comprehensive national health insurance, catastrophic insurance, various regulatory programs, reimbursement reform, direct government delivery of medical care services, various ways of introducing competition into the system, and essentially doing nothing.

The range of possibilities is really quite impressive. Interviews were filled with comments like: "There are lots of things that people are studying." "There are lots of good ideas around." "I honestly don't think there was any option that was not surfaced somewhere along the line." "These things float around all the time." One of my more sharp-tongued respondents dryly observed, when asked if nationalization of railroads was being considered, "Yes, sure, it's being considered. There's hardly a bad idea that isn't being considered. If you think of a bad idea that isn't being considered, call me up collect. I'd like to hear about it."

Incentives and Policy Entrepreneurs

We have spoken of advocates for proposals or for the prominence of an idea. Let us label these advocates policy entrepreneurs.[3] These entrepreneurs are not necessarily found in any one location in the policy community. They could be in or out of government, in elected or appointed positions, in interest groups or research organizations. But their defining characteristic, much as in the case of a business entrepreneur, is their willingness to invest their resources—time, energy, reputation, and sometimes money—in the hope of a future return. That re-

---

[3]For a few previous uses, among many, of the concept of policy entrepreneur, see Jack L. Walker, "Performance Gaps, Policy Research, and Political Entrepreneurs," *Policy Studies Journal* 3 (Autumn 1974): 112–116; Walker, "The Diffusion of Knowledge, Policy Communities and Agenda Setting," in John E. Tropman, Milan J. Dluhy, and Robert M. Lind, eds., *New Strategic Perspectives on Social Policy* (New York: Pergamon Press, 1981), pp. 75–96; and Robert H. Salisbury, "An Exchange Theory of Interest Groups," *Midwest Journal of Political Science* 13 (February 1969): 1–32.

turn might come to them in the form of policies of which they approve, satisfaction from participation, or even personal aggrandizement in the form of job security or career promotion.

Why do they advocate? Or more broadly, what incentives prompt advocacy? What purposes might a given proposal serve? One fairly straightforward possibility is that people sense there is a problem, and they advocate solutions to solve the problem. Some portion of the time, such problem solving does take place. But people in and around government sometimes do not solve problems. Instead, they become advocates for solutions and look for current problems to which to attach their pet solution. What makes the solution a "pet"?

One incentive that prompts advocacy is the promotion of personal interests. This might mean the protection of bureaucratic turf—keeping one's job, expanding one's agency, promoting one's personal career. The legendary battles between the Federal Highway Administration and the Urban Mass Transit Administration within the Department of Transportation are in part battles for bureaucratic turf: protecting and expanding their budgets, employees, and programs. In the case of a lobbyist, advocacy of a proposal might be prompted by the group's interest. The American Medical Association advocated a version of national health insurance in the mid 1970s, for instance, not because they were particularly enthusiastic but because they felt they should be a part of the discussions in order to protect the interests of their members. In the case of a politician, advocacy has electoral benefits. Members of Congress become active in order to claim credit for some accomplishment or to gain publicity. Presidential candidates need policy proposals to make their campaigns credible. These considerations are akin to what James Q. Wilson calls "material" incentives—direct, personal, concrete gain is at stake.[4]

Second, people sometimes advocate proposals because they want to promote their values, or affect the shape of public policy. Advocates of comprehensive national health insurance, for instance, generally have a rather well-articulated vision of a complete package of social insurance programs. Their ideology about the proper role of government in social insurance prompts them to advocate national health insurance as a part of that package. The activists who comprised the first Reagan administration had a vision of smaller government, balanced budgets, and lower taxes. Their ideology prompted them to advocate the curtailment of domestic spending that became a major hallmark of Reagan's first year in office. Advocacy sometimes serves Wilson's "purposive" incentives.

Finally, some of these entrepreneurs are what we might call policy groupies. Much like people who participate and join for "solidary" incentives, some entrepreneurs simply like the game. They enjoy advocacy, they enjoy being at or near the seat of power, they enjoy being part of the action. They make calls,

---

[4]James Q. Wilson, *Political Organizations* (New York: Basic Books, 1973), Chapter 3. See also Peter B. Clark and James Q. Wilson, "Incentive Systems: A Theory of Organization," *Administrative Science Quarterly* 6 (September 1961): 219–266. My discussion of incentives is quite similar to their material-purposive-solidary typology.

have lunch, write memos, and draft proposals, probably for the other reasons we have discussed as well, but in combination with the simple pleasure they take in participating.

Origins, Mutations, and Recombinations

We have just discussed the variety of incentives that lead entrepreneurs to advocate their favorite proposals. Much as we argued in Chapter 4, however, a concentration on origins tells only a small fraction of the story. In fact, many, many proposals are possible—a theoretical infinity of them. This policy primeval soup does not closely resemble a rational decision-making system with a few well-defined alternatives among which decision makers choose. Instead, for the reasons just discussed, a very large number of proposals are considered somewhere along the line. The process is evolutionary, a selection process in which some of these ideas survive and flourish. With this reasoning, the origins become less important than the processes of mutation and recombination that occur as ideas continuously confront one another and are refined until they are ready to enter a serious decision stage. Thus the order ideas are tried out sometimes approaches randomness, but the key to understanding the process is knowing the conditions under which ideas survive.

Many theorists of evolution have come to distinguish between mutation and recombination.[5] According to some current thinking, evolution proceeds not so much by mutation, or the sudden appearance of a wholly new structure, as by recombination, or the new packaging of already familiar elements. Similarly, creative activity usually involves recombination of old elements more than fresh invention of new ones.[6] New musical or artistic forms are found, on analysis, to be new combinations of familiar forms. Likewise, breakthrough scientific discoveries usually build on a lot of previous research.

So it is with the evolution of public policy ideas. Wholly new ideas do not suddenly appear. Instead, people recombine familiar elements into a new structure or a new proposal. This is why it is possible to note, "There is no new thing under the sun," at the very same time change and innovation are being observed. Change turns out to be recombination more than mutation. One of my respondents captured this change process in a particularly apt analogy, ar-

---

[5]This distinction goes by different names with different authors. Some describe a process of crossing-over, for instance, not recombination, to label an exchange of previously existing genetic material. Inversion is another form of genetic change, in which previously existing chains of cells are turned end-to-end. But the general distinction between mutation and recombination is maintained in some form. For a general discussion, see John Maynard Smith, *The Theory of Evolution,* 3rd ed. (Baltimore: Penguin Books, 1975), Chapters 3–5. See also Dawkins, *The Selfish Gene,* op. cit., Chapter 3, especially pp. 32–33. For a more technical treatment, see John H. Holland, *Adaptation in Natural and Artificial Systems* (Ann Arbor: University of Michigan Press, 1975), Chapter 6, especially p. 110.

[6]For example, Koestler argues that an act of creation involves "bisociation," or the combination of diverse but familiar elements in unexpected ways. See Arthur Koestler, *The Act of Creation* (London: Hutchinson, Danube Edition, 1969), especially Chapters 1 and 23.

guing that the elements that go into a policy change can be understood better than how they came into contact and were combined with one another:

> It's like the right combination of gases at the creation. You don't know exactly how the creation took place, except that the right combination of elements was present. The gases sort of swirled around until the right ones came into contact and created the right molecular structure.

Ideas, Not Pressure

Political scientists are accustomed to such concepts as power, influence, pressure, and strategy. If we try to understand public policy solely in terms of these concepts, however, we miss a great deal. The content of the ideas themselves, far from being mere smokescreens or rationalizations, are integral parts of decision making in and around government.[7] As officials and those close to them encounter ideas and proposals, they evaluate them, argue with one another, marshal evidence and argument in support or opposition, persuade one another, solve intellectual puzzles, and become entrapped in intellectual dilemmas. This mode of working through problems and proposals, in contrast to working through them by lobbying muscle or mobilization of numbers of people, is particularly true of the policy community we are discussing in this chapter. As John Maynard Keynes said, "The ideas of economists and political philosophers, both when they are right and when they are wrong, are more powerful than is commonly understood. Indeed, the world is ruled by little else. . . . I am sure that the power of vested interests is vastly exaggerated compared with the gradual encroachment of ideas."[8]

Governmental officials often judge the merits of a case as well as its political costs and benefits. By most informed accounts, for example, the arguments of academic economists in favor of airline deregulation really did play a major role in its passage. One of my respondents, in fact, took me through the arguments marshaled by the airlines against deregulation, and showed me how their arguments were "simply destroyed" during the course of the hearings. Another portrayed the originally skeptical senators as being persuaded by the arguments and evidence, rather than by some lobbying campaign or the anticipation of electoral consequences. Then the arguments were carried over into the trucking and rail cases, once airline deregulation had passed. When I asked one respondent why there was movement in the trucking case, despite the formidable opposition of the regulated truckers and Teamsters, he replied, "Well, I hate to say it, but by God, every once in a while in this town, somebody stands up and says something because it's right. You have to allow for the possibility that something is being talked about because it's the right thing to do." Its "right-

---

[7]For a discussion of the difference between politics as learning and as power or influence, see Hugh Heclo, *Modern Social Politics in Britain and Sweden* (New Haven: Yale University Press, 1974), pp. 304–322.

[8]John Maynard Keynes, *The General Theory of Employment, Interest, and Money* (New York: Harcourt Brace, 1936), p. 383.

ness" was in dispute, but his point is well taken: People often advocate proposals or become persuaded "on the merits."[9]

Policy making is often a process of creating intellectual puzzles, getting into intellectual binds, and then extracting people from these dilemmas. Items might be held off of a public policy agenda for a considerable amount of time while such puzzles are being solved. The key break in the logjam over an interstate highway system, for instance, was an idea—the notion of earmarking funds. Everyone wanted to do something about traffic congestion and clogged highways, but nobody wanted to pay the bill. When the Clay Committee appointed by President Dwight Eisenhower advocated an earmarked trust fund so that the interstate system could be financed from user charges (a fuel tax), the dilemma disappeared and the idea very quickly found its way into enactment.

Preoccupation with rising costs creates a similar bind for health policy makers. As they have wrestled with cost control, they have developed theories to explain the persistence of the problem. These theories concentrate on the fact that because insurance pays, neither providers nor patients have much incentive to reduce costs. The widespread acceptance of this theory has then implied that some solutions gain acceptance more easily than others. Various regulatory programs, and allowing greater marketplace competition to act as a regulator, for instance, seem to show some promise for extracting health policy from its basic dilemma. By contrast, more insurance, while seriously considered during the Carter years, was not enacted in the end. Indeed, some observers argued that the administration's insistence on hospital cost containment as a precurser to national health insurance locked the administration into a logical bind: If cost containment proposals were not adopted, as happened eventually, the administration could not very well advocate national health insurance after arguing that cost containment was a necessary first step.

Even if argumentation is nothing more than rationalization, it is still important. Some events may be governed by lobbying influence or by judgments about clout at the polls, but governmental officials still try to reason their way through problems. Lobbyists marshal their arguments as well as their numbers. The regulated truckers and Teamsters, for instance, known in popular lore for their pressure tactics, employ many experts and analysts who worry constantly about refuting the calculations and arguments of their opponents concerning the likely effects of deregulation. Representatives of barge owners feel their cause really is seriously damaged by arguments about environmental effects of rivers and harbors projects, so they go to considerable lengths to show that water navigation is environmentally sound. One bureaucrat stated the point nicely after referring to a refurbished lobby for intercity buses as a "very dynamic organization." I asked how he judges the dynamism—whether by volumes of letters, or what:

---

[9]For an excellent discussion of the translation of academic economists' arguments into deregulation proposals, see Martha Derthick and Paul J. Quirk, *The Politics of Deregulation* (Washington, D.C.: The Brookings Institution, 1985), Chapter 2.

No, there are not a lot of letters. It's mostly in the sophistication of their talk when they come in to see you. They talk about the number of people that buses carry, the kinds of financial problems they face. They really make a good case.

Superior argumentation does not always carry the day, to be sure. But in our preoccupation with power and influence, political scientists sometimes neglect the importance of content. Both the substance of the ideas and political pressure are often important in moving some subjects into prominence and in keeping other subjects low on governmental agendas.

Finally, sometimes ideas fail to surface in a policy community, not because people are opposed to them, not because the ideas are incompatible with prevailing ideological currents, but because people simply find the subjects intellectually boring. Among my health respondents, for instance, the subject of fraud and abuse did not receive much attention. Over the four years of my interviewing, the highest proportion that discussed any facet of fraud and abuse as a prominent agenda item was 11 percent. This occurred despite the fact that it received a great deal of press play during the same period, and despite the fact that legislation was passed on the subject. A major reason for this lack of interest, it seemed to me, was that policy makers just found the subject boring: messy, unlikely to produce much cost savings, and, most important, not really tied to their intellectual preoccupations with things like market structures, third-party payment, and the contributions of high technology to burgeoning medical care costs. These policy communities are a bit like academic disciplines, each with their own theories, ideas, preoccupations, and fads.

The tendency to concentrate on interesting subjects and avoid boring ones has important implications. First, one who advocates a position tends to oversell it. If a specialist qualifies his or her analysis appropriately, others will lose interest. As one observer put it:

> If you try to sell an idea by saying, "Well, this might work but on the other hand, there are problems with it, but the data show this, but there are problems with the data, so we have to qualify it, but nevertheless I think we should perhaps try this out," you won't get anywhere. You have to go in there and say, "This is the greatest thing to come along in years."

Second, to the extent that policy communities are swept by intellectual fads, attention to subjects will naturally decay as well as advance. Part of the atrophy is due simply to the fact that the subject becomes commonplace, routine, and boring. Attention then turns to subjects that are more interesting. The problem may not be solved, concern with it might still be just as important, approaches to the problem might still be as valid as they ever were, but the idea just isn't novel any longer.

Softening Up

To some degree, ideas float freely through the policy primeval soup. But their advocates do not allow the process to be completely free-floating. In addition to starting discussions of their proposals, they push their ideas in many different forums. These entrepreneurs attempt to "soften up" both policy communities, which tend to be inertia-bound and resistant to major changes, and larger publics, getting them used to new ideas and building acceptance for their proposals. Then when a short-run opportunity to push their proposals comes, the way has been paved, the important people softened up. Without this preliminary work, a proposal sprung even at a propitious time is likely to fall on deaf ears.

The respondent quoted at the beginning of this chapter expressed the point well when he described the years and years of discussion that it would take to obtain serious consideration of his landmark proposal. But this respondent was not alone in my interviews by any means. Consider the following expressions of the same idea:

> It takes a long time to educate people. And then once you get them educated, you have to build up some power to do something. Educating people is very time consuming and energy consuming.

> What you have in these things is a group of dedicated advocates who work long hours and expend a lot of energy to get an idea talked about.

> A proposal like airline deregulation has to go through a gestation period. It takes a number of years.

> All the talk over the last several years in congressional hearings and elsewhere has been a deliberate attempt to create a climate that will allow you to introduce change.

There are many common language expressions of the same idea, phrases like "greasing the skids" and "getting your ducks in a row."

Case histories underline the same point. The passage of Medicare, for example, was the culmination of years of agitation—publicizing the health and financial problems of the aged, introducing draft bills, making speeches, and holding hearings. Discussion of some version of public passenger rail service started back in the 1950s; enactment did not come until 1970. Receptivity for Health Maintenance Organization legislation was built throughout the 1960s by a drumfire of prominent talk about a health care crisis that was then channeled into the HMO debate. Deregulation proposals in transportation were enacted only after years of academic economists "educating" various policy makers and activists about the issue, followed by years of presidential initiatives that "failed" but paved the way for eventual success.

Who are policy entrepreneurs trying to soften up? Some of the time, they speak of educating the general public. Presidential speeches, for instance, are used to "bring the public along," in the words of one bureaucrat. Repeated attention to medical care costs serves to heighten general public sensitivity to the problem. A second target is a more specialized public, peculiar to a particular issue. As with the general public, the purpose of the softening up is to insure that the relevant public is ready for a certain type of proposal when its time does come. Railroad groups try to educate shippers, to make them sensitive to the ways that public policy decisions affect their interests. National health insurance advocates try to create an aura of inevitability so that physicians will become accustomed to the idea of insurance even if they don't like it. The final target is the policy community itself. Even specialists might not be sensitive to a problem or aware of a given proposal, so entrepreneurs try to educate their fellow specialists. One health policy activist, noting that even specialists were not working on long-term care, said, "It's a difficult thing to get people to concentrate on, and we haven't got them to concentrate on it very much yet. But we'll still work on it. We'll plug away at it. It has to come as an issue."

Entrepreneurs use many different means of educating, often several of them at once. On the Hill, introducing a bill can "get people to talking," and "get people to face the issue," in the words of a lobbyist and a congressional staffer. Holding congressional hearings can also dramatize a problem or a proposal. Senator Kennedy's repeated hearings on drug problems, for instance, while not necessarily aimed at a given legislative outcome each time they were held, paved the way for eventual serious consideration of food and drug regulatory reform. Or as a congressional committee aide told me about medical fraud and abuse legislation, "Members sat through those hearings that showed really fantastic things—people ripping off the public with the greatest of ease, intermediaries who were either inept or co-opted. It was a real education for them. Then when it came around to fraud and abuse legislation, they were not going to poopoo the problem as something that wasn't there."

Bureaucrats have their channels as well. Prominent appointees and civil servants make many speeches around the country. As one told me, "All of us have a lot of speaking engagements around the country—the administrator, the deputy, me, and others here. If we're promoting something, we make sure it shows up in all the speeches we make." Bureaucrats and analysts constantly issue studies, reports, and other papers, some mandated by statute and some done on their own; these can play a part in preparing the policy community for some future direction, even though no immediate result is evident. Reports of presidential commissions, White House conferences, and advisory panels to presidents and secretaries can serve the same purpose. Some of the softening up is quite specialized, but some of it is aimed at rather general audiences and carried through the mass media. As one high-level bureaucrat summarized the effort, "You have to create the right climate to get people to focus on the issue and face the issue. The lead time for that sort of thing is two to six years."

Softening up sometimes consists of floating trial balloons. A bureaucrat tries out an idea by slipping a paragraph into a secretary's speech to see what the reaction is. Or a senator introduces a bill, not because it will pass that year but because he tests the water and gauges the state of receptivity to an idea. Many of these trial balloons don't survive the scrutiny. As a journalist put it. "You let an idea float up, and see how it goes. If it's shot down, it's shot down." Thus Senator Edward Kennedy's idea of a doctor draft and Congressman James Howard's idea of financing mass transit through a corporate income tax never got very far. But advocacy may have been worth the effort anyway; attention was focused on specialty maldistribution and transit financing, and on themselves. Some trial balloons are taken more seriously; people notice the idea, debate it, or at least file it away in their minds for future reference. One of my respondents summarized the process beautifully: "There's an idea floated, and it gets thrown in the wastebasket. Then it comes back. Somebody fishes it out of the wastebasket and floats it again."

Some of the bill introduction and speech making without immediate results have the purpose of keeping an issue alive in lean times.[10] Long-time advocates of national health insurance, for example, characterize the parade of bills, proposals, and analyses of the 1940s, 1950s, and early 1960s in those terms—"in there just for the purpose of keeping something alive," as one put it. My analysis of subjects of congressional hearings revealed many, many topics that were not prominent in the interviews, indicating that somebody, somewhere was keeping issues alive and floating their ideas, even though they were not at the moment very hot items. As one committee staffer said of an admittedly losing effort, "We'll probably report it out of the committee, and they'll tear us apart on the floor. But that's to be expected." The issue gets attention anyway, the point is made, and the proposal is aired once more in the hope that it will eventually pass. Another respondent said, "It isn't futile to try and to lose because at least it brings attention to a problem."

Softening up seems to be necessary before a proposal is taken seriously. Many good proposals have fallen on deaf ears because they arrived before the general public, the specialized publics, or the policy communities were ready to listen. Eventually, such a proposal might be resurrected, but only after a period of paving the way. One political appointee stated the importance of this preparation extremely well:

> A lot of preconditioning has to happen. This town does not respond instantaneously to a new idea. There has to be a lot of preconditioning, a lot of maneuvering in the first place. There's a lot of talk going on right now about prevention, the limits of medical care, and so forth. Nothing specific, no specific proposals, but just a vague feeling. Suddenly, maybe tomorrow, maybe six months, maybe longer, out of the wind will come someone with an idea. It doesn't make a lot of difference where it comes from. The critical thing is that the preconditioning has taken place.

Despite the fact that ideas sweep policy communities like fads, a phenomenon we discussed in Chapter 5, government does not act on ideas quickly. To become a basis for action, an idea must both sweep a community and endure. This situation is frustrating to those who promote the idea, but reassuring to those who value stability. Using transportation deregulation as a case in point, a Carter administration appointee provided an apt summary:

> The Ford administration deserves due credit. The Ford administration laid the groundwork for this, softened up opinions, got people interested in the issues. Then we slugged it out. But it does take that period of softening up first. You can go up to the Congress and you can hit them over the head with a baseball bat

[10]Polsby's discussion of the Senate as incubator makes a similar point. See Nelson Polsby, "Strengthening Congress in National Policymaking," *Yale Review* (Summer 1970): 481–497; reprinted in Polsby, ed., *Congressional Behavior* (New York: Random House, 1971), pp. 3–13.

once, then you have to allow them a period of time to recover from that before you can hit them again. It takes a while.

CRITERIA FOR SURVIVAL

We have conjured up a picture of ideas floating about in the policy primeval soup. But, as we have hinted, they don't simply float. They bump into one another, they combine with one another; some survive, some die out, and some survive in a form quite different from their origins. Even if the beginnings are somewhat haphazard, the survival is not. As in any selection system, there is a pattern to the elements that endure. Let's now reflect on the characteristics that enhance the odds of an idea's survival.

Some of the criteria for survival, such as technical feasibility and value acceptability, are internal to the policy community itself. Specialists develop a sense for the "right" type of policy direction and for the technical characteristics that make a proposal viable. Specialists must also anticipate what might happen should the proposal be advanced in the larger political arena. They concern themselves with the cost of a proposal, for instance, in anticipation of a budgetary constraint. They ask themselves whether the proposal stands a prayer of passage on the Hill, and whether it will meet a test of public acceptance. Proposals that fail to meet these criteria—technical feasibility, value acceptability within the policy community, tolerable cost, anticipated public acquiescence, and a reasonable chance for receptivity among elected decision makers—are not likely to be considered as serious, viable proposals. If a proposal initially fails one or more of these tests, it might be reworked or combined with something else, and then floated again. A proposal that survives usually satisfies these criteria.

Technical Feasibility

Even faulty ideas can be trial balloons. But eventually, advocates of a proposal must delve deeply into details and into technicalities, gradually eliminating inconsistencies, attending to the feasibility of implementation, and specifying the actual mechanisms by which an idea would be brought into practical use. It is a bit difficult to specify precisely what policy makers mean by technical feasibility, but they all sense, as they react to a proposal, whether it is "worked out," "staffed out," "worked through," or "ready to go." Many a good idea is sent back to the drawing board, not because it isn't a good idea, but because it isn't "ready" or "all worked out." As one bureaucrat said, "You don't want some stupid fatal flaw to come to light on the first day of hearings and have the whole thing discredited." Or as a researcher put it, "It's important to do your homework, to be prepared, to do in-depth research, and don't sell people on something that won't work." Or to quote a congressional staffer who would have liked to tackle a particular issue, "A lot of people advocated it. We seriously considered doing it in the bill, but we had to drop it because we didn't have enough time to work up a proposal on it in the press of the other things."

Feasibility, as policy specialists talk about it, is heavily involved with implementation. The word "actually" constantly comes into their conversation as they discuss feasibility. "Will it actually accomplish what we want to accomplish?" "Can it actually be administered?" Proposals for nationalizing rail roadbed form a case in point. One solution to the problem of roadbed deterioration discussed during the 1970s was nationalization of the roadbed only, and then allow many users to run trains over the common roadbed, much as trucks, buses, and cars use highways. This proposal was discarded for several reasons, including a serious doubt in the minds of many railroad specialists that the analogy to highways was apt, that the idea could technically be implemented. Several respondents told me in some detail about the difficulties of constructing switching and signaling equipment that would be compatible with rolling stock, how roadbed and rolling stock must go together in an integrated package, and thus why a proposal to separate roadbed from trains would be extremely difficult and costly to implement.

Attention to the technical aspects of a proposal can become extremely detailed. As one presidential staffer put it:

> Just attending to all the technical details of putting together a real proposal takes a lot of time. There's tremendous detail in the work. It's one thing to lay out a statement of principles or a general kind of proposal, but it's quite another thing to staff out all the technical work that is required to actually put a real detailed proposal together.

A serious proposal eventually receives that detailed attention, and is worked on until the obvious bugs are ironed out. As an informed observer summarized the development of one committee chairman's proposal for transportation financing:

> His first proposal, as it was reported in press releases and so forth, was all garbled up. It just seemed to be a bundle of earth-shaking ideas, and we sat here looking at it, trying to figure it out, chuckling to ourselves, and noticing that it was quite a can of worms. Gradually, this has evolved into at least a coherent package. I'm not sure I favor it all, but at least it is coherent.

Attention to the details of implementation does not necessarily result in enacted programs that work. Policy makers do not always anticipate all of the consequences that will flow from their actions, issues are often extremely complex, and in retrospect even advocates of a proposal may conclude that it was a futile attempt right from the beginning. To be seriously considered, however, policy makers believe that a proposal will work if enacted, even if the idea seems far-fetched in hindsight. Without that belief in its technical feasibility, the proposal is not likely to survive to the point of serious consideration.

Value Acceptability

Proposals that survive in the policy community are compatible with the values of the specialists. Obviously, all specialists do not have the same values, and in the instances of disagreement among the specialists, conflicts spill over into the larger political arena. But in some respects, the bulk of the specialists do eventually see the world in similar ways, and approve or disapprove of similar approaches to problems. One respondent told me that a proposal that had received a great deal of press attention was not being taken seriously among the specialists because "it doesn't really represent any mainstream thinking." Their thinking is composed not just of ordinary liberal-conservative dimensions, but also of such concepts as equity and efficiency. Proposals that don't fit with specialists' values have less chance of survival than those that do.

Some of the participants' values are composed of their view of the proper role or size of the federal government vis-à-vis the states and localities, and their view of the proper size of the public sector vis-à-vis the private sector. Their views on these issues directly affect the alternatives they propose or oppose. Those we usually classify as liberals support larger government roles while those we usually classify as conservatives oppose them. Within the health area, for example, a knot of ideological liberals believes in more ambitious social welfare programs in general, and in more ambitious national health insurance in particular. They have a view of the proper package of social insurance that every advanced country should offer its citizens, and they work to fill in the gaps in that package, piece by piece, as the appropriate opportunities arise. First they support social security pensions, then the expansion of death benefit and disability coverage, then the enactment of Medicare and Medicaid, and then the same advocates for all of those initiatives push for eventual enactment of comprehensive national health insurance. As one of them told me, "Ours is not really a response to a perceived need, but it's ideological, if you will. People like me have this concept of what ought to be done in the area of social insurance, and we want to fill in the logical gaps in that program."

This component of ideology, based on the participants' view of the proper size of government, has a cross-national aspect. Some writers argue that a distinctive ideology or political culture dominates American politics, one that places much more emphasis on the virtues of private sector activity and the evils of government than the thinking that dominates the politics of other industrialized countries.[11] Programs that are commonplace in other countries, such as nationalized railroads, national health insurance, and public ownership and operation of sizable portions of the housing stock, are not even considered live options in the United States, according to this argument. One of my transportation respondents illustrated graphically the different mind set:

> I was just talking to somebody from Sweden. In Sweden, they designed their system so that they would have various modes of passenger transportation all coming into the same terminal, and various modes of freight transportation all coming into the same terminal. They coordinate these things very nicely. When I asked this man how they do that, he replied, "How else would you do it?"

[11]For example, see Samuel P. Huntington, *American Politics: The Promise of Disharmony* (Cambridge, MA: Harvard University Press, 1981), Chapter 2: Louis Hartz, *The Liberal Tradition in America* (New York: Harcourt Brace, 1955), Chapter 1: and Anthony King, "Ideas, Institutions, and the Policies of Governments," *British Journal of Political Science* 3 (July and October 1973): 291–313 and 409–423.

If there is such a national culture or dominant ideology, it affects different policy arenas differently. In this study, health seems to be affected by the ideological biases in the American political culture much more than transportation. Fully 36 percent of my health interviews contained an unprompted, prominent reference to such ideological biases, compared to only 7 percent of transportation interviews. The health interviews contained many references to a distinctive American distrust of governmental solutions, such as the following:

> There are possible solutions that would never fly here. This country is built on private initiative, and that runs very deep in our thinking.

> Personal lifestyle is a matter of personal choice. I hope the federal government won't get in the business of telling me whether I can smoke or drink or what to eat.

But transportation interviews had far fewer such references, suggesting that transportation is a less ideologically laden arena. One transportation respondent confirmed this impression in his own experience:

> Compared to a lot of government activity, transportation is relatively insulated from emotional content. It's true that you get a lot of protest about pollution and you do get emotional protest against certain highway projects. But almost everybody sees the need for good transportation, and they are willing to put money into it. There is no Republican or Democratic position on transportation, no liberal or conservative view. You don't get bound up in a lot of ideological conflict. I say that because I came over here from the Department of Defense. Over there, there is a large emotional and moralistic content to everything you do. Shall we have a strong national defense, peace, and all that.

Debates over nationalization illustrate the point. Nationalization does not have serious agenda status in either health or transportation. Only 7 percent of the transportation interviews included a prominent mention of railroad nationalization. There was some flurry of interest, particularly in the idea of nationalizing roadbeds, during the Penn Central crisis, but it quickly died. Similarly, socialized medicine, in which providers would be employees of the government, was prominently discussed in only 3 percent of the health interviews.

On the face of it, these figures might argue that a dominant national ideology that emphasizes the virtues of limited government controls the agenda in both health and transportation. But digging a bit deeper, it becomes apparent that the arguments used in the two policy areas are sharply different. In health, particularly in response to my questions about why some version of a national health *service* is not seriously considered, in contrast to the widely discussed national health *insurance,* people often responded in terms of national political ideology, culture, or symbolism:

> Our ethic is personal initiative, and when the government tries to do anything, people cry socialism.

> If you think things are bad now, see what happens when the government controls everything. I don't think that a health service would be acceptable to most of the population.

> I think the words are too frightening.

As one source close to the American Public Health Association wryly observed of many members' advocacy of a national health service, "Well, it's not exactly the shot that's been heard round the world."

There was a similar reaction in transportation when nationalization was mentioned; respondents talked about "national traditions" and "general opposition to the idea." But these general mentions were overshadowed by a much more pragmatic discussion about the disadvantages of nationalization: high cost, such problems with roadbed nationalization as incompatibility with rolling stock, the skimming of profitable traffic by large corporations that would leave common carriers with the dregs, and the administrative problems that would overtake the system. A typical response was the following: "There is no great political clamor for nationalization. The primary reason is that it is expensive, and we may be able to do the job much more inexpensively." When asked why nationalization did not win out during the Penn Central crisis, another respondent summarized the general thinking:

> The administration's opposition to nationalization was not over the philosophy of nationalization or anything like that. It was not an ideological thing. The problem for the administration was that they didn't want to put the funds into it. Nationalizers want funds, and very large quantities of funds. The question is really over money, not ideology. Nationalization isn't unthinkable. That's not it at all. But it won't resolve the underlying problem.

Thus, to the extent that a dominant ideology affects public policy outcomes in the United States, it does not do so very simply. The differences between health and transportation suggest that ideology may be more at work in some domains than in others, more at work under some circumstances than others. In some cases, we might be tempted to attribute great power to a dominant national ideology, when it may not really be at work at all.

We have been discussing ideology as if it were completely conceived as people's attitudes toward the size and role of the federal government, vis-à-vis the states and localities and vis-à-vis the private sector. But the ideologies of government officials or people close to them have other components, including the theme of equity. Proposals sometimes come to be prominent on governmental agendas because they would serve to redress inequities, imbalances, or unfairness. Governmental officials and those around them sometimes perceive an inequity so compelling that it drives the agenda. Even if a principle of equity is not a driving force, fairness or redress of imbalance is a powerful argument used in the debates for or against proposals.

One example of the principle of equity as a driving force is the case of the government's renal dialysis program.[12] As soon as the technology for convenient dialysis was perfected, it became clear that some people were receiving this life-giving treatment and others were not. The selections of patients to re-

---

[12]For an account of the progress of the issue, see Richard A. Rettig, "The Policy Debate on Patient Care Financing for Victims of End-Stage Renal Disease," *Law and Contemporary Problems* 40 (Autumn 1976): 196–230. An interesting classroom exercise that plays out the policy dilemmas is in Ronald Brunner, *The Kidney Problem* (Boston: Intercollegiate Case Clearing House, 1977).

ceive treatment were made on the basis of ability to pay, qualification for experimental study groups, proximity to the few centers where dialysis was being performed, and the happenstance of personal health insurance coverage. Gripping stories appeared in the popular media about "death committees" of physicians that were charged with deciding whose lives should or should not be saved. Such a fundamental, dramatic difference of treatment was more than decision makers' values could bear. The Senate passed a short rider introduced right on the floor which provided that renal dialysis and kidney transplants be financed by Medicare, and the House quickly followed suit. So compelling was the inequity that had thrust this item onto the agenda that Congress really did not consider the cost of the program in any detail, a cost that exceeded a billion dollars within a few short years. As one knowledgeable respondent summarized the forces that led to such sudden agenda status and passage, "When there is serious inequity, that is politically and socially unstable. Once a technology is developed, everybody will want it." The moral pressure to avoid letting people die, when a procedure was available to save them but for its cost, was simply irresistible.

There is even more discussion of equity in transportation than in health. Overall, equity considerations were important in 28 percent of the interviews. But they were prominently discussed in only 13 percent of the health interviews, as compared to 45 percent of the transportation interviews. In addition, 20 percent of the transportation interviews contained some side mention of equity, compared to only 8 percent of health interviews.[13]

Much of the discussion of equity in transportation concerns comparisons across the various modes. Railroads complain that waterways have an unfair disadvantage because of the free use of the Corps of Engineers' navigation projects, and they claim that truckers are not paying their fair share of highway construction and maintenance. Buses complain that the huge amount of taxpayers' money poured into Amtrak unfairly diverts traffic from buses. Without taking a position here on the validity of various claims, we can point out that the frequency of such discussion is noteworthy. The different transportation modes operate to some degree in similar markets, placing them in potential competition with one another for the traffic. Yet their technologies differ, the governmental regulatory programs differ, and the government subsidies differ. Inevitably, those who feel at a disadvantage raise questions about inequity, arguing that they are put at an unfair competitive disadvantage because of government action.

A final component of policy makers' values has become a principle of efficiency. They increasingly concern themselves not only with the cost of a program but with the benefits that are being realized from that expenditure, whether these benefits justify the costs, and whether the benefits could be achieved at a lower cost. Some of this concern is attributable to short-run eco-

---

[13]In the case studies, there is no substantial difference between health and transportation. Equity considerations were coded as very or somewhat important in prompting agenda prominence in 9 of the 23 cases.

nomic and budgetary problems. But it also probably reflects a long-range trend toward more economists (and people receptive to their thinking) in government. Economists' language is everywhere: references to cost-effectiveness, tradeoffs, efficiency, cost allocation, and cross subsidy. As one health respondent said of the concern with the efficacy of medical care, "That efficacy issue is coming along, and that's an important development because it puts the cost issue in a new perspective. People are starting to ask what they're *getting* for the cost. Part of the concern about cost is not really about cost *per se,* but rather, are we getting anything for all the money we're spending?"

Sometimes, the concern with efficiency is reflected in formal cost-effectiveness evaluation studies. At other times, the concern is less formal. Respondents would talk about Amtrak in cost-benefit terms, for instance, as in the following passage: "The costs are going to get astronomical, and you're not providing a public service in return for that cost. There are trains running around all over the place and nobody is on them. You have them in place for rail buffs." The same type of reasoning was applied by others to the proposed construction of new subway systems: "People are increasingly coming to the view that urban mass transit is a rathole down which money shouldn't be pissed any more than it has. Take the Washington METRO system. It's a beautiful system, but Jesus Christ Almighty, is it expensive!"

As some of these cases illustrate, efficiency does not always carry the day, particularly as an issue moves from the community of specialists we have been discussing into a larger political arena. Some respondents even argued that political processes systematically favor inefficiency. In the health area, for instance, the pressure to opt for heroic treatment and heroic expenditures to save lives seems nearly irresistible. As one health respondent put it, "The concentration on the cost of Medicare and Medicaid is reflected in the thinking of almost all the people in HEW now. That's as long as they aren't sick. Of course when they're sick, then cost be damned, I want to have the best care, and full speed ahead." Or as a transportation respondent said:

> Economists somehow think that waste is a politically potent issue. But they get to the Hill, and they discover that congressmen favor waste. You know, "What do you mean, waste? You mean small town service is waste? Do you mean servicing the beet growers in my district is waste?" The very place that there is waste is also the toughest thing to handle politically.

Another spoke of large-scale, expensive subway systems: "It has always been apparent to me that subways are not the way to go. But they take so much money, they are so inefficient, that there is a great deal of support for them." Then he added, in an absolute masterpiece of pithy summary, *"For a politician, the costs are the benefits."*

Anticipation of Future Constraints

Specialists in policy communities know that as an initiative's saga unfolds, some constraints will be imposed on proposals that are adopted or even seriously considered. Down the line, decision makers need to be convinced that the budgetary cost of the program is acceptable, that there is a reasonable chance that politicians will approve, and that the public in its various facets—both mass and activist—will acquiesce. Anticipation of these constraints within a policy community forms a final set of criteria by which ideas and proposals are selected. Some ideas fail to obtain a serious hearing, even among specialists, because their future looks bleak, while others survive because specialists calculate that they would meet these future tests.

One of these tests is a budget constraint. Members of a policy community know that somewhere along the line a proposal must be shown to have a tolerable cost, at least a tolerable cost to the federal budget. So they spend untold hours costing out proposals, paring them down to manageable proportions, and floating the slimmed-down version again. If they cannot come up with a proposal that is financially acceptable, the idea may be dropped. As one respondent said of an administration proposal, "They went back and did their cost estimates right, and discovered that it was going to cost a lot more money than they'd figured to do it right. When they discovered that, they became less interested in it." Some proposals never really see the light of day because of anticipated cost. Many health respondents cited long-term care as an example. As one put it:

> Long-term care is a back burner item. I have heard people talk about it for years, but nobody can decide what to do. None of the health insurance proposals take it on. There is a simple reason for that. Nobody can figure out how to handle it, and they're scared to death of trying. The numbers rise so fast when you crank in the demographic facts plus the cost of long-term care, it really boggles the mind when you think of taking on this additional financial commitment. So people play around with the alternatives and they fuss about doing something about home care, but that's about it.

A second test is public acquiescence. Specialists in a policy community know that ultimately their proposals must be acceptable to the public. They may conceive of the public as the bulk of the people in the country, as a more narrow set of activists who have a special stake in the outcomes, or as both. It would be a mistake to argue that proposals more or less well up from the public, but it would be equally in error to argue that advocates ignore public reaction as they design their proposals. The case of health habits is an appropriate example. Health policy makers know that people's own habits—smoking, diet, sleep, exercise—have a great deal to do with both the population's health and the population's medical care bill. Many of them fairly itch to do more in the area of habits, but their experience with public reaction has convinced them that aside from education and warnings, not much more can be done. Public outrage over seat belt interlocks, for instance, is often cited as the major cause of the very quick repeal of a proposal that had actually been enacted.

Sometimes, a broad, general public is being considered; at other times, it is a more specialized public. Proposals to require physicians to work in rural areas, for example, run afoul of anticipated physician opposition. As one respondent observed, "Physicians just don't want to go to Horse's Ass, Idaho, to practice, and there isn't any way you can force them to."

Policy specialists often interpret the support or opposition of elected officials as closely tied to or indicative of public sentiment. The reactions of senators and House members, congressional staffers, the president, and presidential advisors are anticipated as proposals are formed and debated in the policy community. Many ideas are discarded because specialists cannot conceive of any plausible circumstances under which they could be approved by elected politicians and their appointees. Some ideas are kept alive in the hope that the larger political climate will change, even though the ideas might not be currently in favor. Other ideas are actively pushed to the forefront in anticipation of approval by elected politicians. One health committee staffer summarized his problem: "It's a matter of arithmetic. You need eight votes in subcommittee, fifteen in full committee, and fifty-one on the floor." When asked if he dropped ideas when he felt he didn't have the votes, he replied, "Yes, often."

THE SHORT LIST OF IDEAS

A policy community produces a short list of ideas. Through the selection process we have described, some ideas are formulated, survive the process of softening up, and largely satisfy the criteria by which specialists evaluate proposals. There may or may not be a single proposal on which all specialists agree, but at least a set of a few prominent alternatives has risen to the top of the policy primeval soup, ready for policy makers to consider. Ideas have been sharpened and changed, combinations have emerged that serve the purpose better than the original proposals, people have become accustomed to thinking along certain lines, the list of alternatives under discussion has narrowed, and a few ideas have emerged as the leading candidates for further serious consideration.

In the rest of this chapter, we discuss the emerging consensus, the general knowledge that results, and the importance of an available alternative.

The Emerging Consensus: Of Bandwagons and Tipping

Through the processes we have been describing in this chapter, consensus spreads through a policy community. This diffusion among specialists involves two different kinds of subject matter: awareness of problems, and agreement on solutions or proposals. We discussed the awareness of problems in Chapter 5. People who are aware of health policy questions, for instance, come to a rough agreement that rising Medicare costs, overbedding, physician surplus or maldistribution among specialists, and the spread of high-cost technology are serious problems. Some agreement on the short list of alternatives also diffuses in a policy community. Health specialists start to agree that increased emphasis on prevention and on promotion of good health through changed personal habits would be a good idea. Transportation specialists start to reach consensus on the desirability of user charges, and on the necessity of cutting back on funding for Amtrak and Conrail. If most specialists do not reach agreement on one alternative in a given domain of problems, they at least reach some understanding on the fairly narrow set of alternatives from which some authoritative choice might be made.

Within the policy community, and according to the principles of diffusion and acceptance we have discussed in this chapter, something akin to a bandwagon effect often occurs. As two respondents put it:

> It's a very complex process, almost like a snowball. It starts with a voice or two in the wilderness. That voice in the wilderness recruits somebody else. You talk to people and keep hammering at it.

> I know a lot of the important people. These people meet in various places—conferences, parties, and so forth—and they all talk to each other. There is a grapevine. If you have a new idea, you can enter that idea into the grapevine. If it has anything going for it, it will spread.

Gradually, the idea catches on. People in and around government speak of a "growing realization," an "increasing feeling," a "lot of talk in the air," and "coming to a conclusion." After some degree of diffusion, there seems to be a take-off point: Many people are discussing the proposal or idea. At that point, knowledgeable people refer to a "widespread feeling," or, as another respondent put it, "by now, this is orthodox thinking." This process of take-off looks similar to Thomas Schelling's "tipping" model, which is used to describe the process of change in racial mix in neighborhoods.[14] A few minority families move into a previously all-white neighborhood until a "tipping" point is reached, after which the neighborhood progresses very quickly to one in which very few whites reside. In this case, an idea starts with a few people, and its diffusion rises rapidly from those few to the point where the idea becomes commonplace. The more a proposal is discussed, the more seriously it is taken. As Robert Axelrod says:

> Problems that are raised only once are probably not often regarded as serious, and it seems that proposals that are suggested by only one person are not often retained as salient options. So the problems and proposals that are regarded as most significant have been brought to the respondent's attention in many different ways and therefore rarely have distinct sources.[15]

---

[14]Thomas C. Schelling, *Micromotives and Macrobehavior* (New York: W. W. Norton, 1978), pp. 99–102.

[15]Robert Axelrod, "Bureaucratic Decisionmaking in the Military Assistance Program: Some Empirical Findings," in Morton Halperin and Arnold Kanter, eds., *Readings in American Foreign Policy* (Boston: Little, Brown, 1973), p. 160.

As respondents discuss this process of diffusion, it is sometimes unclear exactly to which population they refer. When they refer to a "growing realization" or a "widespread feeling," one often has little but an intuitive feel among *whom* the realization or feeling is spreading. Usually, however, they are referring to the specialists we have been describing in this chapter—researchers, bureaucrats, academics, congressional staffers—all of whom specialize in a policy domain such as health or transportation. Within that set of people, the bandwagon or tipping phenomenon is quite different from a similar phenomenon that one might find in a more political arena. As we will describe it in Chapter 7, tipping in politics is a process of coalition-building; bargains are struck, concessions are given in return for participation in a coalition, and as the bandwagon gains momentum people join out of fear of being excluded from participation in the goodies to be obtained. Here, the process emphasizes persuasion and diffusion: An idea with something to recommend it, according to the criteria for survival, becomes accepted by ever larger numbers of specialists. The diffusion may be fully as explosive as in the political stream, but the process by which the growth takes place is quite different.

"There is no new thing under the sun." (Ecclesiastes 1:9)

People in and around government are fond of calmly and patiently pointing out to the novice that nothing is new. Various respondents described a given proposal with versions of that reaction: "Everybody knows about that." "It's been kicking around for a long time." "That one is as old as the hills." "Everything seems like the same old stuff to me." Perhaps expertise is demonstrated by showing familiarity with an idea, familiarity approaching boredom. In some respects, in fact, there *is* no new thing under the sun. As we pointed out in Chapter 4, everything has its antecedents, trapping one who attempts to track down an ultimate origin into an infinite regress. And as we pointed out in that same chapter, the agenda may show a great volatility at the same time that the alternatives being seriously considered might be quite familiar to the participants.

This familiarity is the logical outcome of the processes we have been describing in this chapter. If alternatives change not by mutation but by recombination, there will always be familiar elements in the new combinations. And if the softening up process is as critical as we have claimed, it would be exceedingly surprising if wholly new ideas suddenly appeared on the scene in the policy primeval soup and immediately received a serious hearing. When the time for action arrives, when the policy window described in Chapter 8 opens, it is too late to develop a new proposal from scratch. It must have already gone through this long process of consideration, floating up, discussion, revision, and trying out again.

Ideas, proposals, or issues may rise into or fall from favor from time to time. One respondent described them as perennials—flowering in one season, then lying dormant, only to flower anew. Or as another put it, "Issues fade in and fade out, but they never, ever go away. They always come back—always." Proposals may not come back in the same form; rather, they are recast, combined with something else, or attached to a problem different from the one they started with. After a subject has been through the lengthy gestation period of most major issues, the alternatives become familiar, the options narrow to a few well-understood possibilities, and a limit is reached on the ability to introduce new material. A new recombination, a new twist—yes—but not wholly new material. Advocates pull old proposals out of drawers, cut and paste them, rehashing old ideas in response to new demands.[16] Consider and sympathize with the exasperation of one respondent who took exception to the reaction of the Carter inner circle to the old, old national health insurance issue: "HEW sent up a package to the White House, and the White House complained that they had worked up the same old hash. Well, there isn't anything around *except* the same old hash."

The Importance of the Available Alternative

In Chapter 1, we distinguished between governmental and decision agendas. Governmental agendas include subjects to which people in and around government are paying serious attention. Decision agendas include only those subjects that are moving into position for some sort of authoritative decision, such as legislative enactment or presidential action. Items are sometimes found on a governmental agenda without a solution attached to them. People might worry about a particular problem without having a solution to it, for instance, and forces in the political stream might prompt attention to an item even though there is no viable proposal connected to it.

But normally, before a subject can attain a solid position on a decision agenda, a viable alternative is available for decision makers to consider. It is not enough that there is a problem, even quite a pressing problem. There also is generally a solution ready to go, already softened up, already worked out. As Paul Light says in his study of the president's agenda, the subject with an "available alternative" is the one that rises on the agenda, crowding out equally worthy subjects that do not have a viable, worked-out proposal attached.[17] One congressional committee staffer told me, when asked how they choose the items they work on from the long list of items they could consider:

> It's partly a matter of what's ready. If there's a bill already drafted, we can go ahead with it fairly easily—tinker with it, amend it, and so forth. If we have to draft a bill, then sometimes it waits, and gets shoved aside in the press of things that *are* ready.

The availability of a viable alternative is not a sufficient condition for a high position on a decision agenda, since many good proposals kick around the system for a long time before the lightning strikes. But the chances for a problem to rise on the *governmental* agenda increase if a solution is attached to the

---

[16]See Polsby, ed., *Congressional Behavior,* op. cit., p. 7.

[17]Paul C. Light, *The President's Agenda* (Baltimore: Johns Hopkins University Press, 1982), pp. 147–149.

problem. The chances for a problem to rise on the *decision* agenda are *dramatically* increased if a solution is attached.

In the health area, for instance, long-term care, the desirability of getting people to alter their own health habits, and persuading physicians to settle in underserved areas are three subjects that could conceivably be prominent on the governmental agenda. But when asked why such major problems were not getting more attention, one bureaucrat replied, "Because we don't know what to do about them." As another health respondent said, "It's difficult to get mileage out of something that we don't have any approach to solving." The lack of a consensus proposal for national health insurance at the beginning of the Carter administration was a major reason for the stall in the first couple of years. Even genuine advocates disagreed fundamentally over how comprehensive the benefits should be, the extent of mandated private as opposed to governmental coverage, the acceptability of deductibles and copayment, and a host of other issues. The proposal, in other words, was not ready to go. In marked contrast, airline deregulation immediately took off. The Ford administration proposals had laid the groundwork, Senators Howard Cannon and Edward Kennedy had agreed on a proposal, and the administration simply adopted that bill wholesale as their own. The alternative was available, worked through, and ready to go.

CONCLUSION

This chapter has considered the processes by which proposals are generated, debated, redrafted, and accepted for serious consideration. Much of this process takes place in communities of specialists. These communities can be quite tightly knit or quite fragmented. Among the consequences of fragmentation are disjointed policy, lack of common orientations, and agenda instability.

We have portrayed the progress of ideas and policy proposals as a selection process in which a large number of possible policy initiatives is narrowed to a short list of proposals that are seriously considered. Getting the policy community receptive to a new idea takes a long period of softening up. Policy entrepreneurs—people who are willing to invest resources of various kinds in hopes of a future return in the form of policies they favor—push their ideas in many ways. They aim to soften up the general public, more specialized publics, and the policy community itself. Only after years of effort are proposals brought to the point where they can be seriously considered. During this consideration, recombinations of already-familiar elements are as important as fresh initiatives: There is nothing new under the sun at the same time that there is substantial change. Ideas themselves turn out to be as important as political pressure.

Proposals that meet several criteria enhance their chance of survival. They are technically feasible—worked out and capable of being implemented. They are acceptable in the light of the values held by members of the policy community. These values include not only notions of the proper role and size of government, but also concepts of equity and efficiency. Specialists in the policy community also anticipate the constraints that their proposals will face. They tailor their proposals to an anticipated budget constraint, they consider whether their proposals will gain the acquiescence of the mass public and specialized publics, and they alter their proposals to gain the approval of elected officials.

The policy stream thus produces a short list of proposals. This short list is not necessarily a consensus in the policy community on the one proposal that meets their criteria; rather, it is an agreement that a few proposals are prominent. Having a viable alternative available for adoption facilitates the high placement of a subject on a governmental agenda, and dramatically increases the chances for placement on a decision agenda.

CHAPTER 7

The Political Stream

Flowing along independently of the problems and policy streams is the political stream, composed of such things as public mood, pressure group campaigns, election results, partisan or ideological distributions in Congress, and changes of administration. Quite apart from what happens in the community of specialists, and quite apart from bringing problems to the attention of people in and around government, such events as a new majority in Congress or a new administration occur. These developments in the political stream have a powerful effect on agendas, as new agenda items become prominent and others are shelved until a more propitious time. The new Reagan administration, for example, set agendas all over town, making some things possible that were impossible before, making other things out of the question, and creating a receptivity to some ideas but not to others.

Let us be clear of our language. When I use the word "political" in this context, I use the word in its colloquial Washington sense. Political science defines "political" very broadly, including just about any activity related to the authoritative allocation of values,[1] or to the distribution of benefits and costs.[2] The intra-Washington definition, implicitly, is more narrow. "Political" factors in such parlance are electoral, partisan, or pressure group factors. As one talks to practitioners of the art, they use "political" motivations, for example, to refer to politicians' attention to voter reactions, their skewering of members of the opposite political party, and their efforts to obtain the support of important interest group leaders. I employ this more narrow usage here.

[1]David Easton, *The Political System,* 2nd ed. (New York: Knopf, 1971), p. 129.

[2]For example, Harold Lasswell, *Politics: Who Gets What, When, How* (Cleveland: Meridian Books, 1958).

Public policy analysis could treat these political events as somehow outside of the policy-making process. The making of public policy, such a notion would run, is the province of specialists, found particularly among bureaucrats, congressional staffers, and researchers. That conception, in my view, would be fundamentally wrong. It is misleading to conceive of policy making as if it were essentially a process such as the one described in the last chapter. To be sure, specialized program development is an important part of the process. But the political stream we are about to describe is also an important, integral part, not at all exogenous to policy making.

In this chapter, we will start with the public and work toward government. We first discuss a vaguely defined but nonetheless important national mood, and consider the place of social movements within that national mood. We then turn to organized political forces, patterns of support for or opposition to the prominence of certain agenda items, within interest groups or other extragovernmental structures. Governmental phenomena occupy our attention last, when we consider such factors as protection of bureaucratic turf and turnover of key personnel brought about by election results. We will end by describing consensus building in the political stream. Throughout, change will be seen as a function of the shifts of important participants (e.g., a change of administration or the influx of new legislators), or as a response to shifts in national mood or interest group configurations.

THE NATIONAL MOOD

People in and around government sense a national mood. They are comfortable discussing its content, and believe that they know when the mood shifts. The idea goes by different names—the national mood,[3] the climate in the country,[4] changes in public opinion, or broad social movements. But common to all of these labels is the notion that a rather large number of people out in the country are thinking along certain common lines, that this national mood changes from one time to another in discernible ways, and that these changes in mood or climate have important impacts on policy agendas and policy outcomes. In the view of close observers, these changes in public opinion are not confined to the policy communities we discussed in the last chapter, nor to the themes that float around in those communities. Instead, talk of a "swing to the right" or an "antigovernment mood" in the country means something much more general. As one health respondent replied when asked why there had been a shift in the direction of emphasizing the virtues of the private marketplace, "I think it is not related to the health field, really. There is a whole environment out there that is moving in that direction."

---

[3]Thanks to John Campbell for this terminology.

[4]Cobb and Elder discuss a "climate of the times." See Roger W. Cobb and Charles D. Elder.,"Communications and Public Policy," in Dan Nimmo and Keith Sanders, eds., *Handbook of Political Communications* (Beverly Hills: Sage, 1981), p. 405.

Governmental participants' sense of the national mood serves to promote some items on their policy agendas and to restrain others from rising to prominence. As for promotion, their sense of national mood is one thing that creates the "fertile ground" that we discussed in Chapter 4. We pointed out there that the seed can come from anywhere, but the key to understanding its germination and growth is whether there is fertile ground or an initial receptivity to the ideas. Many respondents pointed to a general climate of hostility to government regulation as one factor that made it possible for deregulation proposals in transportation to get a sympathetic hearing during the 1970s. As one put it, "These changes involve whole attitudes toward government which affect the administration's success in making new proposals. There was an appropriate mood for deregulation. It could have come earlier, but it didn't because that mood wasn't there." Similar effects were evident in health, as prominent discussion of proposals to increase marketplace competition rose from near zero in the first three waves of interviews to 38 percent in 1979, and as Health Maintenance Organizations, a keystone of this procompetitive approach, rose to 63 percent.

In contrast to this ability of the national mood to promote a higher agenda status for some items, policy makers' perception of the national mood also serves as a constraint, pushing other items into relative obscurity. During the 1970s, the same time that this perceived antigovernment climate promoted deregulation schemes, it demoted proposals for ambitious new spending and additional government regulation. As one congressional committee staffer said, "Add to [the budget constraint] the panic of Proposition 13, and the overwhelming concern with inflation and with wasteful big government. These things affect the debate at every turn, and affect all the actions that you would want to contemplate." Or as another said while describing the government interest in promoting good health habits and the public reaction against initiatives like banning saccharin and requiring seat belt interlocks, "Last year, the health side was pushing on this issue of lifestyle. This year, society is pushing back. The issue really is the limit on government telling people what's good for them." Indeed, prominent commentary among my health respondents on the theme of excessive government regulation rose from 23 percent of health respondents in 1976 to 71 percent in 1979.

Not only do participants feel that they can accurately sense the national mood at any one point in time, but they also feel that they can sense changes in the mood. Most of my respondents in the mid- to late-1970s, for instance, were confident of their characterization of the national mood as conservative— against ambitious new federal programs, in favor of whittling down the size of government, against big expenditures, and against regulation in general terms. In my interviews this was called "the conservative tidal wave in which we are all engulfed" and "a general societal trend." One respondent said, "There's a general antipathy toward government right now. I don't know why that is, but everybody feels it and it has effects." Researchers on public opinion will long debate the validity of these perceptions, but for our purposes the critical fact is that important people held them strongly.

In some measure, such swings in national mood are regarded as inevitable as swings of a pendulum. Politics move left at one point in time, and as surely as a pendulum must swing back, politics will move rightward in turn. The 1970s, for instance, were seen as a reaction to the policy enactments of the Great Society in the 1960s. As one respondent claimed quite directly, "The ideas of the 60s are shot. There's an unease, an uncertainty about what to do, a lack of direction." Said another, "National health insurance would be the biggest social program of all, and there is a healthy skepticism about the social programs of the 1960s." Some of these swings of the pendulum may follow partisan realignments.[5] Others may be feedback cycles; a program is enacted, problems with its implementation emerge, corrections are made, and new problems emerge from the corrections.

We have been speaking of a national mood as a rather vague presence that people in and around government sense, something that is palpable to them but hardly concrete or specific. Where does this mood actually reside, and how do these people sense its content? One fairly clear answer is that the mood does not necessarily reside in the mass public. Operationally, we could take sample surveys of the mass public to discern the popular preferences that make up the national mood or climate, and scholars often do. But to policy specialists and even to politicians, such samplings are a bit beside the point. Referring to the general antiregulation mood, for instance, one respondent argued, "I don't think that there is a great public groundswell in favor of fat in their meat, or in favor of Saturday night specials, or in favor of high-tar cigarettes. In fact, polls show that people overwhelmingly want gun control and some of these other things." Even as my respondents characterized the national mood as strongly antiregulation, for instance, the Gallup poll in 1977 actually showed the public favoring a government requirement for air bags on all new cars.

Similarly, the shifts that we have come to call social movements may not be very widespread in the general public. Ordinarily, social movements need organization and leadership to have a policy impact.[6] Indeed, they may be led by just a few very active people, and have surprisingly few adherents. The consumer movement, for instance, started, grew, and prospered due to the efforts of Ralph Nader, a few other activists, and their allies in Congress.[7] The successful social movements, of course, catch on in the more general public and

[5]See Benjamin Ginsberg, "Elections and Public Policy," *American Political Science Review* 70 (March 1976): 41–49; Barbara Deckard Sinclair, "Party Realignment and the Transformation of the Political Agenda," *American Political Science Review* 71 (September 1977): 940–953; and David Brady, "Congressional Party Realignment and Transformations of Public Policy in Three Realignment Eras," *American Journal of Political Science* 26 (May 1982): 333–360.

[6]For a statement of a "resource mobilization" perspective on social movements, which emphasizes the importance of leaders mobilizing resources, see John D. McCarthy and Mayer N. Zald, "Resource Mobilization and Social Movements," *American Journal of Sociology* 82 (May 1977): 1212–1241.

[7]See Mark V. Nadel, *The Politics of Consumer Protection* (Indianapolis: Bobbs-Merrill, 1971), Chapter 5.

eventually have electoral impacts. Politicians, seeing the electoral payoff, climb on the bandwagon. Such movements eventually add up to the sort of shift in national mood that we have been discussing here. But organizationally, they may not be the broad-based movements that we tend to assume they are.

If the national mood does not reside in the mass public, then where can it be found? And how, specifically, do people in government sense it? I find it difficult to give very precise answers. Generally, governmental officials and those near them have a lot of experience with collections of attentive publics, activists, and political elites out in the country. They hear from interest groups' leaders both in Washington and in the hustings; they read newspaper editorials; they give talks and listen to questions and comments at meetings; they see how public events are being covered in both general and specialized media; and they talk to party activists and other politicos who presumably have their ears to the ground.

The process of sensing a national mood works in two ways. First, elected politicians judge their constituents' mood from such communications as mail, town meetings, smaller gatherings, and delegations of people or even individuals coming to them during their office hours in the district. Second, nonelected officials tend to sense the national mood from what they hear from politicians. It is quite common for career bureaucrats, for example, to discuss the political climate or the national mood in some detail, with the current statements being made on the Hill as the only evidence for their conclusions. They simply assume that politicians have their fingers on the national pulse because it is their business and their livelihood to do so.

The diffusion of an impression of the national mood does not work exclusively in this version of a two-step flow from politicians to nonelected officials. Both sets of people follow the media, for instance, which is filled with commentary on and impressions of the nature of the times. And the national mood may, in some important respects, be an echo of events at the governmental level. Reagan is elected, and everybody assumes that the national mood has swung in a conservative direction. Leading columnists write that the climate is thus-and-so, and this in turn affects the national mood. A president communicates his sense of priorities to the nation, influencing the viewpoints relayed by the general public to their elected representatives.

People in and around government believe quite firmly that something like a national mood has important policy consequences. It has an impact on election results, on party fortunes, and on the receptivity of governmental decision makers to interest group lobbying. A shift in climate, according to people who are actively involved in making or affecting public policy, makes some proposals viable that would not have been viable before, and renders other proposals simply dead in the water. Advocates for the newly viable proposals find a receptive audience, an opportunity to push their ideas. Advocates for the proposals currently out of favor must adapt to their unfortunate situation, present their ideas for consideration as much as is possible under the circumstances, and wait for the mood to shift once again in their direction.

ORGANIZED POLITICAL FORCES

The arena of organized political forces is a more standard stock in trade for political scientists than many of the subjects discussed in this book. Students of politics are comfortable with notions of interest group pressure, political mobilization, and the behavior of political elites. These organized political forces form the second component of the political stream.

In Chapter 3, we reviewed the place of interest groups in the processes of agenda setting and alternative specification. We had occasion then to discuss interest group resources, the frequency of blocking and of promoting activities, and the place of other organized forces like political parties. Thus it remains here to consider how the forces described in Chapter 3 are fed into the political stream, how people in and around government perceive and react to various organized activities.

Central to an understanding of these perceptions and calculations is some concept of consensus and conflict among the organized interests. If important people look around and find that all of the interest groups and other organized interests point them in the same direction, the entire environment provides them with a powerful impetus to move in that direction.[8] But if there is some conflict among the organized forces, then political leaders implicitly arrive at an image of their environment that strikes some balance between those for and those against a given proposal, or for and against the emergence of an item to agenda prominence. Their perception that the balance of support is tilting against a proposal may not necessarily prevent that item from being seriously considered, but it does indicate the price that will be paid for attempting to push the idea forward. On the other hand, support for an item allows it to be pushed, and may be solely responsible in some cases for its rise to agenda prominence, as in the phrase, "The squeaky wheel gets the grease."

There are many examples of this type of assessment in the interviews. On the consensus side, one respondent said of an administration proposal for child health assessment, "It doesn't threaten anybody, it doesn't regulate anybody, and we're doing something for our precious mothers and children." To illustrate the conflict case, consider the Carter administration's proposal for hospital cost containment. One knowledgeable respondent described its lack of support: "To a politician, it's not a very popular bill. They don't hear anything positive from anybody, and they hear a lot of negative." Or as a Hill staffer elaborated:

> The support for this kind of legislation is quite weak compared to the opposition by the interests that are directly affected by it and see a really large stake in it.

---

[8]This discussion is reminiscent of the way legislators make decisions on the floor: by voting with a consensus of the forces important to them. See John W. Kingdon, *Congressmen's Voting Decisions,* 3rd ed. (Ann Arbor: University of Michigan Press, 1989), Chapter 10. For another discussion of the importance of consensus, see Nelson's emphasis on valence issues. Barbara J. Nelson, *Making an Issue of Child Abuse* (Chicago: University of Chicago Press, 1984), Chapter 5.

Hospitals, providers, and those natural opponents of the bill have gone out and enlisted allies like suppliers. The opposition has not only been constant, but it has increased. And the hospitals are still among the good guys, you know, the community leaders. It's tough to go against them.

It is difficult to portray precisely how people in and around government arrive at their notion of where the balance of support and opposition lies. In part, their calculations involve their perception of communication flows. If they hear a lot from one side and not from the other, they assume that the balance lies with the first side. They make this assumption in part because intensity does count for something, and they consider communication to be an index of intensity.[9] In part though, their assessment of the balance turns on their implicit calculation of the various groups' resources. Even if communications were roughly equal in frequency and vigor, one side might be awarded the upper hand, so to speak, because important people believed that the dominant side had superior political resources, such as group cohesion, their advantage in electoral mobilization, and the ability to affect the economy.[10] While the determination of the balance of support and opposition is somewhat imprecise, the fact that decision makers do arrive at an assessment of the balance is not. In most cases, respondents can be quite specific about who is on which side and which side has a greater strength, however they define that strength.

Much of the time, a balance of organized forces mitigates against any change at all. Important interests with the requisite resources are often able to block not only passage of proposals inimical to their preferences but even serious consideration. Advocates of such proposals, looking over the terrain they would have to traverse and the land mines strewn in their path, sometimes decide not to raise an issue at all rather than see their energy and their capital squandered on a losing cause. The costs to their resources and their reputations would be too great.[11] They seem to go through a calculation of intensities with regard to agenda setting similar to those made by legislators as they decide how to vote on the floor.[12] If there is intense opposition to a proposal, an advocate will often back off just like a politician facing intense opposition to a contemplated vote. As a respondent laid out one reason for failing to push a particular initiative, "If too many people get angry, it's not worth it."

[9]For an argument for the importance of intensity in a democratic system, even a majority rule system, see Robert A. Dahl, *A Preface to Democratic Theory* (Chicago: University of Chicago Press, 1956), Chapter 4. For an application, see Kingdon, *Congressmen's Voting Decisions,* op. cit., Chapter 2.

[10]For a fuller treatment of resources important to agenda-setting processes, see Chapter 3 of this book.

[11]See Light's discussion of how the agenda is structured by benefits and the alternatives by costs. Paul C. Light, *The President's Agenda* (Baltimore: Johns Hopkins University Press, 1982), p. 11.

[12]Kingdon, *Congressmen's Voting Decisions,* op. cit., Chapter 2.

One major reason for governmental inertia is the nearly inevitable building of a clientele in favor of an existing program. Once a government program is established, the clientele it benefits organizes into an impressive collection of interest groups whose major purpose is to protect the program from which they draw their sustenance. Not only does this clientele fend off attacks on the program, but it also makes consideration of proposals that might change the program difficult. The highway trust fund, originally established to build the interstate highway system, is an interesting case in point. The expenditures flowing out of that program benefit quite a formidable array of groups, including state highway departments, contractors, construction and maintenance people, truckers, and shippers. This so-called "highway lobby" supports the continuation of the trust fund, opposes proposals to change the fund, and supports a redefinition of the fund's purpose to keep the flow of benefits coming should the original definition prove to be inadequate to that purpose. Thus, as new interstate highway construction has gradually come to an end, more and more attention has turned to the use of federal monies to rebuild and maintain existing highways. This shift in focus is partially rooted in the need for maintenance, but the shift also serves to keep the federal dollars flowing to the program's clients. As one respondent said of the impending end of new construction, "They have to figure out some other way to keep pouring concrete."

To counter this strong inertia, it is common for knowledgeable informants to cite the need for a constituency favoring change, and to prove their point by citing examples in which ideas failed to get serious consideration for lack of such a constituency. As one of them put it to me, "There are a lot of causes in this town, but they don't have the necessary muscle." Many respondents used the Carter administration's hospital cost containment proposal as their leading example of a cause with no supporters. As one said, "Clearly industry is hostile, the doctors are hostile, the hospitals are hostile, and even the labor unions aren't very happy about it. This is a measure that has no natural constituency." Subjects having to do with buses received only fleeting mentions in my interviews for lack of a well-placed, vocal, middle- to upper-class constituency that rides buses, as we pointed out in Chapter 3. There is a complex set of reasons for the low agenda prominence of such items, but one of the major reasons is this deficiency in articulate beneficiaries and supporters.

Yet opposition to change is sometimes overcome. A version of trucking deregulation did finally rise to prominence on the governmental agenda and did pass, despite the formidable opposition of the regulated truckers and Teamsters. As we noticed in Chapter 3, the application of the resources of major interest groups against a proposal does not necessarily carry the day. Swings of national mood and the shifts of administration and of seats in Congress brought about by election results can be sufficient to overcome organized opposition, and to define the political stream as leaning toward change. On other occasions, the collection of organized interests itself changes. The highway lobby, for example, has sometimes been thwarted by the organization of such counter groups as neighborhood freeway opponents and environmentalists. On still other occasions, politicians take on organized opponents in the hope of stimulating support for their positions. So this balance of organized forces, far from constituting a comprehensive explanation for public policy outcomes, is but one element—albeit an important one—in a more complete understanding. Decision makers do take soundings in the sea of organized interests, and they do anticipate the cost they would pay if they were to take on well-organized, vocal opposition.

GOVERNMENT IN THE POLITICAL STREAM

The third major component of the political stream—in addition to swings of national mood and the balance of organized political forces—is composed of events within government itself. Administrations change, bringing with them marked changes in policy agendas. Seats change hands in Congress, creating opportunities to push some proposals and to bury others. Bureaucratic agencies and congressional committees battle for their share of the policy turf, affecting agendas in the process. We examined the importance of each of the governmental actors separately in Chapter 2. It is now time to introduce them into the political stream. Instead of concentrating on each actor individually, as we did earlier, we will now examine two major processes by which these actors affect policy agendas, turnover, and jurisdiction. Agendas are changed because some of the major participants change, and agendas are markedly affected by the drawing of jurisdictional boundaries and by battles over turf.

Turnover of Key Personnel

When it involves governmental actors, agenda change occurs in one of two ways. Either incumbents in positions of authority change their priorities and push new agenda items; or the personnel in those positions changes, bringing new priorities onto the agenda by virtue of the turnover. In Chapter 2, we considered the first of these at some length. We discussed the importance of the president's or a committee chair's priorities, for instance, and noticed that hospital cost containment was high on the health agenda largely because the Carter administration insisted that it stay there. We also noticed that catastrophic health insurance rose abruptly on the health agenda between 1978 and 1979 because of Senator Long's decision to take his Senate Finance Committee into markup sessions. Let us concentrate here, then, on turnover.

The interviews and case studies are filled with examples of the dramatic impact of turnover on policy agendas. The election of 1964, for example, produced a turnover of congressional seats that enabled the Johnson administration to push for and enact a sweeping series of domestic initiatives, including Medicare, Medicaid, aid to education, the poverty program, civil rights bills, and a host of others. The election of 1980, to take another example, which produced the Reagan administration and a Republican Senate, yielded a substantial change in direction, certainly in terms of the items on the governmental agenda and even in terms of the budgetary initiatives and other programs enacted. As one House committee staffer said, "New faces mean that new issues will be raised."

Not only does turnover produce new agenda items, but it also makes it impossible to consider other items that might be thought deserving at another time. The new Reagan administration, for instance, structured the governmental policy agenda to include items on which it placed a high priority, but in the process made it virtually impossible to get other potential initiatives seriously considered. Thus people in and around government worked on such subjects as cuts in domestic spending and school prayer, but did not devote serious attention to such subjects as comprehensive national health insurance. Among the easily recognizable products of a new administration or a shift in ideological or partisan balance in Congress is the rise to agenda prominence of some agenda items. Less recognizable but fully as important is the fact that other items do *not* rise, as a new administration makes their consideration impossible.

As intimated above, one of the most powerful turnover effects is a change of administration. As we noted in Chapter 2, the administration is at the very top of the list of actors in the policy-making arena. The first year of a new administration is clearly the prime time for preoccupation with the subject of change. Fully 83 percent of my health interviews and 81 percent of my transportation interviews in 1977 contained prominent discussion of administration change. At the time of a change of administration, people all over town hold their breath in anticipation, waiting to see what the new administration's priorities will be, what its policy agendas will look like.

We have been speaking primarily of turnover in Congress and change of administrations. The same point applies in other locations. In such regulatory agencies as the Civil Aeronautics Board and the Interstate Commerce Commission, for instance, many observers pointed to the importance of turnover. The CAB pushed along aviation deregulation proposals, for instance, partly because of the appearance of a more receptive chairman during the Ford administration (John Robson), partly because of the vigorous advocacy of Carter's appointee to the same post (Alfred Kahn), and partly because of the turnover of board members. The ICC also moved in the direction of deregulation, albeit more slowly, due in large part to the resignation or retirement of some commission members who had been staunch supporters of government regulation, and then the addition of new, more proderegulation members during the Carter administration. Such events make it tempting to attribute policy change to the actions of certain prominent individuals, thereby adopting a kind of personality model of agenda change. Alfred Kahn, for instance, a very dynamic and personable advocate of deregulation, might be cited as "the" reason for the CAB's change. The driving forces, however, are more structural than that. They involve a more general change in mood toward regulation, and the nomination process that would lead a president to propose and the Senate to confirm someone like Kahn to head an agency like the CAB.

Questions of Jurisdiction

In addition to turnover, the second central governmental process involves jurisdiction. In general, a major impact of constitutions, charters, statutes, and regulations is to establish jurisdictions. In the case of the federal government, administrative agencies and congressional committees have their claims to turf. Their positions are affected by their jurisdiction, agenda setting is affected by battles over turf, and some items are ignored because they are "defined away" by the drawing of jurisdictional boundaries.

There is ample evidence in this study for the maxim, "Where you stand depends upon where you sit."[13] Positions taken in battles over policy directions quite commonly reflect the jurisdictions and interests of the agencies involved. The Office of Management and Budget, for instance, has some enduring orientations that persist, regardless of the turnover of personnel within OMB or the comings and goings of administrations. Because a budget manager is interested in controlling as much of the budget as possible, transportation people can always count on OMB to oppose trust fund arrangements and to attempt to erode existing trust funds. Everybody in government, furthermore, can count on OMB to be interested in cutting budgets, and, in the case of new initiatives, opting for the least expensive program possible. In the battles over many features of the national health insurance proposals during the Carter administration, for example, one knowledgeable respondent explained, "HEW would take the liberal side and OMB would take the conservative side. They were expected to by the people in those organizations."

There are similar battles for turf within executive branch departments. Many respondents within the health area, for instance, attested to a deep and abiding difference in orientation between the Social Security Administration (SSA) and the Public Health Service (PHS). SSA, with jurisdiction over Medicare and hence over the largest pot of money in health, seemed primarily interested in social insurance questions: paying the bills, financing the system, and expanding the benefits. PHS, by contrast, seemed more interested in the structure of the medical care delivery system, reforming that system, and avoiding the incentives for higher-cost care produced by third-party payment arrangements such as Medicare. These differences in orientation sometimes boiled up to the level of the HEW secretary. In the battle over the regulations concerning the renal dialysis program, for instance, PHS pushed for and eventually won a substantial system of networks, regulations, and negotiated fees that SSA opposed. Indeed, such squabbles provided one major impetus for the establishment of the Health Care Financing Administration, which was supposed to collect the various health financing activities—Medicare, Medicaid, and peer review—into one agency.

Similar disputes abound within the Department of Transportation. The various modes—highways, rail, aviation, urban transit—each have their own administrations and hence their own advocates within the Department. Some of

[13]See Graham T. Allison, *Essence of Decision* (Boston: Little, Brown, 1971), p. 176.

the battles between the highway and the urban transit people, for instance, have become fairly legendary. As one informant described the meetings between the two over a limited transfer of highway monies to mass transit:

> You had to sit down people from the highway administration and the Urban Mass Transit Administration to negotiate the regs. They wouldn't talk to each other for two months. They'd get into meetings and they'd sit across the table from each other and scream at each other. The highway people didn't care one iota about UMTA's problems, and the UMTA people didn't care one iota about the highway people's problems. It took eight months before they got out the regs.

Generally, we expect bureaucrats to defend their turf. When they do not, the event is certainly noticed, and can become very significant. In airline deregulation, for instance, the testimony of the CAB in favor of less regulation was a very important event, as one Hill staffer said:

> The committee held three weeks of hearings, the most boring hearings you can imagine. There was airline president after airline president giving all these horror stories and saying that the planes were going to fall from the sky. It was a waste of time. Then the head of the CAB, Robson, came in. He testified that his own agency should have less power than it has now. Wow! An agency administrator himself saying that his own agency ought to be put out of business. It just sent shock waves through the whole system. Shock waves in the industry, shock waves on the Hill.

Under the subsequent chairmanship of Alfred Kahn, buttressed by new members appointed by the Carter administration, the CAB actually implemented a substantial measure of deregulation on its own, without benefit of statutory change. Some of the legislation that was subsequently passed ratified what the CAB had already put into practice. Even the Interstate Commerce Commission opted for some deregulation measures in early 1979—deregulating the movement of fresh fruits and vegetables by rail, deregulating intercity bus transportation for the summer of 1979, giving railroads limited contract authority, and easing entry requirements for trucking. These moves also "sent shock waves" through the system, if my interviews are any indication. The possibility that the ICC might adopt some regulatory reform on its own, without new legislation, was mentioned by only 19 percent of my 1978 transportation respondents as a prominent possibility. That figure had shot up to 74 percent in 1979.

We usually see turf disputes as retarding the possibilities for governmental action. For example, many health respondents believed that the jurisdictional disputes among the congressional health committees and subcommittees often diminished the chances for enactment of important initiatives, and even diminished the chances of a serious hearing of these proposals. Health was divided between the Finance and the Human Resources committees in the Senate, and between Ways and Means and the health subcommittee of Interstate Commerce in the House. Some observers argued that national health insurance proposals developed during the 1970s were hampered by fights between the principals. As one congressional staffer observed:

> First, it's bad enough to have to deal with two committees of Congress. If you think that's bad, dealing with four committees creates real problems. And then the cast of characters involved is even harder to deal with. You have Long, Talmadge, Kennedy, Paul Rogers, Tim Lee Carter, Barber Conable. The egos involved there and the jurisdictional strife are enough to keep the republic busy for 150 years.

Similar comments in the transportation interviews revolved around proposals to develop some sort of integrated trust fund that would combine various modes. Such proposals have run afoul of many things, but prominent among them is the fact that each mode deals with its own congressional committee and its own administrative agency. All of the participants have a stake in preserving current sources of funding and current jurisdictions, which makes the chances of enacting a more integrated approach quite remote.[14]

In addition to jurisdictional disputes leading to stalemate, however, there is another impact, both more subtle and probably at least as frequent. Battles over turf, far from leading to stalemate, often actually promote the rise of an item on the governmental agenda. Congressional committee chairs, for instance, compete with one another to claim credit for some initiative that they sense will be popular.[15] In the rush to beat each other to the punch, a subject may become prominent much more quickly than it would in the absence of this competition.

My interviews included many examples of this positive, rather than inhibiting, impact of jurisdictional fragmentation and competition. In the case of airline deregulation, for instance, Senator Edward Kennedy held hearings in his antitrust subcommittee of Judiciary. His claim to jurisdiction was actually a bit shaky, the primary jurisdiction being with Senator Howard Cannon's subcommittee on aviation. Cannon was "absolutely furious," according to one well-informed observer, and in order to head off Kennedy and protect his own claim to jurisdiction, he held hearings himself. Thus jurisdictional overlap and competition actually promoted, rather than retarded, governmental movement on the issue. Similar events occurred in 1979 on national health insurance. There had been a long-standing rivalry over jurisdiction in health between Kennedy and Senator Russell Long, the chairman of the Finance Committee. Long had some incentive to head off Kennedy and take credit for the movement himself. Once Long scheduled markup sessions, the Carter administration moved its plan

---

[14]Problems involving fragmented committee jurisdictions and bureaucratic infighting are discussed quite frequently in the interviews, but not so frequently as to indicate that they form a major preoccupation of people close to policy making. There are several variables in the code that are relevant to these subjects. The proportion of respondents discussing jurisdictional strife ranges from about a fifth to about a third, a respectable but not strikingly frequent showing. Such problems are coded as somewhat important in 4 of the 23 case studies, not very frequently.

[15]On the concept of credit claiming, see David R. Mayhew, *Congress: The Electoral Connection* (New Haven: Yale University Press, 1974), pp. 52–61.

along more quickly as well. Thus overlapping jurisdictions actually enhanced the chances for serious consideration, as the various players vied with one another for the credit and for the claim to jurisdiction.

This promoting aspect of competition cuts across the legislative and executive branches as well. As bureaucrats see an issue moving on the Hill, for instance, they will often take action first, in order to have some control over the events, rather than simply responding to and implementing legislation that is not of their own making. The threat of legislation to regulate clinical laboratories, for instance, prompted HEW to stiffen their own regulation, which in turn took some of the steam out of the movement for new legislation. One respondent said, "A natural bureaucratic reaction is self-preservation, and one way to do that is to bend with the wind."

So sometimes jurisdictional competition results in stalemate, while at other times it results in greater movement. Under what conditions does each result obtain? The key difference seems to be the perceived or potential popularity of the issue. If the various participants see a current or potential constituency for action out there, or if they see some electoral or publicity mileage in it, competition will enhance the chances of the issue rising on the agenda. If the issue has no such constituency or some opposition, or if it is unpopular, then competition contributes to its downfall. Put another way, competition for jurisdiction simply reinforces the other forces that are already at work. If the complex of political and policy forces are already balanced against an issue, competition for turf will drive the last nail into the coffin. But if that same balance tilts toward the issue, competition will contribute its share to moving the issue along.[16]

Finally, many potential agenda items never are the subject of a given policy maker's attention, largely because they fall into someone else's jurisdiction. They may be agenda items somewhere in government, but not where a given official is located. So an item may be ignored with the rationale that it is being taken care of somewhere else. As Tom Lehrer would say, "That's not my department."[17]

There are specialized agendas within such larger policy domains as health and transportation. Within health, for instance, there are specialists in direct delivery of medical services, food and drug regulation, and biomedical research. These subjects were never high on the general health policy agenda during the years of my study. Despite the tremendous clamor over recombinant DNA research in the biomedical research community, for instance, the subject was never prominent in more than 8 percent of my health interviews. Similarly, the highest-rated variable in the food and drug area was 9 percent, and no direct

[16]Incidentally, competition as an inhibitor and competition as a promoter are mentioned with about equal frequency in the interviews, and coded as important with about equal frequency in the case studies, although the promoter frequency is slightly greater than that for inhibition.

[17]This phrase comes from Tom Lehrer's song in which he "quotes" a rocket scientist as saying, "Once the rockets are up, who cares where they come down—that's not my department."

delivery item ever rose above 11 percent. These items are on a government agenda in some sense, but the set of people occupied with them is confined to one particular location in the panoply of jurisdictions within larger policy domains, and these subjects do not diffuse very widely into the domains' larger communities.

In addition to the importance of specialized agendas within policy domains, some items are not high on the agendas of health or transportation specialists, even though they could easily be in some conceptual sense, because they have their primary location elsewhere in the executive branch or congressional committee structure. Transportation respondents could have talked about energy, for instance, long before the crisis brought about by the 1979 gas lines, but they did not. When asked why not, they often responded by saying that energy was the province of the Department of Energy or of other committees of the Congress than their own. One high-level Department of Transportation bureaucrat told me, when asked in 1978 why energy was not high on a transportation agenda, "I don't know the answer to that. I've been wondering about it myself. There was quite a bit of concentration on it in the Department of Transportation before the Energy Department was created. Now there's some inclination to think that this other operation is supposed to be worrying about that, so we don't have to do as much with it." Similarly, protecting the environment is more the province of the Environmental Protection Agency (EPA) than of the health bureaucracy, despite the clear impact of pollution on health. Indeed, only 4 percent of my health interviews included prominent discussion of pollution that was not prompted by my questions. The tremendous government involvement in health in the form of the veterans' health system also was mentioned very little. As one respondent said, "It's an entirely different universe."

CONSENSUS BUILDING IN THE POLITICAL STREAM

In the policy stream, we discovered in Chapter 6, consensus is built largely through the processes of persuasion and diffusion. If an idea survives scrutiny according to a set of criteria for survival, it diffuses within the policy community.

There is also consensus building in the political stream. However, the processes which set bandwagons in motion are radically different in the two streams. In contrast to the policy stream's emphasis on persuasion, the political stream's consensus building is governed by bargaining.[18] Here, coalitions are being built through the granting of concessions in return for support of the coalition, or as actual or potential coalition members make bargains. Joining the coalition occurs not because one has simply been persuaded of the virtue of that course of action, but because one fears that failure to join would result in

[18]For a thorough discussion of bargaining, see Robert A. Dahl and Charles E. Lindblom, *Politics, Economics, and Welfare* (New York: Harper and Row, 1953), Chapters 12 and 13.

exclusion from the benefits of participation. The proposals have already been discussed and honed in the political stream. The actors are now trying to reach toward a winning coalition. Thus the discussion is more likely to be, "You give me my provision, and I'll give you yours," rather than, "Let me convince you of the virtue of my provision."

Let us be clear once again that the processes are different from the participants, and that we are discussing processes here. In fact, policy specialists do not have a monopoly on persuasion; nor do politicians have a monopoly on bargaining. One often observes politicians persuading and specialists bargaining. We are making this distinction between the two different types of coalition building to draw attention to the differences between the processes in the political and policy streams, not to argue that one process is the exclusive preserve of one type of actor.

Illustrations of these bargaining processes, and their contrast to persuasion processes, abound in the interviews and case studies. In the transportation field, for example, a bargain developed between highway and mass transit advocates that resulted in benefits to both. As interstate highways were being built, urban legislators became increasingly unhappy, both because freeways were distorting land use in the urban areas and because a substantial program was underway which benefited small town and rural areas and not cities. They first pressed for raiding the highway trust fund for mass transit, and found considerable resistance—to say the least—to that idea. The controversy over that tack receded, however, because of a not-so-tacit understanding that the highway advocates would support mass transit appropriations from general funds if mass transit advocates would leave the highway trust fund alone. Each had its funds, and while there were still disagreements around the edges, a powerful coalition was built to their mutual benefit. They had not persuaded one another so much as they had generated a logrolling exchange.

Attempts to build support for national health insurance during the Carter administration provide another illustration of such coalition-building processes through bargaining. The arguments, facts, and proposals had really been aired for many years. Building the administration's proposal thus involved not only persuasion, but assiduous attention to giving people their pet provisions in return for support. One source close to administration thinking said that by inserting maternal and child health benefits and more low-income aid into their proposal, they could attract some liberal support, which would be convenient in terms of denying Senator Kennedy his undisputed claim to liberal adherents. Of course, this strategic consideration was not the only reason for including these provisions. The administration had always made clear their interest in a package of benefits broader than simple catastrophic insurance. Nor did their strategy succeed in the end. But the case does illustrate the bargaining process well.

In the political stream, if one does not pay sufficient attention to coalition building through bargaining, one pays a major price, as the Carter administration discovered. Many health respondents who were well-acquainted with both the issues and the political realities roundly criticized the administration's handling of hospital cost containment. Administration officials told me that they had consulted with important people on the Hill and elsewhere prior to sending up the proposal. But the recipients of the consultation drew a distinction between being told of administration plans or floating proposals, on the one hand, and genuine consultation on the other. As one congressional committee staffer portrayed the difference between hospital cost containment and food and drug reform:

> On the cost containment thing, what the administration meant by consultation was briefing us on what they wanted to do. So our attitude was, "Okay, if that's the way you want to do it, screw you. Go away and write your own bill, and then we'll do with it what we want to do." And we won. On the drug bill, they agreed to let us put it together on the Hill, and we wouldn't go with a bill unless we were satisfied with it, in the sense that we liked the bill in substance and thought it would pass. Because of the way we went through it, everybody's name is on the bill, and we have a real chance of passing it.

Of Bandwagons and Tipping, Again

We talked in Chapter 6 of the explosive diffusion of ideas within policy communities. A good idea catches on, snowballing as it picks up adherents. Sometimes a bad idea does the same. We can also observe explosive growth in coalitions in the political stream, but driven by very different dynamics. Here, a bargaining process is at work; potential coalition supporters are enticed into support by promises of some benefit, and others climb aboard the bandwagon out of fear that they will be left without their share of the benefits, in the event that something should pass.

Initially, participants stake out their positions somewhat rigidly, refusing to compromise on their principles. On national health insurance, for instance, Senator Kennedy and his organized labor compatriots steadfastly held out for a plan of comprehensive insurance, with a rich package of benefits, full coverage of the population, and no deductibles. Years after it was apparent that such an approach would not be viable, they held to it. As one congressional staffer close to the action told me, "You stake out a position, because if you don't, you won't have anything to compromise with." Kennedy tried in 1973–74 with Wilbur Mills to pass a more modest program, but labor insistence on the whole comprehensive proposal derailed the attempt. As one observer said, "You need something to the left of center sometimes, to get people to move over."

The time comes when rigid adherence to one's original position would cost one dearly. These times are the real opportunities for passage, the policy windows that we will discuss in the next chapter, when compromise is in the air. At these times, participants of all types conclude that the bandwagon is rolling, and that they should be active in shaping the outcome. Advocates of change push hard for their proposals. Even enemies of change introduce their own proposals in an attempt to bend the outcomes as much as they can to their own purposes. Informed observers describe such events with phrases like "wanting to be in the game," "trying to be dealt in," and "jumping on before it's too late." Consensus is built, sometimes very rapidly, by cutting in many and diverse interests.

The progress of national health insurance during the 1970s provides a convincing illustration. Up until the first years of the Carter administration, Kennedy and labor had indeed held fast to their comprehensive proposal. At that point, seeing the new administration and a Democratic Congress as their opportunity, they made what many respondents called a dramatic move. As one of them told me, "We decided not to posture any longer" with the comprehensive proposal. They decided instead to back a less ambitious plan that would provide a place for private insurance companies and keep large portions of the cost off the federal budget. As one savvy observer described the change, "Kennedy wants to be in the ball game. If there's going to be a table with people sitting around it and everyone dealing out the goodies, Kennedy wants to be sitting at that table."

Once an issue seems to be moving, everybody with an interest in the subject leaps in, out of fear that they will be left out. In the national health insurance case, Senator Russell Long, chairman of the Finance Committee, introduced several of his own proposals, including one that would provide for catastrophic insurance only, and even held markup sessions on the subject. Many reasons for his action were advanced by knowledgeable informants, but among them was his desire to play a part in the outcome, in the event that the steamroller was moving. As one put it, "He wanted to introduce this as a way to trot it out in case there was any bigger threat that was coming along. This is his way to take the steam out of a comprehensive plan whenever it looked like it might get serious." Even the American Medical Association weighed in with their own proposal. At the time of Kennedy-Mills in the early 1970s, the AMA threw something together in such a big hurry that one source close to the AMA told me, "Our original bill was a laugh—I'll freely admit it." But as another informant put it, "They have to put these bills up just to be able to be in the game in case something is going to happen." So we might distinguish between genuine advocates and pseudoadvocates. The pseudoadvocates, such as the AMA in the case of national health insurance, are not genuinely interested in pushing the cause. They advocate their own plans in the event, likely or unlikely, that an issue of concern to them becomes a serious threat to their interests.

CONCLUSION

Independently of the problems and policy streams, the political stream flows along according to its own dynamics and its own rules. It is composed of such factors as swings of national mood, election results, changes of administration, changes of ideological or partisan distributions in Congress, and interest group pressure campaigns.

Politicians and other participants believe they can sense both a national mood and changes in that mood. The national mood does not necessarily reside in the mass public, but instead is perceived in the attitudes of various more active sectors of the public. Politicians sense the mood from various communications that come to them, including mail, visits, trips home, newspaper coverage, and conversation with constituents. Nonelected officials take their reading of the national mood from politicians. Perceptions of the national mood affect governmental agendas, both by promoting items that fit with that mood and by inhibiting attention to items that do not.

Governmental officials judge the degree of consensus among organized political forces. If there is widespread agreement among those forces, officials either try to go along with them, or at least know what they are up against. If there is conflict among those forces, officials judge the balance of the strengths among them. Strength is perceived partly in terms of frequency or intensity of communications, and partly in terms of the various groups' resources. Often the balance of organized forces mitigates against change, as beneficiaries of current programs attempt to protect their current interests. Change is aided by a constituency in favor of it, and hampered by the absence of such a constituency or by the active opposition of organized interests. However, the balance of organized forces does not always determine outcomes. Indeed, powerful interests are sometimes overcome, and change occurs despite their opposition.

In government, turnover has powerful effects on agendas. A change of administration, a substantial turnover of congressional seats, or a change of top personnel in an administrative agency all change agendas substantially. Agendas are also affected by jurisdictional boundaries. Competition for turf does not necessarily produce stalemate. Indeed, if a popular issue is involved, competition promotes rather than retards action. Another jurisdictional effect is the neglect of some potential agenda items because they are supposedly being handled elsewhere in government. Some subjects are very prominent on specialized agendas without being prominent on more general agendas.

Consensus building in the political arena, in contrast to consensus building among policy specialists, takes place through a bargaining process rather than by persuasion. Once participants sense that there is some movement, they leap in to protect their interests. This entry into the game, sometimes sudden entry, contributes to sharp agenda change, both because various interests receive some benefit from their participation, and because a generalized image of movement is created.

The Political Stream in the Larger Scheme of Things

The political stream is an important promoter or inhibiter of high agenda status. All of the important actors in the system, not just the politicians, judge whether the balance of forces in the political stream favors action. They also judge whether the general public would at least tolerate the directions pursued at the elite level. Without that tolerance, the potential for retribution at the polls is likely to torpedo the idea in Congress.

We have been equating the various political forces—national mood, organized interests, election repercussions, the orientations of elected officials— with each other, and arguing that participants somehow total them up and arrive at a balance, or a notion of the preponderance of pressure in the political stream. But as we have seen repeatedly, the forces are not equal in practice. In particular, the complex of national mood and elections seems to create extremely powerful impacts on policy agendas, impacts capable of overwhelming the balance of organized forces. They bowled over the regulated transportation industries in the case of deregulation, for instance, and the taxpayers' "smaller government" mood similarly resulted in President Reagan's early budget victories over the organized interests that benefit from federal programs.

Once again, however, our distinction between the agenda and the alternatives is useful. This mood-elections combination has particularly powerful impacts on the agenda. It can force some subjects high on the agenda, and can also make it virtually impossible for government to pay serious attention to others. But once the item is on the agenda, the organized forces enter the picture, trying as best they can to bend the outcomes to their advantage, either by affecting the final compromises over the alternatives to be considered or, in some cases, by defeating proposals altogether. Impact on the agenda, again, is different from control over the alternatives or over the outcomes.

CHAPTER 8

The Policy Window, and Joining the Streams

When you lobby for something, what you have to do is put together your coalition, you have to gear up, you have to get your political forces in line, and then you sit there and wait for the fortuitous event. For example, people who were trying to do something about regulation of railroads tried to ride the environment for a while, but that wave didn't wash them in to shore. So they grabbed their surfboards and they tried to ride something else, but that didn't do the job. The Penn Central collapse was the big wave that brought them in. As I see it, people who are trying to advocate change are like surfers waiting for the big wave. You get out there, you have to be ready to go, you have to be ready to paddle. If you're not ready to paddle when the big wave comes along, you're not going to ride it in.

—An analyst for an interest group

The policy window is an opportunity for advocates of proposals to push their pet solutions, or to push attention to their special problems. Indeed, as the quotation above illustrates, advocates lie in wait in and around government with their solutions at hand, waiting for problems to float by to which they can attach their solutions, waiting for a development in the political stream they can use to their advantage. Sometimes, the window opens quite predictably. The scheduled renewal of a program, for instance, creates an opportunity for many participants to push their pet project or concern. At other times, it happens quite unpredictably. Policy entrepreneurs must be prepared, their pet proposal at the ready, their special problem well-documented, lest the opportunity pass them by.

We have just finished a series of chapters that considered separately the various streams flowing through the system. The separate streams come together at critical times. A problem is recognized, a solution is developed and available in the policy community, a political change makes it the right time for policy change, and potential constraints are not severe. This chapter deals with the processes by which the separate streams are joined. We begin by discussing what policy windows are and why they open, and then proceed to describe the coupling of the streams that takes place. Policy entrepreneurs play a major part in the coupling at the open policy window, attaching solutions to problems, overcoming the constraints by redrafting proposals, and taking advantage of politically propitious events. We then discuss the occurrence of open windows: their frequency, duration, and predictability. Finally, we discuss spillovers, a process in which the appearance of one item on the governmental agenda sets up the subsequent prominence of conceptually adjacent items.

WHAT POLICY WINDOWS ARE AND WHY THEY OPEN

In space shots, the window presents the opportunity for a launch. The target planets are in proper alignment, but will not stay that way for long. Thus the launch must take place when the window is open, lest the opportunity slip away. Once lost, the opportunity may recur, but in the interim, astronauts and space engineers must wait until the window reopens.

Similarly, windows open in policy systems. These policy windows, the opportunities for action on given initiatives, present themselves and stay open for only short periods. If the participants cannot or do not take advantage of these opportunities, they must bide their time until the next opportunity comes along. As one congressional committee staffer said of one such opportunity, "You might just say the stars were right." The separate streams we have been discussing in the three previous chapters come together and are coupled at these times. Participants dump their conceptions of problems, their proposals, and political forces into the choice opportunity,[1] and the outcomes depend on the mix of elements present and how the various elements are coupled.

An open window affects the type of agenda we labeled a decision agenda in Chapter 1. As we have been discussing agendas, the *governmental agenda* is the list of subjects to which people in and around government are paying serious attention at any given point in time. We have essentially measured that agenda in this study by asking the participants what the list is. Within that governmental agenda, there is a smaller set of items that is being decided upon, a *decision agenda*. Proposals are being moved into position for legislative enactment, for instance, or subjects are under review for an imminent decision by the president or a department secretary. In the vernacular of the participants, the issue is "really getting hot," which is a step up from saying that the participants are seriously occupied with it. Being on this decision agenda, of course, does not insure enactment or favorable bureaucratic decision, but it is a more active status than being on the governmental agenda.

Policy windows open infrequently, and do not stay open long. Despite their rarity, the major changes in public policy result from the appearance of these opportunities. In 1965–66, for instance, the fortuitous appearance of extra liberal Democratic seats in Congress brought about by the Goldwater debacle

[1]This phenomenon is captured nicely in Michael D. Cohen, James G. March, and Johan P. Olsen, "A Garbage Can Model of Organizational Choice," *Administrative Science Quarterly* 17 (March 1972): 1–25.

opened a window for the Johnson administration that resulted in the enactment of Medicare, Medicaid, the poverty program, aid to education, and all of the other programs collected into Johnson's Great Society initiatives.

Think of a queue of items awaiting their turn on a decision agenda. Somehow, the items must be ordered in the queue. The opening of a window often establishes the priority in the queue. Participants move some items ahead of others, essentially because they believe the proposals stand a decent chance of enactment. During the late 1970s, for instance, various transportation deregulation proposals were in the queue. The Carter administration chose to move aviation ahead of the others, not because it was conceptually the best but because it stood the best chance of passage. Senators Edward Kennedy and Howard Cannon had already agreed on a bill, the Hill had been softened up by a long set of hearings, the regulatory agency (the Civil Aeronautics Board) favored deregulation, and the industry groups were not unanimously opposed. Trucking deregulation, on the other hand, faced the unified and formidable opposition of the regulated truckers and the Teamsters. Change in the much larger and inertia-bound Interstate Commerce Commission, which dealt with both trucking and railroads, also seemed unlikely. Under the circumstances, aviation represented what various respondents called a "soft target" or a "quick hit," at least by comparison with the alternatives.

Health respondents talked similarly about Medicare. As one of the prominent proponents of Medicare beautifully summarized the priority placed on the elderly during the early- to mid-1960s:

> If you stop to think about this, it was a crazy way to go about it, from a rational point of view. Here we took the one group in the population, the elderly, that was the *most* expensive, needed the *most* health care, for whom medical care would do the *least* amount of good, for whom there was the *least* payoff from a societal point of view. But we did it because that's politically what we could run with at the time. It didn't make rational sense to start a health insurance scheme with this sector of the population, but it's where we started anyway.

To take the other side of priority setting, without the prospect of an open window, participants slack off. They are unwilling to invest their time, political capital, energy, and other resources in an effort that is unlikely to bear fruit. Many potential items never rise on the agenda because their advocates conclude it isn't worth their effort to push them. They are so far away from coming to real action—legislative enactment or other authoritative decision—that they are never taken up at all. As one congressional staffer said, "We concentrate on issues that we think are going to be productive. If they're not productive, then we don't have unlimited time here, and we're not going to go into them." If trucking deregulation wasn't a live option, for instance, most participants concentrated on something that was: aviation.

The same reasoning applies to bargaining. When the issue isn't really hot, advocates hold firmly to their extreme positions. But when the issue has a serious chance of legislative or other action, then advocates become more flexible, bargaining from their previously rigid positions, compromising in order to be in the game, as we said in the last chapter. As another congressional staffer put it, referring to the Kennedy-labor stance of holding fast to their comprehensive national health insurance plan and then offering compromises when it looked in the late 1970s like some version of health insurance might stand a chance of passage, "Why should you bargain if there is no realistic chance of getting a bill anyway?" So one stakes out an extreme position early, then compromises when the window opens.

Why Windows Open and Close

Returning to our distinction between the agenda and the alternatives, and speaking rather generally of our three process streams, the agenda is affected more by the problems and political streams, and the alternatives are affected more by the policy stream. Basically, a window opens because of change in the political stream (e.g., a change of administration, a shift in the partisan or ideological distribution of seats in Congress, or a shift in national mood); or it opens because a new problem captures the attention of governmental officials and those close to them. A change of administration is probably the most obvious window in the policy system. In the words of one political appointee, "A new administration comes to town, and they ask, 'What should we do first?' Something right away." The new administration gives some groups, legislators, and agencies their opportunity—an open policy window—to push positions and proposals they did not have the opportunity to push with the previous administration, and it disadvantages other players.

The same is true of turnover of any of the political actors. The rise of a new congressional committee chair, a wholesale change in congressional membership (as in 1966 or 1974), and new members on a regulatory body all open windows for the advocates of proposals that might get a sympathetic hearing with the new cast of characters. Thus the new Reagan administration provided a window for a host of players previously disadvantaged: budget balancers, supply-siders, right-to-lifers, advocates of school prayer, and others. Likewise, new appointees to the Civil Aeronautics Board and the Interstate Commerce Commission during the Carter administration created a receptivity to deregulation initiatives that was not as marked before.

None of these political events—administration change, a redistribution of seats in Congress, national mood shifts—specifies in detail what is to be done. All of them set general themes that need to be filled out with specific proposals. A Carter administration wants to "get government off our backs," for instance, and casts about for ways to do that. Or a taxpayer revolt makes members of Congress wary of expensive initiatives, but does not specify exactly where budget cuts should be made. The advocates of more detailed proposals use these general events and themes to push their own ideas to the fore. In other words, these political events and themes open windows for these advocates.

There are also occasions during which a problem becomes pressing, creating an opportunity for advocates of proposals to attach their solutions to it. For instance, gas lines bring governmental attention to energy shortages, and many transportation interests—mass transit, railroads, and others—argue that their programs should be seen as at least a partial solution to the prominent problem. As a congressional staffer put it, "Energy is the conversation of the year. It used to be the environment. If something was connected to the environment, everyone would genuflect. Now it's energy." Or medical care costs become such a pressing problem that everybody must relate proposals to the search for solutions. Focusing events work this way as well. An airplane crash, for instance, opens a window for advocates of initiatives in aviation safety. If they have their proposals ready, the crash provides an opportunity to argue that the proposal should be enacted.

Once the window opens, it does not stay open long. An idea's time comes, but it also passes. There is no irresistible momentum that builds for a given initiative. The window closes for a variety of reasons. First, participants may feel they have addressed the problem through decision or enactment. Even if they have not, the fact that some action has been taken brings down the curtain on the subject for the time being.[2] Second, and closely related, participants may fail to get action. If they fail, they are unwilling to invest further time, energy, political capital, or other resources in the endeavor. As a bureaucrat said of the Carter administration's effort to pass a hospital cost containment bill, "When they can't get it passed, naturally attention turns to some other things."

Third, the events that prompted the window to open may pass from the scene. A crisis or focusing event, for example, is by its nature of short duration. People can stay excited about an airline crash or a railroad collapse for only so long. Or the pyramiding of resources that caused the window to open may not last long. A new administration, for instance, enjoys its honeymoon for only a few months, and its passing is inevitable. The moment the new president starts to make decisions of any kind—appointments, budgets, legislative proposals— he begins to disappoint some people and to satisfy others. Before those first decisions, everybody is looking to the president with eager anticipation. But the window provided by the honeymoon is most fleeting.[3]

Fourth, if a change in personnel opens a window, the personnel may change again. People in key positions come and go, and so do the opportunities that their presence furnishes. As one transportation committee staffer mused about his interest in changing the funding arrangements for infrastructure construction, "Staffers on this committee have thought about the issues a lot. It might be that we could, over four years' time or so, persuade members of our point of view and pursue this thing actively. But it's quite likely that we'll leave here first. I'm not saying that we're going right away, but it's in the nature of turnover." And they were in fact gone in two years.

[2]Murray Edelman, *The Symbolic Uses of Politics* (Urbana: University of Illinois Press, 1964), Chapter 2.

[3]See Paul C. Light, *The President's Agenda* (Baltimore: Johns Hopkins University Press, 1982), Chapter 2.

Finally, the window sometimes closes because there is no available alternative. In the chapter on the policy stream, we spoke of the need to soften up the system, to have a given proposal worked out, discussed, amended, and ready to go, long before the window opens. The opportunity passes if the ready alternative is not available.

The short duration of the open window lends powerful credence to the old saying, "Strike while the iron is hot." Anthony Downs's issue-attention cycle calls for quick action when the opportunity presents itself.[4] He argues that intense desire to act gives way to a realization of the financial and social costs of action. As one reflective journalist put it, "I have a theory that the really big steps are always taken very quickly or not at all. The poverty program breezed through, and only after it passed did people start to have second thoughts about it. Until the time that national health insurance can be done in a groundswell, very quickly, it won't be done." Thus HEW Secretary Joseph Califano seized the occasion of his first months in office to jam through the reorganization of the department that created the Health Care Financing Administration. He did it so quickly and in such secrecy that only a handful of people knew what was up before the announcement. To prevent leaks, even the graphics to be used in the press conference announcing the move were made up by a friend in another department.

If the window passes without action, it may not open again for a long time. Consider the abject frustration of the official who wanted to cut Amtrak's budget, only to see the effort swallowed by the 1979 energy crisis:

> In April and May we thought we were in real good shape. Then the gas shortage turned the whole thing around. The papers got into it, and there were all these articles about the demands for Amtrak. If the energy crisis had just held off for *five months,* we would have had our proposal approved. But it didn't.

As with the Amtrak case, the opponents of a change also know that the window closes soon. Thus is born the common expression, "Riding out the storm." If one can delay, by studying the issue or by another expedient, the pressure for the change subsides. The longer people live with a problem, the less pressing it seems. The problem may not change at all, but if people can live with it, it appears less urgent. It becomes less a problem and more a condition than it seemed at the beginning.

Perceptions, Estimations, and Misestimations

We have been talking as if one can tell with some certainty when a policy window opens. Sadly for strategists trying to manipulate the process, the world is

---

[4]Anthony Downs, "Up and Down with Ecology—The 'Issue-Attention Cycle,'" *The Public Interest* 28 (Summer 1972): 38–50.

not quite that simple. Some objective features define a policy window, such as a change of administration, a renewal, or the imminent collapse of a major sector of the economy. But the window exists in the perceptions of the participants as well. They perceive its presence or absence, they estimate the likelihood of its future occurrence, and they sometimes misestimate or misperceive. Beyond misperceiving, even highly skilled and knowledgeable people may disagree on whether a window is or will be open because the nature of the beast is complex and a bit opaque.

The case of national health insurance proposals during the first years of the Carter administration nicely illustrates these differences in perception. Advocates of comprehensive national health insurance, particularly the alliance of Senator Kennedy and organized labor, looked upon the years 1977 and 1978 as an open policy window unlikely to emerge again for some time, an opportunity to push their proposals into agenda prominence and even into enactment. They thus entered into a series of negotiations with the Carter people, and even abandoned their previous insistence that the plan be financed through government rather than through mandated private insurance. One of them told me, "You have a president in office who is strongly and publicly committed to national health insurance, and an overwhelmingly Democratic Congress. You just don't see these opportunities come along very often." Another put it more dramatically: "Our feeling is that if this is not done in the next Congress, it will be dead for a decade, and it might even be dead for a generation. All of us feel that this is the time. If we can't bring the interests together now, we won't be able to do it again for a long time."

Others were skeptical that the window actually was open. One well-known health activist told me, "I don't think it's going anywhere, and if it's not going anywhere, it's not something I want to spend any time on." An important congressional committee staffer also expressed his deep skepticism: "What you're going to see is a lot of singing and dancing, a lot of sound and fury, a lot of playing the national anthem, and not much more than that. The fact is that there is no way to finance it, number one, and number two, there is no public demand for it. [Even catastrophic insurance] has by now been priced out of the market." Advocates of comprehensive plans might disagree with these assessments of the budgetary and political realities, but that is precisely the point. In judging how wide a window is open, there is considerable room for disagreement even among reasonable people.

It turned out that the window closed, if it was ever open. Inflation and budgetary deficits, combined with such indicators of taxpayer revolt as California's Proposition 13, made administration officials and members of Congress skittish about large new federal expenditures. Advocates also could not come to agreement, which meant that an alternative was not available. The project was thus left destroyed on the reefs of financial cost, dissension among advocates of various plans, and a lack of time to work out all of the substantive details and political bargains.

Savvy politicians often speak of the importance of timing. As one bureaucrat said, "The important thing is that a proposal come at the right time." What they mean is that the proposal must be worked out beforehand, and must surface and be pushed when the window is open. Missing that window results in a wait until it opens again. Many national health insurance advocates portrayed labor intransigence in 1973–74 as a prominent example. During that brief period, Senator Kennedy and House Ways and Means Committee Chairman Wilbur Mills introduced a compromise national health insurance plan. Many people felt at that time, before the major onslaught of taxpayer revolt and budgetary stringency, that the federal government could afford at least the Kennedy-Mills plan. Weakened by Watergate, Nixon might even have signed it as part of an attempt to save his presidency. But organized labor opposed the Kennedy-Mills plan, substantively because they would not approve of the deductibles and less-than-comprehensive benefits, and politically because they preferred to wait for what they judged would be more propitious times, particularly with a Democratic president. In retrospect, one advocate told me in 1978, "That was a big mistake on the part of labor. They opposed it because it was only a 40 billion dollar bill. Now they're going to be lucky to get something that's 10 or 15 billion." Said another, "In my opinion, it was a terrific strategic mistake. You could have accepted [Kennedy-Mills], and built on it to get to the point where you want to be." A labor participant, however, refused to accept such a characterization, arguing that Kennedy-Mills really was substantively unacceptable. When asked if Kennedy is too prone to compromise for his taste, he replied, "No, other than his brief flirtation with Kennedy-Mills. But he returned to the fold after that." In any event, Kennedy-Mills *may* have been the window that national health insurance advocates were seeking for many years, though there was some disagreement about that. If it was, the time for seizing the opportunity passed, and as it turned out, the experience of the Carter administration and the subsequent election of Ronald Reagan resulted in the window closing for many years thereafter.

COUPLING

In the policy stream, proposals, alternatives, and solutions float about, being discussed, revised, and discussed again. In contrast to a problem-solving model, in which people become aware of a problem and consider alternative solutions, solutions float around in and near government, searching for problems to which to become attached or political events that increase their likelihood of adoption. These proposals are constantly in the policy stream, but then suddenly they become elevated on the governmental agenda because they can be seen as solutions to a pressing problem or because politicians find their sponsorship expedient. National health insurance, for example, has been discussed constantly for the better part of this century. The arguments and information about it are quite well honed by now. But the proposal rises on the agenda when the political stream, in the form of such events as a new adminis- tration or a shift in national mood, opens a window that makes its timing propi- tious.

An excellent example of the constant solution adapting to the changing mo- saic of problems and politics is the case of urban mass transit. When a federal program for mass transit was first proposed, it was sold primarily as a straight- forward traffic management tool.[5] If we could get people out of their private automobiles, we would move them about more efficiently, and relieve traffic congestion in the cities, making them more habitable. When the traffic and con- gestion issues played themselves out in the problem stream, advocates of mass transit looked for the next prominent problem to which to attach their solution. Along came the environmental movement.[6] Since pollution was on everybody's minds, a prominent part of the solution could be mass transit: Get people out of their cars and pollution will be reduced. The environmental movement faded, and what was the next big push? You guessed it: energy. The way to solve the country's energy problem, so reasoned the advocates of mass transit, was to get people out of their cars when commuting. Of course, the cities' need for money and their interest in transferring substantial portions of the cost to the federal taxpayer were driving their advocacy of mass transit all along. But since that driving impetus could not successfully serve as the entire rationale, advocates were obliged to hook their solution onto whatever problem might be prominent at any given moment. As one such advocate summed it up, "There is a continu- ing interest in mass transit. The underlying goals exist and continue along. You want to do something, and you ask, 'What will work this year? What's hot this year that I can hang this on?'"

Thus solutions come to be coupled with problems, proposals linked with po- litical exigencies, and alternatives introduced when the agenda changes. Their advocates hook them onto the problem of the moment, or push them at a time that seems propitious in the political stream. This is why, as one bureaucrat said, "Issues keep reemerging in other forms. You think you'd buried it one year, but it comes up in the next year in a different place. The issues get pack- aged differently, but they are just about the same." One of those advocates do- ing the repackaging agreed: "There is nothing new. We are resurrecting old dead dogs, sprucing them up, and floating them up to the top."

Problem Windows and Political Windows

What does an open window call for? The answer depends on what opened the window in the first place, or, to put it another way, what caused the agenda to change. As noted above, such change usually comes about in response to devel-

[5]See Alan Altshuler, "Changing Patterns of Public Policy," *Public Policy* 25 (Spring 1977): 186.

[6]See William Lilley, "Transit Lobby Sights Victory," *National Journal* (4 March 1972): 39. He says that transit is "able to ride piggyback on the politically hot environmental issue."

opments in the problems and political streams, not in the policy stream. So the two categories of windows—problem and political windows—call for different borrowings from the policy stream. If decision makers become convinced a problem is pressing, they reach into the policy stream for an alternative that can reasonably be seen as a solution. If politicians adopt a given theme for their administration or start casting about for proposals that will serve their reelection or other purposes, they reach into the policy stream for proposals.

Sometimes the window is opened by a problem that presses in on government, or at least comes to be regarded as pressing. The collapse of the Penn Central Railroad, for instance, demanded some sort of response. In the absence of federal government action, service to shippers all over the Northeast would have come to a halt. The Penn Central collapse thus opened a window for advocates of all sorts of proposals relating in more general terms to the financial condition of the nation's railroads: subsidies, deregulation, nationalization, loan guarantees, roadbed rehabilitation, and many others. Advocates attempted to couple their pet solution to the problem at hand.

The prominence of the cost problem in the health area created similar pressures. With the adoption of Medicare and Medicaid, health care costs rose dramatically. When people in and around government fixed on cost as *the* problem of the period, then everything had to be somehow tied to it. Various regulatory programs—Professional Standards Review Organizations, Health Planning, fraud and abuse—were adopted, justified in part by their supposed contribution to saving money. Health Maintenance Organizations were established with the hope that the competition between prepaid practice and fee-for-service practice would introduce competition into the medical marketplace and drive down costs. People became interested in restraining the introduction of high-cost technology and in working on prevention in order to contribute to a reduction of unnecessary expenditures. The problem of rising cost was so pressing and so pervasive in the thinking of health policy makers that it resulted in the consideration and adoption of a large battery of programs connected to it.

In addition to one opened by the emergence of a pressing problem, a window can be opened by an event in the political stream—a change of administration, a shift in national mood, an influx of new members of Congress. Politicians decide to undertake some sort of initiative on a particular subject, and cast about for ideas. Putting themselves in the market for proposals creates a window for advocates, and many alternatives are then advanced by their sponsors. One or more of the proposals worked up and available in the policy stream thus becomes coupled to the event in the political stream that changed the agenda. The problems may not have changed at all; nor did the solutions. But the availability of an alternative that responds in some way to a new political situation changes the policy agenda.

For example, available alternatives are coupled with general administration themes. The Ford administration put out a general call within the executive branch for proposals to reduce unemployment. They received a suggestion to hire unemployed people to maintain rail roadbeds. Rail specialists had been occupied with roadbed deterioration for years, and saw the administration's interest in employment as an opportunity to address the roadbed problem. The Carter administration's desire to undertake an urban initiative is another example. There had been some talk within transportation circles of encouraging intermodal terminals in cities, which would combine rail and bus, intercity and commuter travel. The administration's interest in programs for the cities opened a window for transportation specialists. As one bureaucrat told me, "When the urban initiative came along, we decided that would be a good thing to tack it to." And the proposal for intermodal terminals did indeed become a part of the urban initiative.

The problem windows and the political windows are related. When a window opens because a problem is pressing, the alternatives generated as solutions to the problem fare better if they also meet the tests of political acceptability. Proposals that cannot muster sufficient Hill support or that meet with administration opposition tend to be dropped, even though they might be perfectly logical solutions to the problem at hand. Similarly, when a political event opens a window, participants try to find a problem to which the proposed solution can be attached. The political event even results in the heightened preoccupation with a problem. When Senator Long decided to hold markup sessions on national health insurance in 1979, for instance, prominent references to the problems that created a need or constituency for national health insurance rose abruptly in the interviews, from 3 percent in 1978 to 42 percent in 1979. Discussion of national health insurance was in the air, necessitating attention to the problems it was supposed to address, even though these problems had not changed abruptly during the same time interval.

Seizing Opportunities

When a window opens, advocates of proposals sense their opportunity and rush to take advantage of it. When a commercial airliner collided with a private aircraft over San Diego, for instance, the publicity opened a window for advocates of greater control over private planes. Said a knowledgeable bureaucrat, "That crash provided FAA with a wonderful excuse to expand the traffic control areas. They want that kind of thing anyway." A budgeteer agreed: "Accidents are unfortunate, of course, but you do get more money for facilities when they happen. Proposals for restricting general aviation had been considered and had been rejected, not on the merits but because of fears of objection to them. Then they came up again because the accident opened a little window, in which advocates of these proposals figured they could do something."

Sometimes the rush to hook one's own interests onto the problem or political event of the moment becomes a bit extreme. During the height of environmental action, for instance, the highway interests felt rather bombarded by arguments that highway construction and the encouragement of automobile use were environmentally unsound. In an effort to make highways compatible with environmental concerns, the highway administration studied various environmental issues. A bureaucrat picks up the action:

> They got their people busy and made a big study to calculate what a big problem there would be with horse shit and mule shit if we hadn't invented the car. This was when everybody was hollering about pollution. So they wanted to make this argument that the car has actually helped on the pollution thing because without it the whole country would have a layer of mule shit two feet thick.

When opportunities come along, participants bring their problems to the deliberations, hoping that decision makers will solve them, and also bring their proposals, hoping they will be adopted. Among the energy initiatives advanced during the Carter years, for example, were proposals to levy a steep tax on crude oil, in hope of encouraging conservation, and to exact a windfall profits tax from energy companies in return for decontrol. For transportation actors, both proposals promised to be revenue bonanzas. Mass transit initiatives were proposed for the construction and operation of conventional and unconventional commuter systems. Highway interests talked of constructing "coal roads" to haul the coal on which the administration proposed to rely increasingly. Railroads talked of subsidies to haul coal as well. A multitude of transportation construction projects could be financed: airports, locks and dams, highways, rail roadbeds, bridges, subways. One lobbyist observed, "It looks to be a way of resolving transportation financing problems that is an easier way than fighting over the trust fund." In the flurry of activity, prominent mentions of new sources of financing transportation rose abruptly from 10 percent of my 1978 interviews to 44 percent in 1979.

A similar chain of events took place when the Nixon administration proposed the Health Maintenance Organization legislation in the early 1970s. When it arrived on the Hill, liberals saw it as their chance to insert a multitude of provisions not in the original legislation. As the legislation emerged from Congress, in order to qualify for federal status and support HMOs were required to offer a much richer package of benefits than the administration's bill contemplated, including dental care and alcohol treatment; to allow for open enrollment; and to base membership on whole communities rather than selected groups. The merits of these various provisions could be debated at length, but the net effect, according to many of my respondents, was to load HMOs down with an impossible set of requirements that made it exceedingly difficult to get the program under way.

On reflection, it seems inevitable that such overloading will occur. More solutions are available than windows to handle them. So when a window does open, solutions flock to it. In addition, strategists sometimes deliberately overload an agenda to frustrate all action. If they want to prevent action on a particular item, they load in many other items to compete.

What happens when such an unmanageable multitude of problems and alternatives get dumped into the deliberations? One possibility, indeed not uncommon, is that the entire complex of issues falls of its own weight. Most participants conclude that the subject is too complex, the problems too numerous, and the array of alternatives too overwhelming. Their attention drifts away to other, more manageable subjects. If they are willing to invest considerable resources in the issues, however, then several alternatives are possible. Sometimes, herculean investment will resolve most or all of the problems and dispose of most or all of the alternatives. More likely, some problems and alternatives will drift away from the particular choice at hand, leaving a set behind that is manageable.[7] Those that can be disposed of without a great investment of resources are handled fairly easily. For the remainder, problems are resolved and decisions are made after a fashion, according to processes that are by now familiar in the literature on decision making: bargaining, majority coalition building, and building consensus. The key to understanding which outcome obtains is the level of resource commitment. The more the participants are willing to commit their resources, the more problems can be resolved and the more alternatives can be dispatched.

The working of resource commitment is illustrated nicely by the case of dangerous chemicals spilled from tank cars during railroad derailments. There was a rash of such accidents in 1977–78, the most prominent of them at Waverly, Tennessee. These accidents opened a window, and advocates of quite a wide variety of solutions pushed for their adoption. Some, including the governor of Tennessee, called for nationalization of the rail roadbed; others called for less ambitious repair of roadbed to prevent derailments. Why did the accidents fail to provide the opportunity to enact sweeping programs dealing with roadbed rehabilitation or even nationalization? The answer was that a less expensive alternative was considered at the same time: dealing with the tank cars themselves. Government could require chemical and petroleum companies to make their tank cars less susceptible to puncture. That solution would not require the investment of financial resources that fixing the roadbed would require, and would avoid the inevitable opposition to nationalization and to aiding the railroad "barons." Under different conditions—if there had been a softening up of sentiment for nationalization, for instance—the Waverly accident might have been a window for roadbed upgrading or nationalization.

The outcomes, however, can be quite unpredictable. An administration proposes a bill, then is unable to control subsequent happenings and predict the result. Solutions become attached to problems, even though the problems themselves did not necessarily dictate those particular solutions. Thus a mine disaster sparks legislation not only for mine safety, but also for black lung disease. A railroad collapse results in a measure of regulatory reform even though the regulatory climate may not have contributed in any significant degree to the railroad's financial condition. Since the outcome depends on the mix of problems and proposals under consideration, there is bound to be some happenstance, depending on which participants are present, which alternatives are available, and even what catches people's eyes.

This unpredictability and inability to control events once they are set in motion creates a dilemma for the participants in the process. To the extent that they have any discretion over the opening of a window, they need to ask them-

[7]The following discussion reflects the garbage can model's discussion of resolution, oversight, and flight. See Cohen, March, and Olsen, "A Garbage Can Model," op. cit.

selves before unlatching it whether they risk setting in motion an unmanageable chain of events that might produce a result not to their liking. An administration, for instance, must decide whether pushing for a given proposal might produce legislation from Congress unlike their original intention, or might produce no legislation at all and leave in the wake of the controversy a generalized image of chaos that reflects poorly on the administration. The submission of a legislative proposal becomes a garbage can into which modifications, amendments, wholly new directions, and even extraneous items can be dumped as the bill wends its way through the legislative process. Once the agenda is set, control over the process is lost. Common language references for such a phenomenon include "opening Pandora's box," "the train went off the tracks," and "opening a can of worms." Sometimes participants choose not to open a window at all rather than risk an outcome that would be worse than the status quo.

The General Importance of Coupling

Problems or politics by themselves can structure the *governmental* agenda. But the probability of an item rising on the *decision* agenda is dramatically increased if all three streams—problems, policies, and politics—are joined. An alternative floating in the policy stream, for instance, becomes coupled either to a prominent problem or to events in the political stream in order to be considered seriously in a context broader than the community of specialists. If an alternative is coupled to a problem as a solution, then that combination also finds support in the political stream. Similarly, if an alternative is seized upon by politicians, it is justified as a solution to a real problem. None of the streams are sufficient by themselves to place an item firmly on the decision agenda.

If one of the three elements is missing—if a solution is not available, a problem cannot be found or is not sufficiently compelling, or support is not forthcoming from the political stream—then the subject's place on the decision agenda is fleeting. The window may be open for a short time, but if the coupling is not made quickly, the window closes. A subject can rise on the agenda abruptly and be there for a short time. A president can place a high priority on it, for instance, or a focusing event like an airplane crash can open a window. But the item is likely to fade from view quickly without the critical joining of the three streams. Since it cannot move from governmental agenda status to a decision agenda, attention turns to other subjects.

If no available alternative is produced by the policy stream, for instance, the subject either fades from view or never rises in the first place. In the case of long-term medical care, both the problems and political streams are firmly in place. The present and future aging of the population indicates a problem that will become most pressing, and the "gray lobby" has shown sufficient political muscle to create abundant incentives for politicians to be interested. But advocates have not devised solutions that are affordable and that have worked out the modalities of matching patients to the appropriate facility or other type of care. As one respondent said, "Every problem does not have a good solution. In the case of long-term care, the first time somebody comes up with a viable solution, then it will become a front burner item in short order." A similar argument about the lack of an agreed-upon solution that would work and that would not be too expensive could be made about the problem of bettering the mental health of the population. Indeed, in my quantitative indicators combining the four years of health interviews, no long-term care variable rose above 13 percent of my respondents discussing it prominently, and no mental health variable rose above 5 percent.

On the other hand, if an alternative can be found, the subject really takes off. Construction of an interstate highway system, for example, was stalled for a number of years due to disagreement over the right financing. During the 1950s, when the Clay Commission advocated a pay-as-you-go earmarked fuel tax, planning accelerated rapidly and construction started. The joining of the three streams had been made: the problem of congestion was evident, there was plenty of political reason to undertake the project, and the acceptable alternative came along.

There are very few single-factor explanations for high placement on the agenda. Generally, the rise of an item is due to the joint effect of several factors coming together at a given point in time, not to the effect of one or another of them singly. When I asked respondents why a given subject got hot, they usually replied in terms of interactions among elements, rather than discussing a single factor or even the addition of several single factors together. It was their *joint* effects that were so powerful. Here are some of the expressions of that idea:

> Several things came together at the same time.
>
> There was a confluence of streams.
>
> It was a combination of things.
>
> A cluster of factors got blended into the mix.
>
> It was an amalgam.

Generally, no one factor dominates or precedes the others. Each has its own life and its own dynamics. The combination of these streams, as well as their separate development, is the key to understanding agenda change.

POLICY ENTREPRENEURS

And what makes the coupling of the streams? Enter again our already-familiar acquaintances, the policy entrepreneurs. In the chapters on problems and the policy primeval soup, we described entrepreneurs as advocates who are willing to invest their resources—time, energy, reputation, money—to promote a position in return for anticipated future gain in the form of material, purposive, or solidary benefits. We discussed their incentives for being active, and their activities in the critical softening-up process that must precede high agenda status or enactment.

The entrepreneurs are found in many locations. No single formal position or even informal place in the political system has a monopoly on them. For one case study, the key entrepreneur might be a cabinet secretary; for another, a senator or member of the House; for others, a lobbyist, academic, Washington lawyer, or career bureaucrat. Many people have some important resources, and Chapters 2 and 3 of this book described the resources of each. The placement of entrepreneurs is nearly irrelevant, anyway, to understanding their activities or their successes. One experienced hand described the differences between administrations by saying that the most important actors within his department would shift from one time to another; at various times the undersecretary, the assistant secretary for legislation, or the head of planning and evaluation would be important. As he summarized the point, "I'm not sure that the location of the person makes a lot of difference. You can do a lot outside the formal structure. You'd be amazed at that."

When researching case studies, one can nearly always pinpoint a particular person, or at most a few persons, who were central in moving a subject up on the agenda and into position for enactment. Indeed, in our 23 case studies, we coded entrepreneurs as very or somewhat important in 15, and found them unimportant in only 3. To those familiar with various happenings in health and transportation over the last decade or so, the litany of these people would be very familiar. The following must suffice as examples:

- Paul Ellwood, the head of InterStudy, as a promoter of HMO legislation.

- Abe Bergman, a Seattle physician, who persuaded Senator Warren Magnuson of the virtues of a Health Service Corps, funding for research on sudden infant death syndrome, and legislation to regulate flammable children's sleepwear.

- Ralph Nader, the consumer advocate who started his career on the auto safety issue.

- Senator Pete Domenici, who pushed for the imposition of a waterway user charge in 1977–78, a version of which eventually was enacted.

- Alfred Kahn, the economist who became head of the Civil Aeronautics Board in the Carter administration, and who used that position to implement a deregulation strategy for airlines and to push for legislation as well.

In none of these cases was the single individual solely responsible for the high agenda status of the subject, as our reasoning about multiple sources would indicate. But most observers would also identify these policy entrepreneurs as central figures in the drama.

Entrepreneurs' Qualities

What qualities contribute to the policy entrepreneurs' successes? To distill a list from respondents' observations, qualities fall into three categories. First, the person has some claim to a hearing. Scores of people might be floating around who would like to be heard; of that set of people, only those who have a claim to a hearing are actually heard. This claim has one of three sources: expertise; an ability to speak for others, as in the case of the leader of a powerful interest group; or an authoritative decision-making position, such as the presidency or a congressional committee chairmanship.

Second, the person is known for his political connections or negotiating skill. Respondents often referred to someone like Wilbur Cohen (a prominent specialist in social security and health insurance, and a former HEW secretary), for example, as a person who combined technical expertise with political savvy, and the combination created much more influence than either of the two qualities taken separately.

Third, and probably most important, successful entrepreneurs are persistent. Many potentially influential people might have expertise and political skill, but sheer tenacity pays off. Most of these people spend a great deal of time giving talks, writing position papers, sending letters to important people, drafting bills, testifying before congressional committees and executive branch commissions, and having lunch, all with the aim of pushing their ideas in whatever way and forum might further the cause. One informant said of one of these famous entrepreneurs, "He could talk a dog off a meat wagon." Another spun out a theory that there were strong and weak senators, and strong and weak staffs. When asked what defined strength, he replied, "A strong senator is one who is just there. He is willing to be at the meeting. That may sound funny, but senators are spread so thin that a senator who shows up is one who is important. And the strong staffer is someone who can deliver his senator to the meeting." Persistence alone does not carry the day, but in combination with the other qualities, it is disarmingly important. In terms of our concept of entrepreneurship, persistence implies a willingness to invest large and sometimes remarkable quantities of one's resources.

Entrepreneurs and Coupling

The qualities of a successful policy entrepreneur are useful in the process of softening up the system, which we described in the chapter on the policy stream. But entrepreneurs do more than push, push, and push for their proposals or for their conception of problems. They also lie in wait—for a window to open. In the process of leaping at their opportunity, they play a central role in coupling the streams at the window.[8] As in the surfer image at the beginning of this chapter, entrepreneurs are ready to paddle, and their readiness combined with their sense for riding the wave and using the forces beyond their control contributes to success.

First, though, they must be ready. Space windows are exquisitely predictable, whereas the policy windows are not. Thus policy entrepreneurs must develop their ideas, expertise, and proposals well in advance of the time the window opens. Without that earlier consideration and softening up, they cannot take advantage of the window when it opens. One bureaucrat, advocating a promotion of transportation modes that conserve energy and a penalty on modes that do not, pointed out the necessity for this sort of anticipation: "I think in

[8]The distinction between pushing and coupling is similar to Eyestone's distinction between generator and broker entrepreneurial roles. See Robert Eyestone, *From Social Issues to Public Policy* (New York: Wiley, 1978), p. 89.

government someplace there should be a little group in a back room that is lay-
ing plans right now for how to handle the next Arab oil embargo. You want to
be in a position to take advantage of times like that. Something like an Arab oil
embargo does not present itself too often, and you want to be ready to propose
changes at the point that the opportunity does come along." Waiting to develop
one's proposals until the window opens is waiting too long.

The policy entrepreneur who is ready rides whatever comes along. Any crisis is seized as an opportunity. As the quotation at the beginning of this chapter
points out, proponents of railroad deregulation took advantage of the collapse
of the Penn Central to introduce a modicum of deregulation into the package
that eventually passed. A new administration comes into power, perhaps riding
a shift in national mood, and policy entrepreneurs try to make their proposals
part of the administration's program. A problem captures the attention of important people, and participants hook their proposals onto it, arguing that they
represent solutions, even though advocacy of these proposals originally had
nothing to do with the new problem. One believer in the dangers of ever-higher
technology in medical care described in particularly astute fashion how he rode
the general concern over the problem of cost:

> Cost doesn't matter a lot, but it produces political pressure to do something. I'm
> one of those people riding on the bandwagon of cost. Actually, I don't care
> much about cost. My concerns are about effectiveness, appropriateness, and
> quality of care. But I'm happy to see the political visibility being given to tech-
> nology for whatever reason it's happening, and I'm happy to ride along on it.

During the pursuit of their personal purposes, entrepreneurs perform the
function for the system of coupling the previously separate streams. They hook
solutions to problems, proposals to political momentum, and political events to
policy problems. If a policy entrepreneur is attaching a proposal to a change in
the political stream, for example, a problem is also found for which the proposal is a solution, thus linking problem, policy, and politics. Or if a solution is
attached to a prominent problem, the entrepreneur also attempts to enlist political allies, again joining the three streams. Without the presence of an entrepreneur, the linking of the streams may not take place. Good ideas lie fallow for
lack of an advocate. Problems are unsolved for lack of a solution. Political
events are not capitalized for lack of inventive and developed proposals.

Implications

The role entrepreneurs play in joining problems, policies, and politics has several implications. First, it makes sense of the dispute over personality versus
structure. When trying to understand change, social scientists are inclined to
look at structural changes while journalists are inclined to emphasize the right
person in the right place at the right time. Actually, both are right. The window
opens because of some factor beyond the realm of the individual entrepreneur,
but the individual takes advantage of the opportunity. Besides telling us that
personalities are important, this formulation tells us why and when they are.

Second, calling attention to the special role entrepreneurs play in joining the streams highlights two rather different types of activity. Advocacy is involved, but so is brokerage. Entrepreneurs advocate their proposals, as in the softening up process in the policy stream, but they also act as brokers, negotiating among people and making the critical couplings. Sometimes, the two activities are combined in a single person; at other times, entrepreneurs specialize, as in the instance of one pushing from an extreme position and another negotiating the compromises. This emphasis on coupling shifts our focus from invention, or the origin and pushing of an idea, to brokerage. Mutation turns out once again to be less important than recombination. Inventors are less important than entrepreneurs.

Third, such a free-form process promotes creativity. Periodically, observes cry out for more structure in government decision making. Structures are not tidy, government inefficiency is rampant, and people do not precisely define their goals and then adopt the most efficient solution. It could be, in contrast to such reasoning, that messy processes have their virtues. In a system like the one described here, entrepreneurs must take whatever opportunities present themselves, so they bend the problems to the solutions they are pushing. If goals are defined too precisely, many interesting and creative ideas are left in the lurch. It is certainly better for these entrepreneurs, and possibly even better for the system, if goals are left sufficiently vague and political events continue to be sufficiently imprecise and messy, that new and innovative ideas have a chance.

Finally, we should not paint these entrepreneurs as superhumanly clever. It could be that they are—that they have excellent antennae, read the windows extremely well, and move at the right moments. But it could as easily be that they aren't. They push for their proposals all the time; long before a window opens, they try coupling after coupling that fails; and by dumb luck, they happen to come along when a window is open. Indeed, the coupling we have described does not take place only when a window opens. Entrepreneurs try to make linkages far before windows open so they can bring a prepackaged combination of solution, problem, and political momentum to the window when it does open. They constantly hook these streams together, unhook them, and then hook them in a different way. But the items rise most dramatically and abruptly on the agenda when the windows are open.

One political appointee had a particularly marvelous summary of the coupling process in which entrepreneurs engage:

> In spite of the planning and evaluation machinery we have here, you still have to have a loaded gun, and look for targets of opportunity. There are periods when things happen, and if you miss them, you miss them. You can't predict it. They just come along. You political scientists are worried about processes. You'd like to build some theory to account for what goes on. I don't know about process. I'm more pragmatic. You keep your gun loaded and you look for opportunities to come along. *Have idea, will shoot.*

OCCURRENCE OF WINDOWS

We have discussed the concept of the policy window, the coupling that takes place when a window opens, and the entrepreneurs who are responsible for that coupling. Here, we consider the opening of windows: its frequency or scarcity; the regular, cyclical, predictable opening of some windows; and the unpredictability that remains.

Competition for a Place on the Agenda

Many potential agenda items are perfectly worthy of serious consideration, yet they do not rise high on the governmental policy agenda largely because they simply get crowded aside in the press of business. There is a limit on the capacity of the system to process a multitude of agenda items. Many subjects are ready, with the streams all in place: A real perceived problem has a solution available, and there is no political barrier to action. But these subjects queue up for the available decision-making time, and pressing items crowd the less pressing ones down in the queue. When "bigger" items are not occupying the attention of decision makers, "smaller" items are free to rise in agenda prominence. To rise on the agenda, these "smaller" items—FDA reform, biomedical research, or clinical labs regulation, as opposed to national health insurance or hospital cost containment—need not change at all in terms of their own properties. The removal of the competition is enough to remove the barrier to their serious consideration.

Part of the scarcity of open windows is due to the simple capacity of the system. In both the executive branch and Congress, there are bottlenecks through which all related items must pass. As one respondent replied, when asked why welfare reform and national health insurance could not be considered at the same time, "Both of them have to go through the same committees of Congress, they have to go through the same department, and they have to go through the same people in that department. There is a pipeline for these things, and there's only so much that you can put through it at once." There is simply a limit on the time people in these central positions have available. In an executive branch department, major items must funnel upward through an ever-contracting bottleneck. "The secretary can attend to only so many things, and things compete for his time," observed one high-level civil servant. A staffer for a congressional committee told me that action was put off for a year on a program that was actually up for renewal because they had no available staffer to work on it.

In addition to this simple limit on time and processing capacity, strategic considerations also constrain the number of items participants consider at any given moment. Each of them has a stock of political resources, and husbands that stock. Their resources are finite, and they cannot spend them on everything at once. Even presidents find they can wear out their welcome, and therefore must save their resources for the subjects they consider highest priority. As one bureaucrat observed of a bill that had run into trouble on the Hill, "There are more important things that the administration is going to use its chips for. It's not that their ardor has cooled. It's just that you have only so much limited capital you can expend."[9]

Other strategic constraints involve the dangers in overloading. If the administration, for instance, insists on action on everything at once, their insistence might jeopardize the items on which they could reasonably expect action. In deregulation, for instance, the Carter administration concentrated first on aviation, and let trucking, rail, and buses slide for the time being. If they had filled the plate too full, the controversy surrounding the other modes might have jeopardized the aviation initiative. By limiting consideration to aviation, the opponents of deregulation in the other modes had less incentive to become active and less claim to a stake in the outcome than if the whole package were being considered at once.

In addition to capacity and strategic constraints on the number of agenda items that can be processed at once, there can also be logical constraints. Once people in and around government become occupied with one subject, this preoccupation may logically preclude consideration of others. In their concern over the costs of medical care, for instance, health policy makers tended to impose a hefty budget constraint on every proposal. The cost issue, according to many observers, drove out consideration of proposals that might prove to be costly and pulled others into prominence if they promised cost savings or at least cost neutrality. These logical constraints are particularly sharp when applied to budgets because a severe budget constraint limits the opportunities for new initiatives and thus restricts the availability of many windows. As a bureaucrat put it, "An organization does have a breadth of attention. What is finite is money."

This talk of competition for space on the agenda, however, should not be exaggerated. The capacity of the system is not constant from one time to another, nor is there a fully zero-sum competition for space on the agenda. The agenda can and does expand at some times and contract at others. During a time when reform is in the air, such as 1932–36 or 1965–66, the system deals with many more agenda items than it does during a more placid time. There may be a similar cycle over the life of an administration. The system may absorb more agenda items during an administration's honeymoon period, when many of its resources are at their height, than later in its tenure.[10] Indeed, during the three years of my interviewing in the Carter administration, there were increasing references to competition for a space on the agenda, as if the capacity of the system was shrinking at the same time that the administration was proposing what seemed like an ever-expanding menu of legislation.

Another mechanism that expands the agenda is specialization. The agenda is constrained insofar as items must funnel through the bottlenecks, but many

---

[9]On the need to preserve capital, see Light, op. cit., *The President's Agenda*, Chapter 1.

[10]Ibid., Chapter 2.

items can bypass them. Because of specialization, a bureaucracy or a legislature is able to attend to several items at once, resulting in a smaller need to set priorities among the items. This importance of specialization leads to a more general formulation of the conditions under which the system absorbs more or fewer agenda items. Basically, the system can handle many specific, routine items, but few general, nonroutine items at any given time. The more specific a subject, the more it can be parceled out to specialists, which implies that the whole set of specialists is able to handle several problems at once. More general subjects, however, must funnel up through the bottlenecks in a bureaucracy, or must be transferred from committee to legislative floor, imposing limits on the number of general subjects that can be considered at any point in time. Similarly, the more routine the subject, the more it can be handled by specialists through standard operating procedures, implying that many routine items can be processed at once. The less routine items are bumped up to the bottlenecks, standing in the queue for a secretary or an important congressional committee to handle.

Predictable Windows

Windows sometimes open with great predictability. Regular cycles of various kinds open and close windows on a schedule. That schedule varies in its precision and hence its predictability, but the cyclical nature of many windows is nonetheless evident.

First, some formal requirements create open windows on a schedule: renewals, the budget cycle, and regular reports and addresses. Many governmental programs expire on a certain date and must be reauthorized. As one Senate committee staffer said, when asked why he pays attention to one thing rather than another, "Nine out of ten times, we're occupied with expiring legislation. I know that doesn't sound very inspiring, but, frankly, that's the truth." Not only Congress, but also the executive branch agencies that administer the programs and the people outside of government who are interested find that their agendas are structured by the renewal cycle. In my quantitative indicators, for instance, discussion of health manpower issues—manpower itself, specialty maldistribution, geographical maldistribution, doctor draft—peaked in 1976, and then declined sharply in the subsequent years. Prominent discussion of manpower went from 43 percent of the interviews in 1976 to 11 percent in 1977. The higher frequency in 1976 was due almost entirely to the fact that the legislation was up for renewal then. Once the renewal was accomplished, people had exhausted that subject for the time being, and their attention turned to other health policy issues.

At first, it seems that renewal is on a routine agenda rather than on a discretionary agenda, as Jack Walker calls it.[11] Indeed it is, in the sense that the subjects rise and fall on the agenda according to the renewal cycle. But what is done with the renewal is quite discretionary. Consideration of the program can be nothing more than a routine extension, or it can involve substantial revision,

[11]Jack L. Walker, "Setting the Agenda in the U.S. Senate," *British Journal of Political Science* 7 (October 1977): 423–445.

serious questioning, or even abolition of the program. As one political appointee said of health manpower, "We knew it would come up. That was predictable, but the issues that were going to arise in connection with that renewal were not necessarily very predictable." Thus, knowing when the subject will come up, staffers, interest groups, bureaucrats, and others accumulate possible provisions, amendments, changes, and proposals over the years, and wait for renewal time to raise them.

So the renewal becomes a window giving policy entrepreneurs of various descriptions an opportunity to advance their ideas, raise their problems, and push their proposals. They don't need to affect the agenda because they know the renewal will do the job for them. Instead, they simply need to be ready when the time for renewal comes. One analyst described the expiration of a piece of legislation as "a major entry wedge for us. We want to get in and point the debate in certain directions." Consider Figure 8-1 for a fascinating illustration. Notice that discussion of road and bridge deterioration rose abruptly in 1978 and declined just as abruptly in 1979. Surely, this spike in attention was not due to the objective condition of highways and bridges. They did not sud-

Figure 8-1

Discussion of Highways:
Trust Fund, Bridge Deterioration, and Road Deterioration

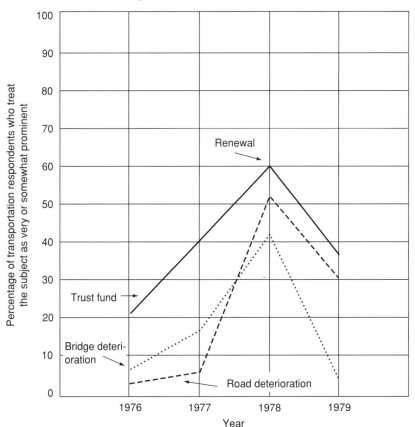

denly deteriorate in 1978 nor rapidly revive in 1979. Instead, the renewal of the highway authorization in 1978 presented people who were concerned about these problems with an opportunity to highlight them and to push for funding that would begin to address them. The renewal was a garbage can into which deterioration, trust fund reform, financing, and many other problems and proposals were dumped.

The renewal cycle sometimes has rather subtle effects. For years, transportation specialists lived with a decision-making process in which various modes were considered quite separately. But a small measure of thinking across modes still was accomplished by changing the scheduling of the renewals. Whether by design or by coincidence, the mass transit and highway bills were put on the same renewal cycle. Even though they were separate bills, Congress and the Department of Transportation still found it difficult—because they occupied their attention at the same time—to consider them without relating them to one another. Not only did this scheduling encourage comparison across the modes, but it also made logrolling exchanges more possible. As one highway committee staffer put it, "When they come up at different times, you get the transit people jumping on the highway people when highways come up, and then the highway jumping on transit when transit comes up. By putting them on the same cycle, maybe you can avoid some of that conflict, when each is getting something in the bill."

In addition to renewals, there are other regularly scheduled windows. The budget cycle, for instance, is a vehicle for everybody who has a hand in it to introduce both funding and program changes. Every year, like clockwork, the budget needs attention, and entrepreneurs all along the line in the process have a chance to affect funding. Scheduled reports and addresses operate in the same way. The president's State of the Union address, for instance, is a classic garbage can. Agencies all over government, staffers in the White House, interest groups, and others all vie for a place in the message. Mention of their particular problem or proposal, even though restricted to a sentence or two, boosts further consideration.

There are also larger cycles, less precisely scheduled but still noticeable in their occurrence and their regularity. Various scholars have written about reform cycles in American politics in which a burst of reform energy is followed by a period during which the system rests, followed anew by another burst.[12] The rest period provides time for reassessment and consolidation, but during this time pressure gradually builds for another period of intense activity directed toward substantial change. The political process does not stand quiescent for too long because there is every incentive for politicians to claim credit for some accomplishment.[13] Claiming credit is promoted by dramatic change, not by the quiet refining of existing programs. Thus politicians find it difficult to tolerate the fallow periods for very long.

[12]See James L. Sundquist, *Politics and Policy* (Washington, D.C.: The Brookings Institution, 1968), pp. 499–505; Thomas E. Cronin, *The State of the Presidency*, 2nd ed. (Boston: Little, Brown, 1980), pp. 18–19; and Arthur M. Schlesinger, *Paths to the Present* (Boston: Houghton Mifflin, 1964), Chapter 5.

[13]See David R. Mayhew, *Congress: The Electoral Connection* (New Haven: Yale University Press, 1974), pp. 52–61.

Attention to national health insurance may operate on such a cyclical basis. A lot of interest revolves around the idea for a while, then interest slackens, only to come to the fore again. It seems that proponents must gear up to push for national health insurance, both because of the formidable opposition and because of the intellectual complexity of the issues. They gear up, they may even be partially successful, as with Medicare, and then they fall exhausted until they are able to regroup and try again. This cyclical dynamic of push, then exhaustion, then renewed push accounts for the regular bursts of interest at fifteen- to twenty-year intervals, starting with Teddy Roosevelt, followed by the New Deal, Harry Truman's comprehensive proposal in the late 1940s, then Medicare in the early- to mid-1960s, and finally the Kennedy-Mills and Carter administration proposals in the mid- to late-1970s.

Scholars and practitioners alike often speak of swinging pendulums. One of them is the swing between periods of reform and quiescence. Another is the swing between liberal and conservative national moods. Many of my respondents in the late 1970s spoke in these terms of the difference between the burst of liberal Great Society legislation in the mid-1960s and the gathering conservatism that culminated in the Reagan election of 1980. As one observer described it, "There's a belief that we've been on a social policy binge, and that it's time for relooking, recouping, drawing in, homey virtues, and self-sufficiency." Or as another said, "In policy as in physics, every action promotes a reaction."

Unpredictable Windows

We have described fairly completely the dynamics within each stream and how the separate streams come together. Sometimes their joining is partly accidental. The separate development of the streams has proceeded to the point where they are each ready for coupling at the same time. A problem is recognized, a solution is available, and the political climate happens to be right, all at the same moment. Or one of the components may be lacking, which results in no or only fleeting appearance on the agenda.

Many respondents noticed a remaining randomness, and pointed to it quite eloquently:

> Government does not come to conclusions. It stumbles into paradoxical situations that force it to move one way or another. There are social forces that you can identify, but what comes out of them is just accident.

> Which idea gets struck by lightning, I can't tell you. I've been watching this process for twenty years and I can't tell you. I can't tell you why an idea has been sitting around for five years, being pushed by somebody, and all of a sudden it catches on. Then another idea with the same kind of advocates, being pushed for those five years, won't catch on fire. You have an element of chance.

Our recognition of a residual randomness does not imply that the entire process is nothing but rolls of the dice. Various constraints—budgets, public acceptance, the distribution of resources—all structure the system in predictable ways. We can also identify the streams and how they come together, and we can say why some items do *not* rise or last on the agenda. We return to the subject of randomness in the concluding chapter.

Many factors promote a subject to high agenda status. If only one of them is missing, then the subject is unlikely to remain high on the agenda, and may even fail to rise in the first place. If any of the factors depends on chance, in other words, the entire process depends on it. To the extent that some policy domains are affected by crisis, for instance, the timing of the crisis—an airplane crash, the collapse of the Penn Central, an Arab oil embargo—is uncontrollable and only partially predictable. To the extent that the process depends on the appearance of an entrepreneur at the right time, the comings and goings of personnel affect the outcomes. Inserting a funding proposal in an appropriation bill, for instance, may depend on the fortuitous absence of an articulate opponent. The inclusion of a provision in an administration proposal may turn on the presence of an advocate among the set of presidential appointees. A given group's interest may not be adequately represented in the Senate because the senator who champions their cause may be lazy, inarticulate, or dumb compared to his opponent.

Sometimes, all the streams are developed and ready, and a willing and able entrepreneur is set to go, but the subject still needs a lever for the entrepreneur to use. Such was the case with the movement of waterway user charges onto the transportation agenda in the late 1970s. The idea of imposing a charge on barge and other inland waterway traffic had been kicking around for years. What made its serious consideration and eventual passage possible in the 1970s was the availability of a hostage—the crumbling Lock and Dam 26 on the Mississippi River at Alton, Illinois. The barge interests wanted that facility replaced so badly that proponents of the user charge could hold it hostage: no user charge, no new facility. Senator Pete Domenici, the leading user charge proponent, linked the issues that way, and President Carter threatened a veto of any funding for Lock and Dam 26 unless it was accompanied by a user charge provision. Without the availability of this hostage, even vigorous entrepreneurs like Domenici, Secretary Brock Adams, and Carter probably would not have been able to pull off the passage of a user charge.

SPILLOVERS

The appearance of a window for one subject often increases the probability that a window will open for another similar subject. Borrowing from Ernst Haas's terminology, let us use the word "spillover" to describe such a chain of events.[14] Taking advantage of a given window sometimes establishes a principle that will guide future decisions within a policy arena. At other times, a precedent spills over from one arena into an adjacent one.

---

[14]Ernst B. Haas, *The Uniting of Europe* (Stanford: Stanford University Press, 1968), pp. 291–299.

Establishing a Principle

Within a given policy arena, such as health or transportation or any of their subarenas, policy changes generally occur gradually, incrementally, in small and nearly invisible steps. But there are times, with the passage of landmark legislation or the adoption of a precedent-setting presidential decision, when a new principle is established. Once that occurs, public policy in that arena is never quite the same because succeeding increments are based on the new principle, people become accustomed to a new way of doing things, and it becomes as difficult to reverse the new direction as it was to change the old. People talk under these circumstances of "establishing the principle," "changing direction," "getting the camel's nose under the tent," "getting your foot in the door," and "setting a precedent."

Establishing a principle does not necessarily imply that policy actually has taken a dramatic new turn, at least in the short run. The step might or might not be quite small; the importance of such events lies in their precedent-setting nature. In the case of imposing a waterway user charge, for example, the actual payment imposed in 1978 on barges for use of navigable waterways was minimal, and was delayed for several years. But the important thing to proponents and opponents alike was that the federal government, for the first time, decided that *some* waterway user charge would be collected. After lamenting the fact that the charge had been watered down considerably over the course of the bill's passage, one proponent nevertheless concluded, "But even at worst, it is an important beach head." Once some version of a user charge was enacted, proponents of greater charges could spend the next several years gradually ratcheting up the charge to the point where they could regard it as equitable and meaningful. So any enactment implied a future quite different from the old regime.

Part of the importance of establishing a new principle lies in its logic: A precedent is set, so future arguments surrounding the policy are couched in different terms. But part of it is political: An old coalition that was blocking change is defeated, and life is never quite the same. That coalition may fight a rear-guard action for years, but is henceforth unable to argue that they are invincible. As one proponent of national health insurance exuberantly claimed:

> The power of the AMA was broken by Medicare. I think that was the greatest accomplishment of Medicare, actually. It was a real crossing of the Rubicon. I'm not saying that the AMA is no longer important. They can slow things down, they can divert people. But they are not *the* sponsor or opponent of legislation any longer. Medicare proved that they can be beaten. Once it proved that, it opened up the way for other programs.

Establishing a principle is so important because people become accustomed to the new way of doing things and build the new policies into their standard operating procedures. Then inertia sets in, and it becomes difficult to divert the system from its new direction. Patients and doctors alike for instance, adapted to Medicare. Elderly patients and their younger children liked having the bills paid, and doctors also came to like the reimbursement. With the onset of

Medicare, major government involvement in financing medical care became acceptable, the accustomed way of doing business. It was then most difficult for opponents to retreat to "socialized medicine" slogans, or to argue that government involvement should be resisted in principle.

Spillovers to Adjacent Areas

Once a precedent is established in one area, it can be used to further a similar change in an area that is like the first in some way. After deregulation was enacted for aviation, for example, proponents of deregulation in the other transportation modes used the experience of the airlines to argue for similar measures for trucking and rail. As we saw in Chapter 1 (Figure 1-2), the agenda prominence for the other modes simply took off between 1978 and 1979. Even airlines were more prominently mentioned, despite 1978 enactment, because respondents who dealt primarily with the other modes were citing the experience of airline deregulation in their arguments both for and against similar measures as applied to them. Similarly, the passage of the first auto safety legislation resulted in a parade of safety legislation in flammable children's clothes, coal mines, and other diverse fields, culminating in the Occupational Safety and Health legislation. Indeed, Ralph Nader's first success with automobiles spread into a very far-ranging consumer protection movement.

Why do such spillovers occur? Part of the answer is to be found in Jack Walker's work on agenda setting in the United States Senate.[15] Following the case of safety, Walker points out that some entrepreneurial senators introduce a lot of legislation and like to claim credit for innovation. Once they saw the publicity and credit-claiming virtues of auto safety, for instance, they picked other safety issues because they saw the same potential. Thus, Congress ran through all the safety issues in very short order because the first of them had "hit" and was a political bonanza for its sponsors. Similarly, once politicians saw the attractiveness of deregulation in the airline case, they turned to the other modes in the hope of cashing in on a similarly popular situation.

But it is important to move very quickly. The window in the first area opens windows in adjacent areas, but they close rapidly as well. Implementation of the first policy eventually takes the bloom off its passage. While airline deregulation produced immediate benefits, such as lower fares, higher load factors, and greater airline profits, the problems only later became evident. Since policy implementation usually uncovers inevitable problems, the precedent-setting ideas must be extended to other areas fast because the argument for doing so may erode as time passes.

Spillover also occurs because the passage of the first principle-establishing legislation alters the coalition structure surrounding the policies. The coalition resisting change is defeated, and the coalition that was built and nurtured to establish the new policy can be transferred to other fights. A coalition had been built for auto safety legislation, for instance, that could be transferred to other

---

[15]Walker, "Setting the Agenda," op. cit.

safety and consumer protection issues.[16] The coalition-building strategy can also be transferred. Proponents of airline deregulation found that it helped tremendously when a few carriers broke the united front of opposition and endorsed the change. Learning from the success of that strategy, they tried to pick off some regulated truckers as well by writing their proposals to benefit the truckers who had come across to their side.

In addition to the incentives for entrepreneurs to seek adjacent arenas and the availability of coalitions to help them, a process of argumentation promotes spillover. The success of the first case provides an argument by analogy for success in the second. In the deregulation case, for example, proponents of trucking deregulation pointed to all of the benefits of airline deregulation, arguing that the same could result if legislation were passed for trucking. If fares were lower, for instance, prices could be lower for shippers because trucking competition would also drive down prices. As a journalist put it in 1979, "It is possible for me to put my kid on a cross-country trip to Los Angeles for $99 to visit Grandma. That's a pretty cheap trip. So the businessman says, 'Maybe we can get the same thing with freight rates.'" It was also harder to make the argument against trucking deregulation because similar predictions of dire consequences in the airline case had not been borne out, at least in the period shortly after its enactment.[17]

Such argumentation requires appropriate category construction. The only way for any issue to progress from one case to another is for the two issues to be placed in the same category. People easily move from one safety issue to the next, for instance, because they all are defined as belonging to the category "safety." But if coal mine safety were defined as belonging to the category of labor-management relations, then it would be much more difficult to carry over the safety reasoning. Similarly, when transportation specialists argued for greater federal funding for highway and bridge maintenance, they often cited the disastrous consequences of letting infrastructure deteriorate in the case of rail roadbeds. The only way one could draw such an analogy was to have a larger category, called "infrastructure deterioration," which could comfortably accommodate both the rail and the highway cases.

Which category one should use is not always obvious. Handicapped activists obtained enactment of legislation requiring mass transit systems to provide equal access to subways. As interpreted in regulations, this legislation literally required retrofitting of existing subways with elevators, an extremely expensive proposition. Categorization had much to do with the issue. If it had been classified as a transportation issue, there were much less expensive solutions (e.g., door-to-door taxi service) that would be more convenient for most handicapped people. But it was classified as a civil rights issue; "separate but equal"

---

[16]Ibid.

[17]Crenson discusses the ways attention to one issue creates attention to others. See Matthew A. Crenson, *The Un-Politics of Air Pollution* (Baltimore: Johns Hopkins University Press, 1971), pp. 170–176.

transit facilities were not enough. The civil rights movement had spilled over into transportation for the handicapped.

The Power of Spillovers

The first success creates tremendously powerful spillover effects. Entrepreneurs are encouraged to rush to the next available issue, coalitions are transferred, and arguments from analogy and precedent take hold. In the deregulation case, for instance, as late as 1977 and 1978 respondents would routinely dismiss the possibilities for trucking legislation, pointing out the formidable opposition coalition of regulated truckers and Teamsters. Yet by 1979, those opponents were clearly on the run and legislation was on the way, due in large part to the passage and apparent success of airline deregulation. Even that sort of blocking coalition could be bowled over by the powerful spillover effect. Deregulation became "The Game in Town," in the words of one analyst, and extended into areas far removed from transportation.

There comes a point when entrepreneurs run through the string, when nothing is left to spill into. As one respondent said of auto safety, "They have done all the things you'd think of having them do—seat belts, collapsible steering columns, and so forth—and are skirting the fringes of new technology with air bags. They're running out of things to do." Similarly, waterway user charges represented the last transportation user charge. There were fuel taxes for highway construction and ticket taxes for airport construction; the "last holdout was the waterway people," in the words of one observer. We noticed that references to airline deregulation actually increased subsequent to its passage, as the issue spilled over to the other modes. In marked contrast, references to a waterway user charge fell dramatically from 1978 to 1979, from 32 percent to 4 percent, because there was nothing left. The string of user charge proposals was played out.

CONCLUSION

The separate streams of problems, policies, and politics come together at certain critical times. Solutions become joined to problems, and both of them are joined to favorable political forces. This coupling is most likely when a policy window—an opportunity to push pet proposals or one's conceptions of problems—is open.

Policy windows are opened either by the appearance of compelling problems or by happenings in the political stream. Hence, there are "problems windows" and "political windows." To return to our distinction between the agenda and the alternatives, the governmental agenda is set in the problems or political streams, and the alternatives are generated in the policy stream.

One key coupling is that of a policy alternative to something else. Entrepreneurs who advocate their pet alternatives are responsible for this coupling. They keep their proposal ready, waiting for one of two things: a problem that might float by to which they can attach their solution, or a development in the political stream, such as a change of administration, that provides a receptive climate for their proposal. Some windows open largely on a schedule; others are quite unpredictable. But a window closes quickly. Opportunities come, but they also pass. If a chance is missed, another must be awaited.

While the governmental agenda is set by events in either the problems or political streams, setting of decision agendas emphasizes, in addition, an available alternative. A worked-out, viable proposal, available in the policy stream, enhances the odds that a problem will rise on a decision agenda. In other words, the probability of an item rising on a decision agenda is dramatically increased if all three elements—problem, proposal, and political receptivity—are coupled in a single package.

Finally, success in one area increases the probability of success in adjacent areas. Events spill over into adjacent areas because politicians find there is a reward for riding the same horse that brought benefit before, because the winning coalition can be transferred to new issues, and because one can argue from precedent.

CHAPTER 9

Wrapping Things Up

This book has considered why some subjects rise on governmental agendas while other subjects are neglected, and why people in and around government pay serious attention to some alternatives at the expense of others. The book is not about how presidents, members of Congress, or other authoritative figures make their final decisions. Instead, we have been occupied with understanding why participants deal with certain issues and neglect others. This chapter summarizes and ties together what we have learned.

Two major predecision processes have occupied us: agenda setting and alternative specification. A governmental agenda is a list of subjects to which officials are paying some serious attention at any given time. Thus an agenda-setting process narrows the set of subjects that could conceivably occupy their attention to the list on which they actually do focus. Obviously, there are agendas within agendas. They range from highly general agendas, such as the list of items occupying the president and his immediate inner circle, to rather specialized agendas, including the agendas of such subcommunities as biomedical research or waterway transportation. Subjects that do not appear on a general agenda may be very much alive on a specialized agenda.

The process of alternative specification narrows the large set of possible alternatives to that set from which choices actually are made. This distinction between agenda and alternatives proves to be very useful analytically, and we have returned to it repeatedly.

Why do some subjects rise on agendas while others are neglected? Why do some alternatives receive more attention than others? Some of our answers to these questions concentrate on participants: We uncover who affects agendas and alternatives, and why they do. Other answers explore the processes through which these participants affect agendas and alternatives. We have conceived of three streams of processes: problems, policies, and politics. People recognize problems, they generate proposals for public policy changes, and they engage in such political activities as election campaigns and pressure group lobbying. Each participant—president, members of Congress, civil servants, lobbyists, journalists, academics, etc.—can in principle be involved in each process (problem recognition, proposal formation, and politics). Policy is not the sole province of analysts, for instance, nor is politics the sole province of politicians. In practice, though, participants usually specialize in one or another process to a degree. Academics are more involved in policy formation than in politics, for instance, and parties are more involved in politics than in drafting detailed proposals. But conceptually, participants can be seen as different from processes.

Each of the participants and processes can act as an impetus or as a constraint. As an impetus, the participant or process boosts a subject higher on an agenda, or pushes an alternative into more active consideration. A president or congressional committee chair, for instance, decides to emphasize a subject. Or a problem is highlighted because a disaster occurs or because a well-known indicator changes. As a constraint, the participant or process dampens consideration of a subject or alternative. Vigorous pressure group opposition to an item, for instance, moves it down the list of priorities or even off the agenda. As an administration emphasizes its priorities, for another example, it limits people's ability to attend to other subjects. Concerns over budgetary costs of an item can also make its serious consideration quite unlikely.

AGENDA SETTING

How are governmental agendas set? Our answer has concentrated on three explanations: problems, politics, and visible participants.

Problems

Why do some problems come to occupy the attention of governmental officials more than other problems? The answer lies both in the means by which those officials learn about conditions and in the ways in which conditions become defined as problems. As to means, we have discussed indicators, focusing events, and feedback. Sometimes, a more or less systematic indicator simply shows that there is a condition out there. Indicators are used to assess the magnitude of the condition (e.g., the incidence of a disease or the cost of a program), and to discern changes in a condition. Both large magnitude and change catch officials' attention. Second, a focusing event—a disaster, crisis, personal experience, or powerful symbol—draws attention to some conditions more than to others. But such an event has only transient effects unless accompanied by a firmer indication of a problem, by a preexisting perception, or by a combination with other similar events. Third, officials learn about conditions through feedback about the operation of existing programs, either formal (e.g., routine monitoring of costs or program evaluation studies) or informal (e.g., streams of complaints flowing into congressional offices).

There is a difference between a condition and a problem. We put up with all kinds of conditions every day, and conditions do not rise to prominent places on policy agendas. Conditions come to be defined as problems, and have a better chance of rising on the agenda, when we come to believe that we should do something to change them. People in and around government define conditions as problems in several ways. First, conditions that violate important values are transformed into problems. Second, conditions become problems by comparison with other countries or other relevant units. Third, classifying a condition into one category rather than another may define it as one kind of problem or another. The lack of public transportation for handicapped people, for instance, can be classified as a transportation problem or as a civil rights problem, and the treatment of the subject is dramatically affected by the category.

Problems not only rise on governmental agendas, but they also fade from view. Why do they fade? First, government may address the problem, or fail to address it. In both cases, attention turns to something else, either because something has been done or because people are frustrated by failure and refuse to invest more of their time in a losing cause. Second, conditions that highlighted a problem may change—indicators drop instead of rise, or crises go away. Third, people may become accustomed to a condition or relabel a problem. Fourth, other items emerge and push the highly placed items aside. Finally, there may simply be inevitable cycles in attention; high growth rates level off, and fads come and go.

Problem recognition is critical to agenda setting. The chances of a given proposal or subject rising on an agenda are markedly enhanced if it is connected to an important problem. Some problems are seen as so pressing that they set agendas all by themselves. Once a particular problem is defined as pressing, whole classes of approaches are favored over others, and some alternatives are highlighted while others fall from view. So policy entrepreneurs invest considerable resources bringing their conception of problems to officials' attention, and trying to convince them to see problems their way. The recognition and definition of problems affect outcomes significantly.

Politics

The second family of explanations for high or low agenda prominence is in the political stream. Independently of problem recognition or the development of policy proposals, political events flow along according to their own dynamics and their own rules. Participants perceive swings in national mood, elections bring new administrations to power and new partisan or ideological distributions to Congress, and interest groups of various descriptions press (or fail to press) their demands on government.

Developments in this political sphere are powerful agenda setters. A new administration, for instance, changes agendas all over town as it highlights its conceptions of problems and its proposals, and makes attention to subjects that are not among its high priorities much less likely. A national mood that is perceived to be profoundly conservative dampens attention to costly new initiatives, while a more tolerant national mood would allow for greater spending. The opposition of a powerful phalanx of interest groups makes it difficult—not impossible, but difficult—to contemplate some initiatives.

Consensus is built in the political stream by bargaining more than by persuasion. When participants recognize problems or settle on certain proposals in the policy stream, they do so largely by persuasion. They marshal indicators and argue that certain conditions ought to be defined as problems, or they argue that their proposals meet such logical tests as technical feasibility or value acceptability. But in the political stream, participants build consensus by bargaining—trading provisions for support, adding elected officials to coalitions by giving them concessions that they demand, or compromising from ideal positions that will gain wider acceptance.

The combination of national mood and elections is a more potent agenda setter than organized interests. Interest groups are often able to block consideration of proposals they do not prefer, or to adapt to an item already high on a governmental agenda by adding elements a bit more to their liking. They less often initiate considerations or set agendas on their own. And when organized interests come into conflict with the combination of national mood and elected politicians, the latter combination is likely to prevail, at least as far as setting an agenda is concerned.

Visible Participants

Third, we made a distinction between visible and hidden participants. The visible cluster of actors, those who receive considerable press and public attention, include the president and his high-level appointees, prominent members of Congress, the media, and such elections-related actors as political parties and campaigners. The relatively hidden cluster includes academic specialists, career bureaucrats, and congressional staffers. We have discovered that the visible cluster affects the agenda and the hidden cluster affects the alternatives. So the chances of a subject rising on a governmental agenda are enhanced if that subject is pushed by participants in the visible cluster, and dampened if it is neglected by those participants. The administration—the president and his appointees—is a particularly powerful agenda setter, as are such prominent members of Congress as the party leaders and key committee chairs.

At least as far as agenda setting is concerned, elected officials and their appointees turn out to be more important than career civil servants or participants outside of government. To those who look for evidences of democracy at work, this is an encouraging result. These elected officials do not necessarily get their way in specifying alternatives or implementing decisions, but they do affect agendas rather substantially. To describe the roles of various participants in agenda setting, a fairly straightforward top-down model, with elected officials at the top, comes surprisingly close to the truth.

ALTERNATIVE SPECIFICATION

How is the list of potential alternatives for public policy choices narrowed to the ones that actually receive serious consideration? There are two families of answers: (1) Alternatives are generated and narrowed in the policy stream; and (2) Relatively hidden participants, specialists in the particular policy area, are involved.

Hidden Participants: Specialists

Alternatives, proposals, and solutions are generated in communities of specialists. This relatively hidden cluster of participants includes academics, researchers, consultants, career bureaucrats, congressional staffers, and analysts who work for interest groups. Their work is done, for instance, in planning and evaluation or budget shops in the bureaucracy or in the staff agencies on the Hill.

These relatively hidden participants form loosely knit communities of specialists. There is such a community for health, for instance, which includes analogous subcommunities for more specialized areas like the direct delivery of medical services and the regulation of food and drugs. Some of these communities, such as the one for transportation, are highly fragmented, while others are more tightly knit. Each community is composed of people located throughout the system and potentially of very diverse orientations and interests, but they all share one thing: their specialization and acquaintance with the issues in that particular policy area.

Ideas bubble around in these communities. People try out proposals in a variety of ways: through speeches, bill introductions, congressional hearings, leaks to the press, circulation of papers, conversations, and lunches. They float their ideas, criticize one another's work, hone and revise their ideas, and float new versions. Some of these ideas are respectable, while others are out of the question. But many, many ideas are possible and are considered in some fashion somewhere along the line.

The Policy Stream

The generation of policy alternatives is best seen as a selection process, analogous to biological natural selection. In what we have called the policy primeval soup, many ideas float around, bumping into one another, encountering new ideas, and forming combinations and recombinations. The origins of policy may seem a bit obscure, hard to predict and hard to understand or to structure.

While the origins are somewhat haphazard, the selection is not. Through the imposition of criteria by which some ideas are selected out for survival while others are discarded, order is developed from chaos, pattern from randomness. These criteria include technical feasibility, congruence with the values of community members, and the anticipation of future constraints, including a budget constraint, public acceptability, and politicians' receptivity. Proposals that are judged infeasible—that do not square with policy community values, that would cost more than the budget will allow, that run afoul of opposition in either the mass or specialized publics, or that would not find a receptive audience among elected politicians—are less likely to survive than proposals that meet these standards. In the process of consideration in the policy community, ideas themselves are important. Pressure models do not completely describe the process. Proposals are evaluated partly in terms of their political support and opposition, to be sure, but partly against logical or analytical criteria as well.

There is a long process of softening up the system. Policy entrepreneurs do not leave consideration of their pet proposals to accident. Instead, they push for consideration in many ways and in many forums. In the process of policy development, recombination (the coupling of already-familiar elements) is more important than mutation (the appearance of wholly new forms). Thus entre preneurs, who broker people and ideas, are more important than inventors. Because recombination is more important than invention, there may be "no new thing under the sun" at the same time that there may be dramatic change and innovation. There is change, but it involves the recombination of already-familiar elements.

The long softening-up process is critical to policy change. Opportunities for serious hearings, the policy windows we explored in Chapter 8, pass quickly and are missed if the proposals have not already gone through the long gestation process before the window opens. The work of floating and refining proposals is not wasted if it does not bear fruit in the short run. Indeed, it is critically important if the proposal is to be heard at the right time.

COUPLING AND WINDOWS

The separate streams of problems, policies, and politics each have lives of their own. Problems are recognized and defined according to processes that are different from the ways policies are developed or political events unfold. Policy proposals are developed according to their own incentives and selection criteria, whether or not they are solutions to problems or responsive to political considerations. Political events flow along on their own schedule and according to their own rules, whether or not they are related to problems or proposals.

But there come times when the three streams are joined. A pressing problem demands attention, for instance, and a policy proposal is coupled to the problem as its solution. Or an event in the political stream, such as a change of administration, calls for different directions. At that point, proposals that fit with that political event, such as initiatives that fit with a new administration's philosophy, come to the fore and are coupled with the ripe political climate. Similarly, problems that fit are highlighted, and others are neglected.

Decision Agendas

A complete linkage combines all three streams—problems, policies, and politics—into a single package. Advocates of a new policy initiative not only take advantage of politically propitious moments but also claim that their proposal is a solution to a pressing problem. Likewise, entrepreneurs concerned about a particular problem search for solutions in the policy stream to couple to their problem, then try to take advantage of political receptivity at certain points in time to push the package of problem and solution. At points along the way, there are partial couplings: solutions to problems, but without a receptive political climate; politics to proposals, but without a sense that a compelling problem is being solved; politics and problems both calling for action, but without an available alternative to advocate. But the complete joining of all three streams dramatically enhances the odds that a subject will become firmly fixed on a decision agenda.

Governmental agendas, lists of subjects to which governmental officials are paying serious attention, can be set solely in either problems or political streams, and solely by visible actors. Officials can pay attention to an important problem, for instance, without having a solution to it. Or politics may highlight a subject, even in the absence of either problem or solution. A decision agenda, a list of subjects that is moving into position for an authoritative decision, such as legislative enactment or presidential choice, is set somewhat differently. The probability of an item rising on a decision agenda is dramatically increased if all three elements—problem, policy proposal, and political receptivity—are linked in a single package. Conversely, partial couplings are less likely to rise on decision agendas. Problems that come to decisions without solutions attached, for instance, are not as likely to move into position for an authoritative choice as if they did have solutions attached. And proposals that lack political backing are less likely to move into position for a decision than ones that do have that backing.

A return to our case studies in Chapter 1 illustrates these points. With aviation deregulation, awareness of problems, development of proposals, and swings of national mood all proceeded separately in their own streams. Increasingly through the late 1960s and early 1970s, people became convinced that the economy contained substantial inefficiencies to which the burdens of government regulation contributed. Proposals for deregulation were formed among academics and other specialists, through a softening-up process that included journal articles, testimony, conferences, and other forums. In the 1970s, politicians sensed a change in national mood toward increasing hostility to government size and intrusiveness. All three of the components, therefore, came together at about the same time. The key to movement was the coupling of the policy stream's literature on deregulation with the political incentive to rein in government growth, and those two elements with the sense that there was a real, important, and increasing problem with economic inefficiency.

The waterway user charge case illustrates a similar coupling. A proposal, some form of user charge, had been debated among transportation specialists for years. The political stream produced an administration receptive to imposing a user charge. This combination of policy and politics was coupled with a problem—the necessity, in a time of budget stringency, to repair or replace aging facilities like Lock and Dam 26. Thus did the joining of problem, policy, and politics push the waterway user charge into position on a decision agenda.

By contrast, national health insurance during the Carter years did not have all three components joined. Proponents could argue that there were real problems of medical access, though opponents countered that many of the most severe problems were being addressed through Medicare, Medicaid, and private insurance. The political stream did produce a heavily Democratic Congress and an administration that favored some sort of health insurance initiative. It seemed for a time that serious movement was under way. But the policy stream had not settled on a single, worked-up, viable alternative from among the many proposals floating around. The budget constraint, itself a severe problem, and politicians' reading of the national mood, which seemed to be against costly new initiatives, also proved to be too much to overcome. The coupling was incomplete, and the rise of national health insurance on the agenda proved fleeting. Then the election of Ronald Reagan sealed its fate, at least for the time being.

Success in one area contributes to success in adjacent areas. Once aviation deregulation passed, for instance, government turned with a vengeance to other deregulation proposals, and passed several in short order. These spillovers, as we have called them, occur because politicians sense the payoff in repeating a successful formula in a similar area, because the winning coalition can be transferred, and because advocates can argue from successful precedent. These spillovers are extremely powerful agenda setters, seemingly bowling over even formidable opposition that stands in the way.

Policy Windows

An open policy window is an opportunity for advocates to push their pet solutions or to push attention to their special problems. Indeed, advocates in and around government keep their proposals and their problems at hand, waiting for these opportunities to occur. They have pet solutions, for instance, and wait for problems to float by to which they can attach their solutions, or for developments in the political stream that they can use to their advantage. Or they wait for similar opportunities to bring their special problems to the fore, such as the appearance of a new administration that would be concerned with these problems. That administration opens a window for them to bring greater attention to the problems about which they are concerned.

Windows are opened by events in either the problems or political streams. Thus there are problems windows and political windows. A new problem appears, for instance, creating an opportunity to attach a solution to it. Or such events in the political stream as turnover of elected officials, swings of national mood, or vigorous lobbying might create opportunities to push some problems and proposals to the fore and dampen the chances to highlight other problems and proposals.

Sometimes, windows open quite predictably. Legislation comes up for renewal on a schedule, for instance, creating opportunities to change, expand, or abolish certain programs. At other times, windows open quite unpredictably, as when an airliner crashes or a fluky election produces an unexpected turnover in key decision makers. Predictable or unpredictable, open windows are small and scarce. Opportunities come, but they also pass. Windows do not stay open long. If a chance is missed, another must be awaited.

The scarcity and the short duration of the opening of a policy window create a powerful magnet for problems and proposals. When a window opens, problems and proposals flock to it. People concerned with particular problems see the open window as their opportunity to address or even solve these problems. Advocates of particular proposals see the open window as the opportunity to enact them. As a result, the system comes to be loaded down with problems and proposals. If participants are willing to invest sufficient resources, some of the problems can be resolved and some of the proposals enacted. Other problems and proposals drift away because insufficient resources are mobilized.

Open windows present opportunities for the complete linkage of problems, proposals, and politics, and hence opportunities to move packages of the three joined elements up on decision agendas. One particularly crucial coupling is the link of a solution to something else. Advocates of pet proposals watch for developments in the political stream that they can take advantage of, or try to couple their solution to whatever problems are floating by at the moment. Once they have made the partial coupling of proposal to either problem or politics, they attempt to join all three elements, knowing that the chances for enactment are considerably enhanced if they can complete the circle. Thus they try to hook packages of problems and solutions to political forces, packages of proposals and political incentives to perceived problems, or packages of problems and politics to some proposal taken from the policy stream.

ENTREPRENEURS

Policy entrepreneurs are people willing to invest their resources in return for future policies they favor. They are motivated by combinations of several things: their straightforward concern about certain problems, their pursuit of such self-serving benefits as protecting or expanding their bureaucracy's budget or claiming credit for accomplishment, their promotion of their policy values, and their simple pleasure in participating. We have encountered them at three junctures: pushing their concerns about certain problems higher on the agenda, pushing their pet proposals during a process of softening up the system, and making the couplings we just discussed. These entrepreneurs are found at many locations; they might be elected officials, career civil servants, lobbyists, academics, or journalists. No one type of participant dominates the pool of entrepreneurs.

As to problems, entrepreneurs try to highlight the indicators that so importantly dramatize their problems. They push for one kind of problem definition rather than another. Because they know that focusing events can move subjects higher on the agenda, entrepreneurs push to create such things as personal viewings of problems by policy makers and the diffusion of a symbol that captures their problem in a nutshell. They also may prompt the kinds of feedback about current governmental performance that affect agendas: letters, complaints, and visits to officials.

As to proposals, entrepreneurs are central to the softening-up process. They write papers, give testimony, hold hearings, try to get press coverage, and meet endlessly with important and not-so-important people. They float their ideas as trial balloons, get reactions, revise their proposals in the light of reactions, and float them again. They aim to soften up the mass public, specialized publics, and the policy community itself. The process takes years of effort.

As to coupling, entrepreneurs once again appear when windows open. They have their pet proposals or their concerns about problems ready, and push them at the propitious moments. In the pursuit of their own goals, they perform the function for the system of coupling solutions to problems, problems to political forces, and political forces to proposals. The joining of the separate streams described earlier depends heavily on the appearance of the right entrepreneur at the right time. In our case study of Health Maintenance Organizations in Chapter 1, Paul Ellwood appeared on the scene to link his pet proposal (HMOs) to the problem of medical care costs and to the political receptivity created by the Nixon administration casting about for health initiatives. The problems and political streams had opened a window, and Ellwood cleverly took advantage of that opportunity to push his HMO proposal, joining all three streams in the process.

The appearance of entrepreneurs when windows are open, as well as their more enduring activities of trying to push their problems and proposals into prominence, are central to our story. They bring several key resources into the fray: their claims to a hearing, their political connections and negotiating skills, and their sheer persistence. An item's chances for moving up on an agenda are enhanced considerably by the presence of a skillful entrepreneur, and dampened considerably if no entrepreneur takes on the cause, pushes it, and makes the critical couplings when policy windows open.

CONCLUSION

The ideas we have explored in the pages of this book have a few important properties which it is appropriate to highlight as we draw to a close. These properties fall into two general categories: the differences between our model of these processes and other notions, and the places of randomness and pattern.

Other Notions

The ideas developed in this book are quite unlike many other theories that could have captured our attention. For example, events do not proceed neatly in stages, steps, or phases. Instead, independent streams that flow through the system all at once, each with a life of its own and equal with one another, become coupled when a window opens. Thus participants do not first identify problems and then seek solutions for them; indeed, advocacy of solutions often precedes the highlighting of problems to which they become attached. Agendas are not first set and then alternatives generated; instead, alternatives must be advocated for a long period before a short-run opportunity presents itself on an agenda. Events do not necessarily proceed in similar order in several different case studies; instead, many things happen separately in each case, and become coupled at critical points.

Other notions have elements of truth, and do describe parts of the processes, but they are incomplete. A pressure model, for instance, does describe parts of the political stream, but ideas are as important as pressure in other parts of the processes. Agenda items do not necessarily start in a larger systemic or public arena and transfer to a formal or governmental agenda; indeed, the flow is just as often in the reverse direction. As we argued in Chapter 4, a concentration on origins does not take us very far because ideas come from many locations, nobody has a monopoly on leadership or prescience, and tracing origins involves an infinite regress. We were drawn to the importance of combinations rather than single origins, and to a climate of receptivity that allows ideas to take off. Also in Chapter 4, we portrayed comprehensive-rational and incremental models as incomplete. Participants sometimes do approach their decisions quite comprehensively and decide quite rationally, but the larger process is less tidy. Incrementalism does describe the slow process of generating alternatives, and often does describe small legislative and bureaucratic changes stretching over many years, but does not describe agenda change well. Thus, in addition to arguing for one way of looking at the policy formation world, we have argued what the world does *not* look like.

On Randomness and Pattern

We still encounter considerable doses of messiness, accident, fortuitous coupling, and dumb luck. Subjects sometimes rise on agendas without our understanding completely why. We are sometimes surprised by the couplings that take place. The fortuitous appearance or absence of key participants affect outcomes. There remains some degree of unpredictability.

Yet it would be a grave mistake to conclude that the processes explored in this book are essentially random. Some degree of pattern is evident in three fundamental sources: processes within each stream, processes that structure couplings, and general constraints on the system.

First, processes operating within each stream limit randomness. Within the problems stream, not every problem has an equal chance of surfacing. Those conditions that are not highlighted by indicators, focusing events, or feedback are less likely to be brought to the attention of governmental officials than conditions that do have those advantages. Furthermore, not all conditions are defined as problems. Conditions that do not conflict with important values or that are placed in an inappropriate category are less likely to be translated into problems than conditions that are evaluated or categorized appropriately. In the policy stream, not every proposal surfaces. Selection criteria make patterns out of initial noise. Proposals that meet such standards as technical feasibility, value acceptability, public acquiescence, politicians' receptivity, and budgetary stringency are more likely to survive than those that fail to meet such standards. In the political stream, not every environment or event is equally likely. Some groups lack the resources that others have, some swings of national mood (e.g., to socialism) are unlikely, and some types of turnover of elected officials are more likely than others.

Second, some couplings are more likely than others. Everything cannot interact with everything else. For one thing, the timing of an item's arrival in its stream affects its ability to be joined to items in other streams. A window may open, for instance, but a solution may not be available at that time in the policy stream, so the window closes without a coupling of solution to problem or politics. Or a proposal may be ready in the policy stream, but the political conditions are not right for it to be pushed, again limiting the coupling possibilities. In addition to timing, germaneness limits the coupling possibilities. Not all solutions have an equal possibility of being discussed with all problems. Instead, participants have some sense of what would constitute an appropriate solution to a problem. There is some room for different solutions being hooked to a given problem or different problems being hooked to a given solution, but participants also set some limits on the appropriate couplings. Finally, the appearance of a skillful entrepreneur enhances the probability of a coupling. Potential couplings without entrepreneurs are less likely because they fail for lack of someone willing to invest resources in them.

Third, there are various constraints on the system, limits that provide a basic structure within which the participants play the games we have described.[1] The political stream provides many of these constraints. Participants sense some boundaries that are set on their actions by the mood of the mass public, and narrower boundaries set by the preferences of specialized publics and elected politicians. As I have argued elsewhere, governmental officials sense these limits and believe they must operate within them.[2] The budget imposes constraints as well. Costly proposals are not likely to be addressed in times of economic contraction or budget stringency, but might be more likely to receive attention in more robust times. Various rules of procedure, including the constitution, statutes, prescribed jurisdictions, precedents, customary decision-making modes, and other legal requirements, all impose structures on the participants. Finally, the scarcity of open windows constrains participants. They compete for limited space on agendas, and queue up for their turn. Even the selection criteria used by specialists in the policy stream anticipate these constraints.

These various types of pattern—dynamics internal to each stream, limits on coupling possibilities, and more general constraints—help us understand why some items never rise on policy agendas. Chapter 1 set forth several such items

---

[1]For a good discussion of constraints, see Roger W. Cobb and Charles D. Elder, "Communications and Public Policy," in Dan Nimmo and Keith Sanders, eds., *Handbook of Political Communications* (Beverly Hills: Sage, 1981), pp. 402–408.

[2]John W. Kingdon, *Congressmen's Voting Decisions,* 3rd ed. (Ann Arbor: University of Michigan Press, 1989), Chapter 12.

in health and transportation in the late 1970s. Some of them, such as long-term care and mental health, remained low, not because participants would not recognize real problems there but because they had little sense for alternatives that might be available as solutions. Some agenda items, such as buses, did not have powerful constituencies behind them in the political stream and failed to receive attention for lack of such advocates. Items such as rail nationalization failed because of powerful opposition. Others were not prominent on health and transportation agendas because systems of specialization and jurisdiction limited their movement. Items like direct delivery of medical care and food and drug regulation were indeed high on certain specialized agendas, but not on the larger health agenda. Finally, some items like environmental impact and transportation safety had been prominent earlier, but were played out by the time of these interviews, according to dynamics we explored when examining why problems fade. Thus this study helps to understand not only the appearance of some items on agendas, but also the failure of other items to appear.

Finally, it should be noted that all of our ideas are probabilistic. I have tried to adhere to such formulations as "the chances are improved or lessened" and "these events are more likely than others." In describing these processes, hard-and-fast rules and the specification of conditions that *must* be met seem less fruitful than a quotation of odds. Constraints, for instance, are not absolutes. Instead, they are conditions that make some events highly unlikely and other events more likely to occur. They do impose structure on the system, but it is structure that still allows room for some gray areas and some unpredictability. A budget constraint, for instance, is subject to some interpretation in the light of knowledge gaps and participants' values, but its operation still does make attention to some proposals at some points in time highly unlikely.

Thus we have made some progress in understanding the vague and imprecise phenomena we wanted to understand at the beginning of our journey. To the extent that our vision is still obscured, the world itself may be somewhat opaque. But further research and thinking beyond what is presented in this book may also allow us to see more clearly.

CHAPTER 10

Some Further Reflections

Now that we have wrapped up the central arguments in the book, let us see how those arguments stand the test of time. This chapter, added for the second edition, does two things. First, I describe some events in the 1980s and 1990s to show that the concepts developed to understand agenda setting and alternative specification are not relevant simply to the time period I originally studied, but remain useful in understanding policy formation. Second, I discuss the original arguments and theories in the light of the literature and commentaries about the book since it first appeared, and present some of my reflections on the picture of agenda setting presented here and on the more general enterprise of modeling these sorts of processes.

NEW CASE STUDIES

This book began with four brief case studies—health maintenance organizations; national health insurance during the Carter administration; deregulation in aviation, trucking, and railroads; and waterway user charges. Throughout the book, we have returned to those case studies to show how the general concepts and theories can be used to understand particular real-world events. Now we come full circle, by presenting three new case studies drawn from the period since the original research was completed.

We concentrate here on the "Reagan revolution" in the federal budget which took place during the first ten months of 1981, the tax reform act of 1986, and the health care initiative of the Clinton administration in 1993. Most observers will recognize these three cases as among the major public policy events of the post-Carter administration years. I will not retell these familiar stories in great detail. Instead, I intend to sketch the events in each case with an eye to using

209

the concepts developed in this book to understand these more contemporary happenings. These new cases allow us both to illustrate the continued applicability of those concepts, and to use those concepts in policy areas other than health and transportation, the areas of the original study.

The Reagan Budget in 1981

The 1980 election produced a major change in post-World War II American politics.[1] Ronald Reagan, sharply more conservative than his Republican predecessors, defeated the incumbent Democrat, Jimmy Carter. Along with Reagan's presidential victory, the Republicans captured majority control of the Senate for the first time since the 1950s, and picked up 33 seats in the House of Representatives. Whether this was the major party realignment that observers had been anticipating for at least a decade was still not clear. But at least within the nation's capital, it seemed as though the new administration and the Republican control of the Senate heralded a new, decidedly more conservative era.

In the terms we have used in this book, the political stream had changed course markedly, in at least two senses. First, the new administration represented quite a sharp turn to the right, and the greater Republican strength in the Congress combined with that new administration created an opportunity (opened a policy window) for markedly more conservative proposals to be considered seriously. Second, many observers thought they detected in the election results a more conservative national mood. The new administration, of course, claimed a popular mandate, as all administrations do. It was not clear, however, that the election outcome resulted from voters' approval of a Reagan platform, or from voters' dissatisfaction with Carter's performance over such events as the taking of American hostages in Iran. Disputes about mandates could rage, but one thing was clear: The political stream had produced a new administration and a greater Republican strength in Congress, which opened a window for sharply more conservative policy directions.

Meanwhile, all through the decade of the 1970s, various conservative policy analysts and activists had been developing and honing their ideas and translating them into proposals that might be advanced when the moment was right. Some of the work took place in academia, some in think tanks like the Heritage Foundation, some in the pages of such publications as *National Review*, some on talk radio, and some in committee hearings, floor speeches, and bills introduced on Capitol Hill. These ideas included work on deregulation, supply-side

---

[1]For a fuller treatment of the events than is possible here, see Allen Schick, "How the Budget Was Won and Lost," in Norman Ornstein, ed., *President and Congress: Assessing Reagan's First Year* (Washington: American Enterprise Institute, 1982); Paul Peterson, "The New Politics of Deficits," in John Chubb and Paul Peterson, eds., *The New Direction in American Politics* (Washington: The Brookings Institution, 1985); and Douglas Arnold, *The Logic of Congressional Action* (New Haven: Yale University Press, 1990), Chapter 7.

economics, changed budget priorities, monetary policy, and privatization of governmental programs, and dealt with the general contours of the federal budget as well as specific federal programs. This conservative "policy primeval soup," to use our term from Chapter 6, was bubbling along, evolving proposals that could actually be enacted at the right time, and softening up the system. This process eventuated in concrete proposals that were ready to go.

A key to the "Reagan revolution" in 1981 was the confluence (we have called it "coupling") of these two streams of politics and policies. The administration entered ready to propose initiatives, and the policy stream had produced the initiatives for them to propose. But what of problems? Developments in the political stream alone could have placed the budget issues on a governmental agenda, but to be on a decision agenda, we would also expect a recognition of the problem(s) being addressed. In this case, the problem was perceived to be the state of the economy. Starting in the early- to mid-1970s, the economy went into a long-term stagnation from which it really did not emerge for two decades. In addition, inflation had been high during the late 1970s, and the federal budget deficit, though puny by 1980s standards, seemed awfully large. So the stage was set for the two major streams in this story, politics and policies, to be joined with the problems stream. Whether "Reaganomics" was the correct solution to these problems was hotly debated, but its advocates saw it that way.

Reagan administration officials were keenly aware of the importance of striking while the iron is hot. As Paul Light says, the president's resources are never greater than right at the beginning of an administration.[2] If that opportunity is not seized, much as we argued in Chapter 8 on policy windows, it disappears and advocates must wait for the next open window.

So the administration officials and their allies on the Hill set about to construct a budget package. It is hard to identify one single policy entrepreneur in such a complicated, large story, but probably the closest was David Stockman. Stockman had been a Republican member of Congress from Michigan, was active in the Reagan campaign of 1980, and became the Director of the Office of Management and Budget in the Reagan administration. He had been involved in budget battles while in Congress, and knew a good bit about both the substance and the strategies of budget-making.

The package which the administration officials and their allies on the Hill assembled represented a considerable departure from business as usual. While it left entitlement programs largely alone, it cut taxes substantially, increased defense spending, and decreased discretionary domestic spending. In a remarkable display of party unity on several different votes in 1981, Republicans in both the House and Senate voted for the package virtually unanimously and in the House, enough Democrats voted for it to see it passed. That unity held for both procedural and substantive votes on both revenue and expenditure bills.

[2]Paul Light, *The President's Agenda* (Baltimore: Johns Hopkins University Press, 1982).

One institutional factor was critical in enabling this success: the reconciliation mechanism. Without entering a lengthy discussion of the congressional budget reform of 1974, we need only note here that prior to that reform, Congress had no formal way to make budgets. There was no formal way in Congress to compare expenditures to revenues, decide the size of the deficit or surplus in the coming fiscal year, or set priorities among expenditure categories. Part of their 1974 reform was a device called "reconciliation," which allowed the administration in 1981 to roll all expenditures into one bill, with an up or down vote on that one bill. The importance of having this mechanism available can hardly be overstated. Without it, expenditures would have been broken down into separate appropriations bills, and the issue in each case would have been, "Shall we cut highways, or public health, or rivers and harbors, or education?", or whatever the program at hand might be. Constituencies supporting each of these programs would have been able to defeat cuts if the bills had been taken up seriatim. But by rolling all of the expenditures into one bill, as the administration and its supporters on the Hill did, the issue was, "Shall we have larger or smaller government?" Once this mechanism allowed the issue to be framed that way, the politics changed dramatically, because the various constituencies for the separate programs were not able to define the issue as one of support for highways, health, harbors, education, and the like.

Although it isn't central to our story, the aftermath was remarkable. The passage of the expenditure and revenue bills in 1981 has affected federal government agendas down to the present day. The annual federal budget deficit skyrocketed. The total national debt quadrupled in twelve years. One result was the overwhelming importance of the deficit in every subsequent debate over every program. If respondents in my original study in the late 1970s pointed to the importance of a budget constraint, as we noticed in Chapter 5, they hadn't seen anything yet. That constraint became a constant preoccupation in Washington, precipitating plan after plan to bring the deficit under control and making bold innovations that would require substantial new expenditures simply out of the question. Whether this result was an intention of the original Reagan budgeteers to put heavy pressure on domestic spending or a product of the venerable law of unanticipated consequences was not clear. But the result of a substantially more stringent budget constraint was unmistakable.

The general outlines of the model which we developed in this book are evident in this case. The political stream had produced a sharp change of administration and party strength on the Hill, which opened a policy window. The policy stream had been developing conservative proposals in many areas for some years, which could be incorporated into a budget package. Those proposals could be connected to a number of economic problems that people perceived developing in the 1970s. The entrepreneurs in this case cleverly took advantage of the open window and the available institutional feature of reconciliation to push through a substantial, non-incremental change in budget priorities.

The Tax Reform Act of 1986

Complaints about taxes are hardy perennials in American politics.[3] After all, the country was born in a taxpayer revolt, and has been in one ever since. But the contemporary taxpayer revolt really took off with the passage of Proposition 13 in California in 1978. As the movement of taxpayer anger spread like wildfire across the country, state after state and locality after locality either passed or grappled with similar tax rollback initiatives. That anger was fueled, furthermore, by the publicity given to millionaires who had manipulated loopholes in the tax code to avoid paying their fair share. So while the anger was directed at the levels of taxation, it was also directed to some degree at equity and fairness.

At any rate, the national mood, as we have termed it in this book, seemed to take a decidedly anti-government, anti-tax turn. This trend, combined with the administration and congressional changes we discussed at the beginning of the previous case study, meant that the political stream was primed for changes in the federal tax code. The electoral and partisan politics of the situation even resulted, as the events unfolded, in a sort of bidding war between the parties, neither of them wanting to allow the other to claim credit for tax reform.

What about the problems stream? By the mid-1980s, a number of problems relevant to taxes came to be recognized as pressing. As we noted in the last case study, the budget deficit loomed large. That deficit affected thinking about taxes in one of two ways. Some argued that there was a revenue shortfall and therefore that government should raise taxes. Others argued that the economy was not growing at a sufficiently robust rate, and that tax reform was needed either to change the incentives to stimulate growth, or to reduce taxes still more to prime the pump.

Another rather different conception of the problems was also at hand. Many knowledgeable people had come to believe that the federal tax code had become inordinately complex, and that tax loopholes which had been incrementally added over the years were both sapping revenue and creating serious inequities. This conception of the problem with taxes resonated with the public as well, and people became angry about fairness as well as about levels of taxation.

Eventually, as the situation developed, participants neglected the budget problems, reasoning that reform of the tax code was not the place to balance the budget. Some of those participants insisted that taxes not be raised in the name of reform; others insisted that the budget deficit couldn't stand any further loss of revenue. The result was a general agreement that any reform must be "revenue neutral," neither raising nor lowering revenues. So participants turned

---

[3]This case study of the 1986 tax reform act relies on the descriptions of the events in Timothy Conlan, Margaret Wrightson, and David Beam, *Taxing Choices: The Politics of Tax Reform* (Washington: CQ Press, 1990); and in Jeffrey Birnbaum and Alan Murray, *Showdown at Gucci Gulch* (New York: Random House, 1987).

from tax reform as a way to balance the budget, and concentrated on problems of fairness and efficiency in the tax system. In any event, regardless of the conceptions of problems that brought people to the issue, there was a widespread sense that the country had some serious tax problems.

As to the policy stream, a lot of prior work had been done. Various economic analysts had spent years developing proposals for tax reform. These ideas included proposals for a "flat tax," which would reduce opportunities for deductions in return for a single and lower flat tax rate on incomes. Its advocates even argued that a flat tax would be less regressive than the current hodgepodge of deductions and tax expenditures. Many other ideas were in the works among the specialists who studied the incidence and consequences of the tax system. Among the actors we have labelled "policy entrepreneurs," Senator Bill Bradley (D-NJ) had made tax reform a major project for several years, and had introduced a comprehensive package of reforms in 1982 which he called a "Fair Tax," co-sponsored by Representative Richard Gephardt (D-MO). On the Republican side, Representative Jack Kemp (R-NY) had introduced reform bills as well, co-sponsored first by Senator William Roth (R-DE) and then by Senator Robert Kasten (R-WI).

A lot of what we have called "softening up" had gone on for some years—developing proposals, generating public discussion about the inequities and inefficiencies of the tax system, introducing bills, holding hearings, making speeches, and writing books and articles. Despite the remaining differences among the various plans, this softening-up process had produced some central agreements on the desirable approaches. Most advocates of reform came to favor a broadening of the income tax base, which would include eliminating or lessening the impact of many deductions and making more sources of income subject to taxation. To accompany this broadened base, tax rates would be reduced and both the rate structure and the system of deductions, credits, and exemptions would be simplified. All of this would take place within the constraint of revenue neutrality. Again, despite remaining differences, all of the approaches devised by the specialists and by the entrepreneurs were connected to the goals of greater simplification, fairness/equity, and efficiency.

In this sequence of events, President Reagan's administration actually came to the issue quite late, in 1984–85. President Reagan himself seemed most interested in driving down individual income tax rates, and the prospect of cutting the top marginal tax rate in half during his administration appealed mightily to him. Electorally, strategists in his administration were concerned that the Democrats would make an issue of tax reform in the 1984 campaign, and wanted to counter with something of their own. Then after the 1984 election, they hoped that Republican tax reform would cement a long-awaited partisan realignment.

So after a public flourish of announcement of President Reagan's intentions, Secretary of the Treasury Donald Regan and a very small set of experts at Treasury labored secretly through most of 1984 on a reform proposal. The result, dubbed "Treasury I," eliminated many deductions, reduced the number of tax brackets, and lowered tax rates. It was an economist's dream of simplification, equity, and efficiency. Unfortunately from a partisan point of view, it also gored the oxes of a lot of Republican constituencies, which sent up red flags in the White House staff, particularly with the Chief of Staff, James Baker. After the dramatic switch in jobs in early 1985, in which Regan became White House Chief of Staff and Baker became Secretary of the Treasury, Baker and his new team produced "Treasury II," which was not quite so pure and more politically palatable. Both Treasury I and Treasury II, while different from each other and from Bradley-Gephardt and Kemp-Kasten in many important particulars, still shared the general approaches of broadening the tax base, reducing marginal rates, and simplifying the tax code, and shared the general goals of greater equity and efficiency.

By the mid-1980s, then, all three streams—politics, problems, and policies—were positioned to join. Politics involved taxpayer anger over what people saw as high taxes and the unfairness of the rich profiting from loopholes. Problems included concern over the budget and over the greater and greater price the country was paying in efficiency and equity from the incremental complications of the tax code. And importantly, the evolution of proposals in the policy stream had reached the point of significant agreement at least on general approaches and even on important specifics. If our theory is right, the situation of confluence among the three streams should make it likely that the issue gets on a decision agenda, not simply a governmental agenda, and that major legislation actually is passed.

Indeed, Congress did crank up an impressive process of hearings, committee meetings, and coalition-building, and did pass the Tax Reform Act of 1986. But despite our quoting good odds for that outcome, based on our theory, nothing about passage was automatic. Indeed, tax reform was declared dead by knowledgeable observers at several points along the way, only to rise from its deathbed and struggle on toward passage. Authoritative descriptions of the events are filled with the despair of reform advocates at several points along the way, exultation of the opponents, glee of the lobbyists who thought their special provisions in the tax code were exempted from change, unravelling of coalitions behind reform, and eleventh-hour rescues by the two committee chairs, Daniel Rostenkowski (D-IL) of the House Ways and Means Committee and Robert Packwood (R-OR) of the Senate Finance Committee. That perilous run down the rapids of reform, with sharp rocks standing ready to wreck the fragile vessel at every turn, reminds us of the fluidity and unpredictability of the process and prompts us to be satisfied with probability rather than certainty in our predictions, explanations, and understandings.

This sequence of events also provides an occasion for reflecting on what models of the policy process do *not* work well. Savvy insiders predicted the demise of tax reform, first, because they depended on a model of interest group pressure. Think of the phalanxes of special interests lined up to undo reform in the name of perfecting it, driven by the imperative of protecting their tax preferences. A pressure group model would surely predict the wreck of tax reform, but it turned out to be wrong. A second commonly-held model of policy processes, incrementalism, would have argued that change takes place piece-by-piece, incrementally, not in large leaps. This ultimately successful effort was clearly aimed at effecting an ambitious, non-incremental change. A third model, majoritarian politics of a partisan sort, also fell short, because the coalitions cut across party lines and formed and re-formed in a much more fluid way than a party model would lead one to expect. A fourth model, the power of ideas, had some resonance, since the economists and lawyers who hatched the original proposals and consulted with the leading policy entrepreneurs reasoned through their proposals and arrived at quite a high degree of consensus about what should be done. Still, ideas themselves were not enough to drive the process. Ideas in the policy stream needed to be combined with events in the politics stream, much as the drive for deregulation which we have recounted earlier in this book combined ideas about natural monopoly and the inefficiencies of regulation with the political impulse to "get government off our backs." It turns out that the model presented in this book, which stresses the confluence of separate streams of problems, policies, and politics at critical junctures, facilitated by entrepreneurs alert to the prospects of coupling divergent forces, helps us quite a lot in understanding these events. This model also does noticeably better than several plausible alternative models.[4]

This understanding of agenda setting and policy formation also points to some intriguing twists on usual ways of thinking about policy-making. The process by which policies were coupled with problems and politics in this case study turns out to be fascinating. The politics of the issue, readers will recall, concentrated mostly on tax reduction, and only to some extent on tax reform. But once the window was opened, a lot of other alternatives became viable as well. The final bill did reduce taxes some, but in conformity with both the administration's and Senator Bradley's approaches, the entire set of discussions and bargains was premised on the notion that the bill would be "revenue neutral," that it would neither raise nor lower federal revenues. So every tax reduction had to be matched with a closed loophole or a tax increase somewhere else. In general terms, the final package did eliminate or reduce a number of tax preferences on both individual and corporate returns and reduced individual tax rates, and when it lost revenue from the individual side, it raised revenue from the corporate side.

The important thing to notice is that the bill's provisions came from the policy community and from the workings of the policy stream, which had emphasized tax simplification, lessening loopholes, and greater equity and efficiency. Advocates for those goals managed to hook their proposals to the political stream's anger over taxes, even though the final reform act was only partially related to that anger. Pressure for tax *reduction* was converted into legislation on tax *reform*. Once the policy window opened in the mid-1980s, the tax package became a giant garbage can, to use the language of this book. Many proposals were considered, the consensus that had developed in the policy stream

---

[4]Conlon, et al, *Ibid.,* Chapter 9, discuss various alternative models that might be applied to this case, and find each of them incomplete or wanting. They also refer explicitly (p. 15) to the usefulness of the model presented in this book.

around tax simplification and equity held particular sway, and the outcome was only an inexact response to the politics and problems streams.

The concepts developed in the first edition of this book help us to understand two major features of this case study. First, we can see why the agenda changed, and why ambitious reform became possible. The three streams all came together at that time, which made this sort of action quite likely. Second, the theory alerts us to the couplings that can take place. Enacted proposals don't always respond exactly to the perceived problems or to the content of political events. In this case, government did not simply respond to taxpayer anger by lowering taxes, or to the problem of the deficit by raising revenue. Instead, the policy stream had produced a rough consensus on the shape that tax reform should take, centered on simplification and equity, and entrepreneurs in that stream used the opportunity presented by the politics and problems to push for and eventually adopt their proposals.

Health Care Reform during the Clinton Administration in 1993

Taxes aren't the only hardy perennials; health care is too.[5] Serious proposals for comprehensive national health insurance in the United States go back past Medicare, past Harry Truman, past the New Deal, at least to Teddy Roosevelt. We started this book with a case study about one of the many times that people really thought they would act on it but didn't, national health insurance in the Carter administration years. The issue heated up again at the beginning of the Clinton administration.

In this case, the governmental agenda was problem-driven. To return to the "big three" concerns that health policy specialists have—cost, access, and quality—few people had serious qualms about quality, but they were very much concerned about the other two.[6] Cost of health care had been rising sharply ever since the late 1960s. Both cost to government (with Medicare and Medicaid particularly) and cost of health care in general far out-paced the rise in the cost of living. The consequences were clear: major constraints on the rest of the federal government's budget, serious financial problems for state governments, major dislocations in the economy at large, big trouble over fringe benefits at bargaining tables across the country, and real concern about whether health care was absorbing more than its share of both government and private expenditures.

But cost was not the only problem. Uneven access to health care, high-quality though it was, also was recognized as a serious problem. During the early 1990s, the figure of 37 million Americans without health insurance was drummed into the national consciousness by media stories about the relevant studies. The problem of gaps in insurance coverage was exacerbated by unemployment during the stubborn recession at that same time, so that people were

[5]The descriptions of the events in this case are drawn from contemporary press accounts and from several conversations with people involved in and knowledgeable about those events.

[6]The "big three" categories are discussed above, pp. 119-120.

losing their insurance by being thrown out of work or by changing jobs. The insurance industry itself, grappling with its own cost problems, had also started practices like experience rating and denying insurance for pre-existing conditions, which made it impossible or very costly for other individuals to obtain insurance. Hospitals were shifting the cost of charity care to patients with insurance. Congressional hearings and the mass media were filled with heart-rending accounts of people unable to obtain the care they needed, obtaining that care too late, or being faced with horrendous bills without insurance.

Different observers came to different opinions about whether cost or access was "the" problem. But it did seem as though there were enough problems out there to prompt government officials to pay attention to health care. So the problem stream produced a place on the governmental agenda.

The political stream was not as clear. On the one hand, attention to the problems which I just discussed produced a political incentive to attend to health care. One of the signal events that prompted politicians to sit up and take notice was the 1991 election of Democratic Senator Harris Wofford in Pennsylvania. Wofford had been appointed to replace John Heinz, a Republican incumbent who was killed in a plane crash in April. Wofford faced a very stiff Republican challenge in a November special election from former governor and U.S. attorney general Dick Thornburgh. Many observers attributed Wofford's victory in the special election to his campaign ads portrayed him looking straight into the camera and saying, "If criminals have the right to a lawyer, I think working Americans should have the right to a doctor." Bill Clinton took a page out of that campaign, making health care reform a major theme in 1992.

But the politics weren't all on the side of action. For one thing, the taxpayer revolt which we discussed above put a major damper on any new expensive federal programs. Second, since most Americans did have health insurance, it was unclear to them how they would benefit from reform. They also were suspicious of government initiatives, partly as a result of a generalized cynicism about government that had been spreading through the body politic since the mid-1960s. Third, the infighting among interest groups in this area is especially fierce. Politicians don't take on health care issues without running a serious risk of crossing such powerful interests as the insurance industry, physicians, hospitals, labor unions, small business, and big business, each with very well-organized lobbies and well-placed constituencies. In trying to build a program in that interest group environment, it's quite easy to step into quicksand and pay a hefty electoral price.

On the other hand, most interest groups agreed by the late 1980s that something should be done. Big business in particular seemed increasingly interested in reform. So the political stream at least tolerated action.

In the early 1990s, however, the policy stream was in disarray. There remained sharp, fundamental differences about which approach to take, even among vigorous advocates of reform. Some of those advocates preferred a single-payer national health insurance system, in which the government would be the only health insurer for the entire population. They reasoned that such a system, patterned after the programs in many Western European countries and

Canada, would be the only effective way to guarantee access to all and to get a grip on rising cost.

A second group of advocates preferred "managed competition." For some years, a group of analysts, businessmen, insurance executives, and providers had been meeting in Jackson Hole, Wyoming at the home of Paul Ellwood—the same Paul Ellwood who was the leading policy entrepreneur in the case of Health Maintenance Organizations which we described in Chapter 1. The Jackson Hole group, the most prominent of the managed competition advocates, proposed a system in which large organizations of consumers—employers and individuals—would band together to purchase health care plans from providers, most of whom would be organized into HMOs or HMO-like entities. They believed that such a system would regulate costs by competition among providers seeking the business of the organizations of consumers, and would provide universal access by including those currently not insured in the purchasing alliances. This system would base most insurance on employer plans, as the current system does, rather than replacing employer-based insurance with a government program.

Yet a third approach still in play provided for more incremental changes in current arrangements than the first two approaches. Some renditions of this approach would require or encourage individuals to purchase specified types of insurance, and provide those who could not afford insurance with government vouchers (or reimbursements or payments) that they could then use in the regular medical care market. A different approach would extend Medicare to the uninsured, but not to the entire population.

For each approach, there were also hybrids under active consideration. There was a lively dispute, for instance, between those who wished to combine managed competition with cost regulation in the form of premium caps or global budgets and those who wished to leave cost containment strictly to the forces of market competition. So there was a welter of plans under active consideration, some toward the government regulation end of the spectrum, others toward the market competition end, some fairly pure forms of the three approaches and others mixed forms.

It is important to emphasize that these approaches each were preferred by advocates of change, not opponents. In other words, there were sharp, fundamental differences among advocates, and no consensus in the policy community about which proposal to support. This was quite unlike the case of airline deregulation at the beginning of the Carter administration, for instance, when advocates in Congress and elsewhere had already ironed out their differences and agreed on a plan. In that case, which we described in Chapter 1, the proposal was ready to go when Carter took office, and his administration simply appropriated it as their own. At the beginning of the Clinton administration, there was no such consensus among advocates about the shape of a national health care plan. There wasn't even as much consensus as had developed about general approaches to tax reform in advance of the 1986 act, which was described in the previous case study.

If the theory presented in this book is right, that situation should have placed health care prominently on the governmental agenda in 1993, because of the general agreement on the urgency of the problems. But its place on a decision agenda would be expected to depend on a greater consensus in the policy stream, at least on a general approach to a new reform proposal. Absent that consensus, one would have expected a lot of governmental attention to health care, but not a lot of concrete action, and not a positioning on a decision agenda. As of President Clinton's inauguration in January of 1993, that's about where things stood.

At the beginning of his administration, Clinton named his wife, Hillary Rodham Clinton, to head a task force on health care. That task force, made up of administration appointees, high-level career bureaucrats, congressional staffers, and specialists from outside the government, was to develop the administration's proposal, and in the process, try to forge a consensus among the advocates of reform. Naming Mrs. Clinton, who was not previously known as a specialist on health care issues, was a particularly high-stakes move. It signalled unmistakably the priority the administration placed on the issue, the investment of prestige and credit they were making, the political cost if the effort were to fail, and the gain if it were to succeed. It put the issue right up front.

As of this writing at the end of 1993, the task force had completed its work and the administration had unveiled its proposal. Health care under the administration's plan would be an amalgam of various approaches, would keep Medicare intact, but would mainly be employer-based. All Americans and legal residents would be guaranteed a standard benefits package, regardless of age, pre-existing conditions, income, or employment status. Employers would be required to offer their employees and their families health insurance with the minimum package of benefits, with employers paying 80 percent and employees paying 20 percent of the premiums. The proposal counted on major cost savings by relying on competition among providers for the business of large regional purchasing alliances made up of employers and consumers, by realizing savings in Medicare, and by streamlining the administration of health insurance, for example by providing one set of forms and reimbursement procedures for all insurers. As a backup, providers would be required to live within a budget, mandated by caps on increases in insurance premiums pegged to inflation. Unemployed and poor people would also get insurance, and small businesses' costs would be capped as a percentage of payroll. These provisions for low-income individuals and small businesses would be paid for partly by the savings produced by competition among providers and the changes in administration and in Medicare, and partly by new taxes on cigarettes and alcohol. While the federal government would require universal access, standard benefits, and cost control, the states would be left free to run programs within their borders in a variety of ways. This flexibility for states could conceivably provide a way to finesse the fundamental disagreement between single-payer and managed competition advocates: Some states could adopt one, other states could adopt the other, and still others could devise mixtures or alternative arrangements.

As of the end of 1993, it was not clear that this proposal would be enough to bring the policy stream on line and move the issue to the decision agenda. One possibility was that the Clinton plan would be seen as an overly complicated, ambitious, and untested approach, and would be subjected to a withering attack from small business, insurance, and other opponents from which it would never recover. Another plausible scenario had it that the country would basically go for an employer-based system, perhaps with some version of purchasing alliances, but without some of the mandatory features of the Clinton plan. One subplot in that story speculated that President Clinton would even bend in his insistence on universal coverage, possibly under the guise of a phase-in scheme, in order to get a bill passed. Another speculation was that despite all the work at developing a plan and trying to develop a consensus, the bundle would unravel because of continued disagreement over the fundamental approach, and nothing major would happen. The most that might pass in this story would be some incremental adjustments in the regulation of current private health insurance, and possibly some extensions of current government programs. But there was a good chance that nothing would happen at all, given the potential for fierce opposition and the dim prospects for negotiating an agreement even on a scaled-back plan. Several other scenarios were possible, and the situation seemed highly fluid as we entered 1994.

The concepts presented in this book, while not providing a hard-and-fast prediction about the outcome in this case, still identify some of the major forces at work, and show which of those forces prompt higher agenda status and which still need to be brought into line to move the issue farther forward. In short, in 1993 the problems were recognized, the politics at least tolerated action, but the hang-up was the policy stream. A prominent place on the governmental agenda was therefore assured, a policy window was open, but movement onto the decision agenda and eventual enactment depended on a process of consensus-building among the advocates and specialists around a particular package of policies. Such consensus is better built before the window opens, however, and the opportunity may have passed before agreement could be reached.

What the New Case Studies Tell Us

This is not the place to re-state the theory developed in the body of this book. We have already done that in Chapter 9. But these case studies of the Reagan budget, the 1986 tax reform act, and the Clinton health care initiative tell us that our concepts work quite well in helping us to understand and explain events beyond those that were originally studied in the 1970s. Not only are these three cases drawn from the 1980s and 1990s, but they also go beyond the areas of health and transportation that formed the empirical base of the original study. Thus it seems that we have quite a useful general theory of agenda setting, alternative specification, and policy making.

THOUGHTS ABOUT THE MODELING

The passage of the time since 1984, when this book first appeared, has allowed me to reflect on the concepts which were developed in the first edition, and has allowed many readers of the book to comment in print and in person. I use this last section of this chapter to present some thoughts about those concepts and about the general modeling enterprise involved.

Elements of Structure

The processes described in this book are portrayed as highly fluid. The formation of policy agendas and the determination of the alternatives from which final choices are made are not tidy and tight. Neither scholars nor practitioners are able to predict with great certainty what will happen, and often find themselves surprised. They find that the best they can do is to quote odds, sometimes quite reliably and sometimes less so.

This fluidity has led some readers of this book to conclude that the processes are essentially random, that the separate streams that run through the system are joined fortuitously, and that the results come about by sheer dumb luck.[7] That conclusion does not correspond with the argument I have presented, and misstates the way the processes actually work. As pointed out at the end of Chapter 9, there is actually quite a bit of structure in the process.[8] I discuss there the structures within each of the streams, structures by which the streams are joined, and general constraints on the system.

In my view, the model developed in this book is structured, but there also is room for residual randomness, as is true of the real world. But it is not true that the model developed in this book portrays the processes as essentially fortuitous or random. For instance, none of the following factors are random: which participants are invited to a meeting, which solutions are in the queue with what timing, whether a solution is available at the time that a problem is pressing, what makes some problems more pressing than others, which proposals survive in the policy primeval soup and which die away, and which proposals get joined to which problems. I could cite several additional examples. The point is that neither the dynamics within each stream nor the connections among the streams are essentially fortuitous or random. Everything cannot be connected with everything else.

---

[7]For a wide-ranging and thoughtful critique of the modeling used in this book, which covers randomness as well as several other issues, see Gary Mucciaroni, "The Garbage Can Model and the Study of Policy Making: A Critique," *Polity,* Vol. XXIV, No. 3 (Spring, 1992) pp. 459–482. I do not always agree with Mucciaroni, as is evident in these pages, but his article does state some conventional concerns about the garbage can model quite well.

[8]See above, pp. 206-208.

The processes are also constrained in a number of ways that have been discussed, which provides yet more structure. What we have called the national mood, and the more long-term content of the political culture and traditions, make some policies possible and other policies impossible. Budgets constrain outcomes, sometimes quite severely and at other times not as severely. The state of the economy sometimes allows for more expansive federal programs than at other times. Some groups and socio-economic classes have more political resources at their disposal than others, which introduces class and group biases into the system and which limits the possible alternatives and agenda items. So the model is constrained by many things. It is structured in the same sense that a river is fluid, but its banks usually restrict its movement. The process cannot flow just anywhere.

One reason that some readers find it difficult to appreciate the structure in something like the garbage can model is that its structure is not familiar. A Marxist-style class structure, for instance, or a bureaucratic hierarchy, or a constitutional order are all more familiar. But that doesn't mean that the sort of model developed in this book has no structure; it's just an unfamiliar and unorthodox sort of structure.

Some fascinating developments in contemporary theory-building about patterns in complexity have parallels to the garbage-can style of theorizing. Gabriel Almond and Steven Genco wrote some time ago that in order to capture a lot of political phenomena, we would have to think of them as clouds, not clocks; we would come to prefer fluid metaphors to mechanical ones.[9] As it happens, one of the major recent developments in the natural sciences, chaos theory, concentrates on just such fluid processes.[10] Hard-nosed scientists like physicists and mathematicians are modeling such processes as cloud formation, eddies and whirlpools, swirls of smoke rising, and patterns of turbulence left in the air behind planes and trucks. And in their telling, there *is* pattern in such phenomena, pattern that can be reduced to mathematical formulation.

In addition to chaos theory, scientists of various descriptions—physicists, biologists, chemists, computer scientists, economists, political scientists, psychologists—have been working on models of complexity and evolution which have intriguing similarities.[11] Scholars from all of these disciplines share an interest in trying to understand dynamic processes and in modeling changes in systems over time. It turns out that these diverse processes have a lot in com-

[9]Gabriel Almond and Stephen Genco, "Clouds, Clocks and the Study of Politics," *World Politics* 29 (1977): 489–522.

[10]For a popular treatment of chaos theory, see James Gleick, *Chaos: Making a New Science* (New York: Penguin, 1987). For textbook treatments, see Pierre Berge, Yves Pomeau, and Christian Vidal, *Order Within Chaos* (New York: Wiley, 1984); and Gregory Baker and J. P. Gollub, *Chaotic Dynamics: An Introduction* (New York: Cambridge University Press, 1990).

[11]For an excellent and readable treatment of these developments, see Mitchell Waldrop, *Complexity: The Emerging Science at the Edge of Order and Chaos* (New York: Simon and Schuster, 1992). Waldrop describes work which surrounds the Santa Fe Institute, which includes the work on complex adaptive systems done by John Holland.

mon, and that various models developed to understand them also look similar in many respects. In these "complex adaptive systems," as John Holland calls them, agents interact with one another as they continually adapt to changing environments and anticipate change as well, control is distributed rather than centralized, and there is continual Darwinian selection. These principles of evolution and adaptation are being applied in a strikingly wide variety of contexts and disciplines.

These theories of complexity, chaos theory, and the garbage can model share a number of properties, as I see it. First, they all find pattern and structure in very complicated, fluid, and seemingly unpredictable phenomena. One can even specify a mathematics to those patterns in some cases. The structures emerge from local rules, rather than being imposed from on high in some sense. Second, there is a residual randomness left after one identifies as much structure as one can, so that there is surprise and unpredictability. At various junctures in their development, these processes essentially call random numbers, sometimes with large effects and sometimes with small effects. Often random errors cancel each other or average out under the influence of natural selection, but sometimes they do not.

Third, these models are historically contingent. What happens at one time depends on what happened previously. It's not true that the flapping of a butterfly's wings determines subsequent weather patterns half-way around the globe, as one famous illustration of chaos theory would have it, because so many other things are going on at the same time. But system directions still depend heavily on initial conditions, and develop in different ways depending on which way they happen to start. If one can specify what the initial conditions in a process are, and if one has good information about those conditions, then one can predict outcomes more reliably than if one does not know of the initial conditions. To the extent that the initial choices are random, however, then there is an inherent unpredictability, except that once the system starts in one direction rather than another, it is unlikely to reverse itself and start down the path previously foregone.

Processes like agenda-setting do seem to be a bit unpredictable. Even savvy insiders are sometimes surprised by major developments. The reasons for this unpredictability can be found in the properties of these systems which I have just discussed. The choice of initial conditions may be random. There is a residual randomness in subsequent steps, even after one has accounted for as much structure as one can. Apart from randomness, the process of evolution involves continual adaptation to changing environmental conditions and continual anticipation by the agents as they adapt to each other, resulting in continual surprise and novelty. But none of this unpredictability implies that we are unable to model the processes rigorously or to understand a lot of what happens. Indeed, the experience of various kinds of contemporary theory-building about complexity and chaos argues quite to the contrary.

Another supposed source of randomness is sometimes alleged to be the importance of titanic individuals. "Great men" happen to come along and dominate events. But this concentration on individuals is uncomfortably idiosyncratic and neglects patterns in events. Our treatment of policy entrepreneurs in this book argues that much of the process is governed by large events and structures not under any individual's control. But entrepreneurs take advantage of those events and work within those structures, which is the way we include the importance of both individuals and structures. The quotation at the beginning of Chapter 8 which describes entrepreneurs as "surfers waiting for the big wave" summarizes the point beautifully. Individuals do not control waves, but can ride them. Individuals do not control events or structures, but can anticipate them and bend them to their purposes to some degree.

Perhaps the best way to state the matter of structure and randomness is as follows: within the structure we can specify in the model and observe in the real world, processes like agenda-setting and alternative specification retain a degree of randomness. There actually is a lot of complexity and fluidity in this real world, and a model of that world should capture that complexity. One reason that a probabilistic model, such as the model used in this book, is more satisfying than a deterministic one is its recognition of that residual randomness. In fact, I tried my best along the way to specify necessary and sufficient conditions and to figure out some tight laws of causation. I found that there were too many exceptions, and that the specifications got unduly complex. I concluded that we do better to quote odds.

Finally, some readers of this book have been concerned with the degree to which the model is empirically testable. I find it reassuring on that point to note that there are a number of plausible alternative models in the scholarly literature, each with intelligent and energetic adherents. I have discussed a number of them in this book, in Chapters 4 and 9.[12] These alternative models do not have the same properties as the garbage can model, and as we have seen, they don't work as well in a number of respects. The process doesn't seem incremental, for instance, or hierarchical, or tightly rational, or driven simply by power and pressure politics, or tracked into simple chronological stages. We have noticed, for example with our case study of the Tax Reform Act of 1986, that prominent and plausible alternative models don't seem to fit real events as well as the model developed in this book. But the presence of credible alternative models in the literature, and their applicability to some parts of the process if not to the whole process, indicates that the garbage can structure is not simply truistic or tautological.

Aside from strict testability, it is also heartening that many researchers and students have found this book interesting and useful, and that practitioners have found that these descriptions "ring true." In addition to testable propositions, this book provides useful categories, realistic descriptions of these phenomena, and concepts that help to understand and explain events. It seems productive in a number of respects to look at the policy world in roughly this way.

---

[12]In Chapter 9, see particularly pp. 205-206 above.

Sudden, Sharp Change

Chapter 6 of this book on the "Policy Primeval Soup" portrays the development of policy proposals as evolutionary, akin to biological natural selection. Long periods of gestation take place before proposals emerge from this policy stream. Ideas are floated, translated into proposals, discussed in various forums, revised and honed, and floated again. Gradually, some ideas that don't meet certain criteria for survival die away, and others prosper. This seems to be similar to a Darwinian, gradualistic evolutionary process. One virtue of picturing the process of proposal development this way is that we avoid an infinite regress. We focus on a more productive theoretical preoccupation: not on where ideas come from, but what makes them catch on and survive in certain communities at certain times.

But we have also noticed sudden, dramatic change. The indicators of change we have used often exhibit sharp spikes upward and sharp declines, rather than gradual incremental changes. The case studies show similar sudden and sometimes unanticipated changes. Even very knowledgeable insiders are sometimes surprised. Public policy changes in very large leaps, as in the New Deal of the 1930s, the Great Society of the mid-1960s, and the Reagan revolution of 1981. These spasms of reform are interspersed with periods of rest and stasis, as if the participants are exhausted from their exertion and catching their breath. But in any event, this does not look like Darwinian, gradualistic evolution.

It could be that different evolutionary models apply to different parts of the process. Development in the policy stream might well resemble the long process of natural selection, in which ideas are tried, revised, tried again, and gradually emerge to prominence or die away. But the agenda-setting process might be much less gradualistic, for reasons we have discussed in this book.

One major recent change in evolutionary theory has been the development of the concept of "punctuated equilibrium."[13] According to this concept, biological evolution has actually proceeded in fits and starts, and not as gradually as Darwin originally thought. Systems seem to settle into an equilibrium for a time, then suddenly change, then settle into a new equilibrium. There is no one stable equilibrium that these systems seek; rather, there are several possible equilibria, and systems lurch from one to another.

As Frank Baumgartner and Bryan Jones point out in their excellent discussion of the issue, agenda-setting looks like punctuated equilibrium.[14] As we have noticed in this book, subjects "hit" suddenly. Attention is focused first on this problem and then on that problem, but attention is fleeting. A policy window opens, the opportunity for action presents itself only for a short time, and then the window closes. The historical development of an issue proceeds in jumps and step-level changes, not in gradual and incremental fashion.

---

[13]Niles Eldredge and Stephen Jay Gould, "Punctuated Equilibria: An Alternative to Phyletic Gradualism," in Thomas Schopf, ed., *Models in Paleobiology* (San Francisco: Freeman Cooper, 1972).

[14]Frank Baumgartner and Bryan Jones, *Agendas and Instability in American Politics* (Chicago: University of Chicago Press, 1993), Chapter 1.

In my view, both gradualistic evolution and punctuated equilibrium seem to be at work in different parts of the process. The agenda changes suddenly and non-incrementally, which makes agenda-setting look like punctuated equilibrium. But the alternatives are developed gradually, and a more Darwinian concept of evolution may be useful to describe that part of the process. So we are able to solve the puzzle presented by sudden and substantial change, at the same time that "there is no new thing under the sun." Agenda change is there, but specialists gradually recombine familiar elements into new proposals. Gradual development in the policy stream, furthermore, is one of the reasons that entrepreneurs must work on their proposals over a long period of time, and not simply invent them instantaneously. When the window opens, it is too late to work up proposals from scratch; proposals must be ready long before that.[15]

To be a bit more conceptually adventuresome, perhaps these systems evolve or develop, and do not necessarily settle into equilibria at all. Perhaps continual change, not equilibrium, is the hallmark of agenda-setting. If that turns out to be a fruitful way of looking at these processes, then we need models that use alternatives to equilibrium-seeking as their core assumption. These models would emphasize development and adaptation, not inertia and stasis. The recent theoretical developments in complexity which I described above may herald quite a new way of thinking about events like those discussed in this book. These models of complex adaptive systems do not necessarily seek equilibrium. There is development, adaptation, and evolution, and in Holland's language, "perpetual novelty." Adaptation is the key to understanding these models, not equilibrium. And one of the attractive properties of these recent approaches is that they can be fully as rigorous and even as mathematical as much of our usual modeling.

The Independence of the Streams

The model developed in this book portrays largely independent streams of problems, policies, and politics running through the system. Each of these streams has a life of its own, and runs along without a lot of regard to happenings in the other streams. Proposals are hatched in the policy stream whether or not they are solving a given problem; politics has its own dynamics independent of the policy proposals being developed by specialists. Then the streams are joined at critical junctures, which are the times when the greatest agenda change occurs.

But how independent are these streams, actually? After all, people often do in fact try to "solve problems," which means that the problems and policy streams are connected. Or as I say in Chapter 6,[16] among the criteria by which some proposals survive and others fall by the wayside is the anticipation by

---

[15]In foreign policy, alternatives may be developed suddenly in crises. See Robert Durant and Paul Diehl, "Agendas, Alternatives, and Public Policy: Lessons from the U.S. Foreign Policy Arena," *Journal of Public Policy,* 1989, 9:179–205.

[16]See above, pp. 131-139.

policy specialists of likely events in the political stream, which indicates that the policy and political streams are related to some degree. Paul Sabatier's advocacy coalition framework is partly an attempt to see these streams, particularly the policy and political streams, as more closely related than I have portrayed them here.[17]

Even on reflection, I still think these streams flow along largely on their own, each according to dynamics not much related to the others, and that the critical event to understand is how these largely independent streams come together. First, as for connections between the problems and policy streams, participants surely do sometimes attempt to solve problems, and the development and the content of proposals are driven by their conceptions of the severity and type of the problem. But policy proposals are also developed for reasons other than to solve a given problem. Bureaucrats develop proposals to protect or expand their turf, for example; interest groups do so to promote their economic interests; people advance proposals to further their ideologies; and so forth. Furthermore, even when participants develop proposals to solve a given problem, it often is true that another problem comes to be pressing, and the proposal originally developed to solve Problem A is transported to solve Problem B. Mass transit is successively advanced to solve problems of traffic congestion, pollution, and energy consumption, for instance, or tax reform is substituted for tax reduction. If we were not to distinguish between the problems and policy streams, and recognize that they each have their own origins and dynamics, we would not be able to understand what happens in such cases and why various couplings are possible.

As to the policy and political streams, I still find it useful to portray them as independent of one another, but then sometimes joined. First, they are independent in the sense that they tend to involve different people. Policy communities are made up of specialists in particular areas, with detailed knowledge and technical expertise; political communities include elected politicians and those around them. Second, these different sets of people have different preoccupations. The policy community concentrates on matters like technical detail, cost-benefit analyses, gathering data, conducting studies, and honing proposals. The political people, by contrast, paint with a broad brush, are involved in many more issue areas than the policy people are, and concentrate on winning elections, promoting parties, and mobilizing support in the larger polity. There is even some distrust between the two types of participants. Policy people often see politics as screwing up their work and neglecting the "merits" of an issue; politicians see policy people as insufficiently interested in pragmatic electoral and legislative realities.

[17]See Paul Sabatier, "Policy Change over a Decade or More," in Paul Sabatier and Hank Jenkins-Smith, eds., *Policy Change and Learning: An Advocacy Coalition Approach* (Boulder: Westview Press, 1993); and Paul Sabatier, "An Advocacy Coalition Framework of Policy Change and the Role of Policy-Oriented Learning Therein," *Policy Sciences* 21 (1988): 129–168.

These are not completely hard-and-fast distinctions. Politicians often traffic in the world of ideas and become immersed in policy detail; and policy specialists often plan campaign and legislative strategy along with the politicians. But in the main, I have observed differences. The two streams involve different people with different backgrounds and training, different orientations, and different preoccupations. And the signal events in the two streams are different. With politics, those events are elections, mass movements, party realignments, and the like; with policy specialists, they are more likely to involve important conferences, visible studies, a new and unexpected position taken by a prominent expert, congressional hearings staged by staffers, and analysis papers with conceptual breakthroughs.

But we do need to understand how independent streams become joined. In this book, I have portrayed them as joining during the times of open policy windows. I think that one amendment to that formulation is reasonable: There are some links between these streams at times other than the open windows and the final couplings. Policy entrepreneurs anticipate political constraints as they develop proposals, for instance, or politicians seek the counsel of policy specialists as they work up campaign themes. Couplings are attempted often, and not just close to the time of final enactment. But the independence of the streams is still noticeable in the real world, and postulating that independence in building theories still has its uses. I continue to like the phrase "loosely coupled" to describe these sorts of systems.

The Importance of Institutions

Various versions of the "new institutionalism" have been prominent in political science over the last couple of decades.[18] The notion is that government is not simply pushed and pulled around by societal or economic forces, but has its own autonomy. Government isn't simply the product of the class structure, for instance, or the handmaiden of public opinion or pressure groups. In this telling, institutions, constitutions, procedures, governmental structures, and government officials themselves affect the political, social, and economic systems as much as the other way around. One need not assume that the state is some sort of reified unitary actor to appreciate the importance of governmental actors and institutions themselves in the setting of policy agendas.

We have noticed a number of manifestations of this importance of institutions in the case studies. Adoption of the Reagan budget in 1981 depended critically on the reconcilation procedure, for instance. The tax reform of 1986 would not have been possible without an ability to hold some bargaining sessions in secret and the availability of restrictive floor rules. To add to these examples, Frank Baumgartner and Bryan Jones note that there are many different institutional "venues" in which policy advocates can push their proposals.[19]

---

[18]For a review essay, see James March and Johan Olsen, "The New Institutionalism: Organizational Factors in Political Life," *American Political Science Review,* 78 (1984): 734–749.

[19]See Baumgartner and Jones, *op. cit.*

Some of these venues are niches in the federal government, but many of them are in the states and localities. The institutional feature of federalism complicates an analysis of agenda-setting, because there are multiple agendas possible for the same subject matter at a given time. But federalism also enhances possibilities for innovation—if a new idea isn't possible in one venue, it might be possible in another, and entrepreneurs can shop for the most favorable venue.

The importance of institutional arrangements and government autonomy puts a distinctive slant on agenda-setting. In one early and influential picture of agendas, Roger Cobb and Charles Elder postulate that there is a "systemic" agenda in the public and a "formal" or governmental agenda.[20] Agenda-setting in this view is a process in which items start in the public, in the systemic agenda, and move to government. That might well be the way the process works some of the time. But the notion that government is at least somewhat autonomous alerts us to the possibility that a governmental agenda might not simply be composed of items previously on a systemic agenda. Instead, government might generate its own agenda through its own processes, and its interaction with the public might involve mobilizing support, rather than reacting to public opinion, interest groups, or social movements.

Institutions at least constitute important constraints on policy-making. Governmental forms and procedural requirements make some outcomes possible and other outcomes unlikely. Furthermore, models that concentrate on governmental responsiveness to political, social, or economic forces might be quite incomplete. Government structures and governmental actors might be sufficiently autonomous that they both act on their own and affect their environment as much as they are affected by it. Actually, examples of both state autonomy and the state as a reflection of society can be found in cases of agenda setting. Scholars need to avoid opting for one or the other view, and to do more work on specifying the conditions under which and the ways in which policy making works from the top down or the bottom up.

Policy Formation

The processes by which public policies are formed are exceedingly complex. Agenda-setting, the development of alternatives, and choices among those alternatives seem to be governed by different forces. Each of them is complicated by itself, and the relations among them add more complications. These processes are dynamic, fluid, and loosely joined.

This book tries to weave a rich tapestry of some of this world, in which the details are laid bare at the same time that the larger picture is clarified. I hope that readers find that tapestry both interesting and useful, that the book furthers our understanding of these important phenomena, and that it continues to do so a decade and more after it first appeared in print.

---

[20]Roger Cobb and Charles Elder, *Participation in American Politics: The Dynamics of Agenda-Building* (Boston: Allyn and Bacon, 1972).

Appendix on Methods

Aristotle could have avoided the mistake of thinking that women have fewer teeth than men by the simple device of asking Mrs. Aristotle to open her mouth.

—Bertrand Russell

This research employed several methods, including interviews with federal government officials and those close to them; case studies of policy initiation and noninitiation; examination of such publicly available records of the agenda as congressional committee hearings and reports, presidential addresses, party platforms, and reporting of issues in the press; and public opinion surveys. The two major sources, however, were the interviews and the case studies.

I chose to concentrate on two federal policy areas, health and transportation. I studied more than one policy domain to insure that generalizations about policy processes would not be due to the idiosyncracies of one case or policy area, and to open up new avenues for theory building by observing contrasts. I decided not to examine more than two areas primarily because the researcher needs to be somewhat conversant with the substantive issues involved in the areas under study, and spreading oneself too thin would be a real danger.

Three criteria—breadth, change, and contrast—guided the choice of the policy areas. First, they should be sufficiently broad in scope that various items could flow on and off the agenda. If we were to narrow our attention to a given case study or even a set of them, such as the start of Health Maintenance Organizations or the passage of airline regulatory reform, we could develop an understanding of the rise and fall of these particular issues on the agenda, but we would not know whether the generalizations would apply to other cases. We would also have little sense of how these items compete with others for the attention of important policy makers. But this study centered precisely on that competition. Agenda setting is a selection process, after all, by which people in and around government implicitly attend to some subjects in the population of potential agenda items rather than others. Health and transportation were suffi-ciently broad domains that potential agenda items could be observed to flow on and off the agenda, competing with one another at given points in time. Also, within domains as broad as health or transportation, varieties of issues can po-tentially surface. So there are some regulatory, some distributive, and some re-distributive issues in the study; some new and some routine; some with large budgetary impacts and others with small; and so forth.

The second criterion required some potential for change during the period of observation. We were likely to learn more from a panel study if items rose and fell on the agenda than if items remained stable. Health and transportation were sufficiently dynamic, having some potential for change during the years I con-ducted the interviews.

Third, these two areas were selected because they exhibited some substan-tively interesting contrasts. With few exceptions, they are in different depart-ments and different congressional committee jurisdictions, so outcomes are not affected solely by the same personnel or organizations. The two areas are sub-stantively different: Health deals with social services, social welfare, and social insurance, while transportation deals heavily with the world of commerce, fi-nance, and the economy. While that distinction is not iron-clad, the two areas do seem to have different substantive centers of gravity, greater than would be evident in a comparison of health and welfare or a comparison of transportation and communications. There is good reason to characterize health as being more ideological in content and more partisan in its politics than transportation. Health also has a larger budget and a much larger recent inflation in expendi-tures than transportation, particularly due to the expansion of such entitlements as Medicare and Medicaid. Finally, the interest group structure seems more fragmented, particularly by mode, in transportation than in health. Rail is quite a different world from air, for instance, but the American Medical Association and other health-related interest groups carry across most of that area.

Thus the domains of health and transportation provided the advantages needed for the research—breadth, change, and contrast. Of course, other do-mains might be equally as interesting, and, in strict terms, one cannot be en-tirely confident that generalizations apply to other domains. But these areas serve my purposes well, and the ideas derived from a study of them should be interesting well beyond the confines of health and transportation policy.

THE INTERVIEWS

I conducted four waves of interviews with people in Washington, all involved with health or transportation, during the summers of 1976, 1977, 1978, and 1979. I conducted 247 interviews over the four years, 133 in health and 114 in transportation. Twenty-one percent of the interviews were with congressional staff, either committee staff or people in such staff agencies as the Office of Technology Assessment and the Congressional Budget Office. Thirty-four per-cent of the interviews were with respondents in the executive branch, including

Table A-1

Numbers of Interviews, by Year and Policy Area

	1976	1977	1978	1979	Total
Health	40	36	33	24	133
Transportation	28	32	31	23	114
n	68	68	64	47	247

upper-level civil servants, political appointees in departments and bureaus, presidential staff, and regulatory agency people. The remaining 45 percent of the interviews were with people outside of government, including lobbyists, journalists who wrote on health or transportation, consultants, academics, and researchers. Many respondents carried over from one year to the next; others were replacements. The interviews proved to be extremely rich in perspectives on the processes I was studying, in information on the substantive policy issues in health and transportation, and in a blend of general reflections on policy making combined with technical detail. They usually lasted nearly an hour, rarely under a half hour, sometimes up to two hours.

Respondents were chosen by two methods. First, I identified certain key positions, such as staff members on the major congressional committees of jurisdiction, career civil servants close to top-level political appointees in the relevant departments, and representatives of obviously important interest groups. Second, I used a snowballing technique by which respondents were asked to identify others I should see, and the sample was thus expanded: My aim was to reach important, influential people in the policy communities of health and transportation, or people in close contact with top decision makers who could serve as knowledgeable informants for me, not necessarily as respondents. In other words, they were important to me not necessarily because they themselves were the decision makers, although many of them certainly were, but because they could inform me about the events and the perspectives of people in the key locations. Thus I fairly often aimed for people who were in close contact with key decision makers, but were not the decision makers themselves. I also wanted to obtain a reasonable coverage within the communities of health and transportation: congressional as well as executive branch respondents; nongovernmental as well as governmental people; informants with various perspectives, self-interests, and attitudes. This sort of selection seemed more appropriate to my purposes than some statistical sampling procedure. The number of interviews by year and policy area is presented in Table A-1. The distribution of the interviews across locations in the policy system is presented in Table A-2.

Since this was a panel study, I attempted to follow the same respondents in the same positions through the four years. While there was substantial continuity, two kinds of change were inevitable: replacement and musical chairs.

Table A-2
Distribution of Interviews by Position

Position	Position at time of interview	Either current or former position
Hill staff, either committee staff or staff agency	21%	29%
Executive Office of President staff and political appointees in departments	10	15
Civil servants in departments and bureaus	24	38
Interest groups	17	17
Journalists	10	10
Researchers, academics, and consultants	18	22
Total %	100%	131%*
n	247	247

*Total percent in column two is greater than 100% because some respondents were counted twice. For example, while 24% of the interviews were held with current civil servants in departments and bureaus, 38% were held with people who had been departmental civil servants either currently or at some time in the recent past. The figure is the percentage of 247.

When people dropped out of the sample completely from one year to the next, I attempted to replace them with their rough equivalent in position. As to magnitude, 21 of the 68 respondents in the second year were not in the first year's sample, due primarily to the change of administration. Then 8 of the 64 respondents in the third year were not in either the first or second year. None of the fourth-year respondents were new. In addition to replacement, some stayed in the sample but shifted positions from one year to another—the musical chairs change. Of those interviewed more than once, 22 percent changed positions at some point during the four years of the study.

The smaller number of interviews in 1979, due to lack of replacement, could potentially affect comparisons across the years. But first, there was little shift in the distribution of respondents across positions. Similar proportions of the sample in 1979 were from the Hill, downtown, and outside of government, even though the sample was smaller. Second, I picked the sharpest changes in both policy areas between 1978 and 1979 for the complete samples, took a subset of respondents who had been in both the 1978 and 1979 samples, ran the same tables for this subset, and then compared the tables for this subset of respondents who had been in both years to the tables for the whole samples. The result in each case was that there was virtually no difference between the complete sample and the subset that had been in both years. Thus the shifts in agenda status that occurred between 1978 and 1979 were not due to the change in the composition or the size of the sample.

Figure A-1

Interview Questions

1. What major problems are you and others in the health (transportation) area most occupied with these days?
   a. Have you listed them roughly in order of importance?
   b. Has there been much change during the last year in the problems that those concerned with health (transportation) are paying attention to? If yes, why has that change take place?
2. Why do you think these particular problems are the ones that receiving attention—how did they come to be the hot issues?
3. Let me shift now, and ask you not about problems, but rather about programs. What are you and other people in the health (transportation) area currently working on, in the way of new approaches or new programs—what's on the front bumer?
   a. Have you listed them roughly in order of priority?
   b. Has there been much change during the last year in the proposals that those concerned with health (transportation) are working on? If yes, why has that change taken place?
4. Why do you think these particular initiatives are being serious considered—how did they come to be the hot proposals?
5. If you were to look down the road a bit, which problems and proposals for government programs in the area of health (transportation) do you think will be prominent, say, two years from now and five years from now?
6. I want to ask you about some specific things. (Note: At this point in the interview, I had a list of items prepared that varied from one year to the next. The list included developments during the previous year that I had followed in the press and wanted to learn more about, and items that could have received attention but apparently had not. To the extent that time permitted, I asked about each item that had not yet been discussed and that I thought the respondent would know about.)
7. Is there anything else that you think I might be interested in?

   The interviews were designed to track the content of the agenda and seriously considered alternatives over time, and to explore explanations for the placement of items on the agenda or the prominence or lack of prominence of possible alternatives. The interview included questions about which problems occupied the respondent and others in the policy area, why they were occupied with these problems, why some problems (named by me) that could have occupied them were not the focus of attention, which proposals or alternatives were currently on the front burner and why, and why some proposals (again named by me) were not under serious consideration. Figure A-1 contains the wording of the questions. I always asked Question 1 as it appears in Figure A-1. Answers to that question were generally quite full, giving not only the prominent subjects on the agenda but also much of the information called for in Questions 1a through 6. So I would ask the other questions in Figure A-1 only as they were needed. The order they were asked varied according to the flow of the conversation and where they could be most gracefully introduced. I also felt free to insert other questions, probes, comments, and exchanges with respondents as appropriate.

As I went back to such involved people year after year, I compared one year to the next, and could trace the dynamics of attention to agenda items and alternatives. If a problem or proposal was prominent in one year's interviews but not in the next, I ascertained why it fell by the wayside. If a new problem or idea had come to the fore within the year, I asked where it came from and why it was currently being seriously considered. I conducted all interviews myself, assured respondents that nothing they said would be for attribution, and took notes rather than taping. All 1976 and 1977 interviews were in person. In 1978 and 1979, I conducted interviews with those I had seen before by long-distance telephone.

The interviews yielded several kinds of useful information. First, they could be coded to describe the agenda at a given point in time, and then could be used to trace the rise and fall of items on the agenda. Trucking deregulation could be shown as having been discussed much more seriously by my transportation respondents in 1979 than in 1978, for instance, and the attention of health respondents to the subject of Professional Standards Review Organizations could be shown to have declined gradually over the four years. Because the measurements were taken independently in each of the four years in a panel design, I was not obliged to depend on the recall of participants, which occasionally is faulty. Several transportation respondents in 1979, for instance, with the tremendous growth in mentions of energy prompted by the spring gas lines, stoutly maintained that they had been working on the problem all along. They may well have been devoting some time to energy among other subjects, but their own interviews of the previous years showed far less attention to the problem and far lower priority on the agenda than they claimed in their 1979 interviews. One health respondent captured the advantage of the design in his second interview: "I don't recall what I said last year, so you have structured the experiment properly."

Second, it is possible using the interview data not only to describe the state of the agenda and to describe changes, but also to investigate why some subjects rise to greater prominence than others and why the changes take place. Inspection of the changes themselves sometimes provides clues to explanation since changes move together with some event or indicator known to the researcher independent of the interviews. But the respondents' accounts of the reasons for change or the reasons for prominence or neglect of certain subjects is often very revealing itself.

A third use of the interviews was to explore some rather general theories of the policy formation process. In the main, I kept the interviews concentrated on the subjects of prominence since, as I argue elsewhere, an issue-by-issue interview strategy would yield better information than one that asked the respondents to generalize about the process.[1] But I also encouraged respondents to

---

[1] John W. Kingdon, *Congressmen's Voting Decisions,* 3rd ed. (Ann Arbor: University of Michigan Press, 1989). Chapter 1.

discuss any general reflections they had on the processes involved, and these reflections sometimes contributed to my thinking in interesting ways.

CODING

The interviews are put to many nonquantitative uses, as is evident throughout the book. But in analyzing the data, I would make implicit quantitative statements like "Many more respondents talked seriously about this subject in 1978 than in 1977," and "That factor was hardly ever mentioned." I thus concluded that some coding of the interviews would be desirable, even if it were crude and fragile. First, the coding would provide a measure of agenda status for a given item. If respondents mentioned a given subject, and if they discussed that subject in a way that indicated they and others were giving it some serious attention, then we would say it was relatively high on the agenda. On the other hand, if the subject was never discussed, we would say it was not high on the agenda. In addition, the coding could be used to rate the importance of various hypothesized influences on the agenda. If respondents rarely mentioned a given factor in the course of talking about why items were or were not prominent on the agenda, we could take that as some evidence for the conclusion that the factor was less important, at least in these respondents' eyes, than a factor they discussed more frequently and with greater intensity.

Thus to measure agenda status, coders combed through each interview, searching for mentions of a host of items. There was quite an elaborate code, about two hundred potential items in each of health and transportation, each of them a variable in the data set. They ranged in importance and breadth from major health items like medical care costs to narrow subjects like CAT scanners, and, in transportation, from deteriorating transportation infrastructure to trucking backhauls.

When a given subject was mentioned, the coder would locate the variable for that subject in the code, and judge which value it should have according to the scheme in Figure A-2. If the respondent indicated that government officials or those close to them were paying a lot of attention to the problem, that it was a major focus of attention occupying a lot of time and energy, coders would classify it as "very" prominent. Coders used this category only rarely, not more than five or six times an interview and often less. If the problem didn't have

Figure A-2
Coding Categories for Potential Agenda Items

1.	Very prominent; spontaneously mentioned
2.	Very prominent; in response to a question
3.	Somewhat prominent: spontaneously mentioned
4.	Somewhat prominent; in response to a question
5.	Little prominence; spontaneously mentioned
6.	Little prominence; in response to a question
9.	Never mentioned in the interview

that status, but still was of some prominence, if it took up more than a negligible amount of the attention, time, and energy of government officials or those close to them, coders would classify it as "somewhat" prominent. If the subject was mentioned as a side issue, lurking in the background or on the back burner, coders would classify it as having "little" prominence on the agenda. If they went through an interview and never found a mention of the item, the last category was used. In addition, the categories noted whether the subject had been spontaneously mentioned—in other words, whether the respondent had discussed the subject without any prompting about that subject from me—or whether the respondent discussed the problem only after I had asked about it.

Rating the importance of a given influence on the agenda—president, Congress, interest groups, media, etc.—involved a similar procedure. There was no battery of standard interview questions on these hypothesized influences, so the coding (very important to not important) refers to whether and how the respondent talked about each influence in the context of talking about the policy agenda and the alternatives under consideration. This procedure has the advantage of being unobtrusive. Rather than asking directly about a given actor, we notice how much that actor is mentioned when respondents are discussing the substance of agendas, alternatives, and changes.

All interviews were coded by two different coders working independently of each other. When they agreed, we used that consensual judgment. With the inevitable disagreements between them, we took a sample of the disagreements, identified the sources of disagreement, resolved the differences in the sampled cases, and then established patterns by which we were resolving disputes. For instance, we discovered that we very frequently would "bump up" a value. If one coder had not used a given variable and the other had, we discovered that the first coder—recognizing that a given passage contained a mention of the item—would accede to the second most of the time. Or if one rated a given subject as "somewhat" prominent and another "little," we found ourselves on reflection agreeing that it should be rated "somewhat" prominent most of the time.

In addition to "bumping up" the values in the case of intercoder disagreements, collapsing the variables contributed to a resolution of the problem. Almost all of the data analysis in this book is based not on the full array of categories in Figure A-2 but rather on a collapsed version of those categories that combines 1 and 3 into a single category labeled "very or somewhat prominent," and 2, 4, 5, 6, and 9 into a single category called "prompted, little, or no prominence." (Incidentally, for ease of style, the cumbersome "very or somewhat prominent" phrase has been replaced in the text of the book by the simple reference "prominent.") The collapsing of categories was done for reasons independent of the coding disagreements, essentially because the small numbers and the other data fragilities would make the finer gradations suspect. But the consequence of this combination rule is that intercoder disagreements *within* the collapsed categories no longer have the significance they would have if the full array were being used. If one coder said "very" and the other said "somewhat," for instance, the disagreement is of less concern when those two categories are combined into one.

When the joint effect of the collapsing and the rule of "bumping up" is used to calculate the error in the data due to intercoder disagreements, the result is quite encouraging. We found that we were resolving the differences between the coders in favor of the higher value 76 percent of the time. That means if we simply bump up *all* of the values in the case of disagreements, we make a mistake in 24 percent of the disagreements on the average. We then need the rate of disagreements. In the set of variables that included all potential agenda items for health in 1976, for instance, there were disagreements between the coders which spanned the collapsed categories in 9 percent of the cases.[2] Thus the rate of error remaining in the data set after we collapse the categories and bump up the values in the case of disagreements is $.24 \times .09 = 2$ percent. If we do the same calculation variable-by-variable, rather than for the whole set of variables, only 9 percent of the variables have an error rate higher than 5 percent, and the very highest error rate for a single variable is 10 percent. If we perform the same calculations for transportation agenda items in 1977, to take another example, the cross-category disagreements are again at 9 percent, making the overall error rate again 2 percent. By variable, only 8 percent of the variables had error rates greater than 5 percent, and only one variable had a rate greater than 10 percent (at 13 percent).

So the way we resolved all disagreements between coders was to choose the higher value, both for the agenda-item variables and for the hypothesized influences on the agenda. If there were to be a bias as a result of the combination of coder judgments into a value for a variable, that bias would be in the upward direction. Thus, when we say that a given influence on the agenda was not considered very important by these respondents or that a given subject was not prominent in their discussions of the agenda, we can be quite sure that the result is not due to a failing in our coding procedure. If either independent coder thought the subject deserved higher, that coder's judgment prevailed. And even the upward bias is minimal, about 2 percent averaged across the whole data set, under 5 percent for over 90 percent of the variables, and virtually never over 10 percent. There is more error when I use gradations that are finer than the collapsed categories, but I rarely refer to those.

The result is two central types of measures. One is a rating that respondents give to the importance of several hypothesized influences on agenda setting. We can see if they frequently discuss such actors as the president or mass media as if they have important impacts on the agenda. The other is our central measure of agenda status itself. If many respondents talk about a given subject in a serious way, we conclude that the subject occupies a higher place on the agenda than if few respondents discuss it. Please note that the usual unit of analysis is the interview (n = 247), or in other words, the respondent for a given year. Note too that we do not use these figures to establish whether a given item is "on the agenda" or not. Agenda status is not an either-or property,

---

[2] A "case" as defined here is the interview for a given variable. There were 40 health interviews in 1976, and 187 agenda-item variables. Thus n = $40 \times 187 = 7480$. Of those cases, there were 695 disagreements spanning the collapsed categories (e.g., using Figure A-2: 3 vs. 9, 1 vs. 5, 3 vs. 4, but not including 1 vs. 3, 5 vs. 9, or 4 vs. 6). Thus the rate of disagreement = 695/7480 = 9 percent.

Table A-3

Changes in Mentions of Catastrophic Health Insurance

Prominence	1976	1977	1978	1979
Very or somewhat prominent, spontaneous	23%	14%	33%	92%
Of little or no prominence, or prompted by interviewer	78	86	67	8
Total %	101%	100%	100%	100%
n	40	36	33	24

Chi-square significance level = .0000

Note: The figure in each cell of the top row is the percentage of the health respondents in the indicated year who were coded as having discussed catastrophic health insurance in a way that indicated they view it as being very or somewhat prominent on the agenda.

and it would be foolish to set, say, 50 percent mentions as some sort of cutoff, below which one would say that a subject is not on the agenda. Rather, agenda status is a matter of degree, and we use the figures consistent with that conceptualization. We use the figures comparatively, indicating that a given item is more prominent in 1978 than in 1977, for instance, or more prominent than another item within the same year.

Finally, there should be a word about how agenda change is operationally defined. Take Table A-3 for illustration. Because of the small number of interviews, I adopted a convention that I would not consider movement to be a change at all unless there was at least a shift of 20 percentage points between any two years *and* the chi-square for the table had a significance level of at least .05. Many changes, of course, were more dramatic than that, as the one in Table A-3 (92% − 14% = 78%, and a significance level of .0000). But at a minimum, a shift would have to meet both of these criteria to be considered a change at all.

CASE STUDIES

The interviews and general reading in the areas of health and transportation also provided many extremely instructive case studies of policy initiation that research assistants and I fleshed out with analysis of government documents, contemporary reports, trade publications, scholarly articles, and other publicly available written sources. These instances of the origins of government programs and of the nonappearance of other potential programs ranged in scope

Figure A-3

The Case Studies

Health

National health insurance
Medicare
Medicaid
Hospital cost containment, Carter administration
Health Maintenance Organizations
Health manpower
Health Service Corps
Health planning (Health Systems Agencies)
Professional Standards Review Organizations
Clinical laboratories regulation
Establishment of the Health Care Financing Administration

Transportation

Highway trust fund; interstate highway act
Airport trust fund; airport development
Mass transit funding
Waterway user charges
Rail recovery acts: Regional Rail Reorganization Act of 1973 (3-R); Rail Revitalization and Regulatory Reform Act of 1975 (4-R); Conrail
Nationalization in rail
Amtrak
Auto safety, concentrating on 1960s
Air safety
Regulatory reform in aviation
Regulatory reform in trucking
Regulatory reform in rail

and visibility from such high-visibility ones as national health insurance and railroad reorganization to such low-visibility ones as federal blood policy and patron security in mass transit facilities. These case studies proved to be quite useful since they provided concrete instances of the processes under study, and since they had a dynamic quality which would not be explored using static methods of observation that concentrate on one point in time.

The cases serve mostly nonquantitative purposes in this analysis. I used them to obtain a better understanding of the processes involved, to develop some theories of agenda setting by aggregating models based on individual cases, and to illustrate the generalizations. But I also reasoned, as in the case of the interviews, that at least some counting might be useful as a check against impression. I might want to say, for instance, that a given factor hardly ever seems to be important.

We identified the 23 cases listed in Figure A-3 as the units of analysis. I make no claim that these cases somehow represent all possible cases of initiation over the last three decades in health and transportation. However, there are quite a few of them, they are among the major cases discussed by my respondents, and most observers would probably name them as being among the major recent initiatives in these policy areas. A couple of them were prominent proposals, but were not enacted. Most were enacted. There were other cases in my interviews which, though fascinating, were not included in the quantitative data base because information on them was too fragmentary.

Our coding of the case studies was similar to that for the interviews. In this instance, we were working only with influences on the agenda, not the substantive topics that could be agenda items, since each case would, in effect, name its substantive topic. There were two coders for each case, working independently of each other, who read through the materials we had gathered, and, on the basis of the whole file of materials, would judge the importance of each of the hypothesized influences on the emergence of the case into agenda prominence. A given factor was rated as "very" important if the coder judged it to be really quite critical in moving the issue or subject into prominence or in retarding its movement into prominence on the agenda. These were the key factors, and this "very" important category was not used more than five or six times per case. A "somewhat" important factor was still important, but not in the first rank. It contributed in some important way to the appearance or nonappearance of the item on the agenda, but didn't seem to the coder to be as important as those in the "very" important category. A factor of "little" importance was minor, a kind of side factor that may have had some relevance but hadn't contributed something major to the agenda. Finally, some factors simply had "no" apparent relevance to the case at all.

Because there were small enough numbers in this instance, we resolved *all* disagreements between the coders for the case studies by going over each one. On the basis of all the interview and noninterview information we had at our disposal, the coders and I arrived at a collective decision about what the appropriate rating should be for a given case study. We therefore did not resort to such combination rules as are described for the interviews, but rather took our collective decision as the value for the variable in the final data set.

NONINTERVIEW MEASURES OF AGENDA STATUS

In addition to tracking the agenda by using the interviews, I gathered information from alternative sources that could be taken as measures of agenda status. If a congressional committee were holding hearings on a subject, for instance, that subject was considered on the agenda. The same could be said for mentions in the president's State of the Union address, coverage in the press, or mentions in public opinion polls. So for the four years under study, looking again only for material related to health or transportation, a research assistant and I gathered and analyzed (1) the subjects of congressional hearings and committee reports, (2) presidential messages, including the State of the Union address, (3) national public opinion data from the University of Michigan surveys and the Gallup polls, (4) 1976 party platforms, and (5) entries in the *New York Times* index.

These sources proved to be of varying usefulness. Public opinion polls simply didn't have much information that could be related to a governmental policy agenda in health or transportation. Party platforms proved to be a grab bag of promises, mostly very vague, which could hardly be a guide to policy making. Parties may have some place in agenda setting, a possibility we explore in this book, but platforms were not very helpful in defining a policy agenda. The *Times* index is an amazing jumble of the trivial and the important that would take a massive coding job to disentangle properly. The two other sources, presidential messages and congressional hearings and reports, do have some useful material, partly because they are more directly related to a governmental agenda than the other sources are.

One finding that becomes immediately clear is that there are many, many hearings and reports on topics that do not rank very high as priority agenda items in the interviews. Indeed, 75 percent of the subjects of hearings or reports in health and 73 percent in transportation concern items that are discussed as being very or somewhat prominent on the agenda by fewer than 20 percent of my respondents in the same year that the hearing was held or the report was issued. There are many hearings on topics that are obviously important to somebody but that my respondents, even those on the committee, simply would not judge to be of great public policy importance. They might have limited constituency importance, for instance, or be the pet project of a committee chairman or staffer, or a routine renewal.

But it could be that the pattern of hearings and reports in a given year might be related to the interviews in another year, not to the interviews in that year. If the hearings and reports included many subjects that then became hot topics in my interviews in the following year, for instance, that could hint that Congress is leading the rest of the policy community. If the hearings and reports followed my interviews, on the other hand, it could be that the rest of the policy community generates an agenda that is subsequently adopted on the Hill. So I examined lagged relationships of the same generic sort as the nonlagged ones, but in this case I compared 1976 hearings and reports to 1977 interviews, 1977 interviews to 1978 hearings and reports, and the like, lagging the relationship by one year. With a few minor wrinkles, the general finding is that the lagged relationships turned out roughly the same as the nonlagged relationships. The hearings and reports were neither leading nor following the interviews. We examine the substantive implications of that finding in the body of the book.

The main methodological message appropriate to this appendix, however, is that hearings and reports data are not a great deal of help in measuring the prominence of an item on the agenda. On occasion, a really high priority item does not look important because there happened to be no hearing or report on it that year, or because it is lost in the welter of other hearings and reports. More often, many low-priority items appear in the hearings and report record, and it is impossible to tell from the documentary evidence whether they were truly important agenda items or not. One would either weight all items equally, which would obscure their obvious differences, or weight them differently without persuasive ways of estimating the proper weights. In the main, I wanted to ascertain which subjects were occupying the attention, time, and energy of important governmental and near-government people, and, for my purposes, there was no substitute for asking them directly.

INDEX